Although my students motivate me to teach with passion, I want to express my gratefulness to my family for inspiring me to write. Together, we have hiked up a few mountains but I'm grateful for that one trek up that particular mountain in Colorado. Since that mountaintop encounter with the Lord, I have begun to see the spiritual realities that concern my origin and my inheritance in Jesus Christ. At the same time, God has been gracious to reveal the spiritual realities that oppose me. To my amazement, this wondrous and at times arduous journey to grasp my spiritual heritage is really not just for me, it's for my family—even to a thousand generations. And so this book is written for my loving family and my extended family, the Body of Christ.

Spiritual Reality

Coming to Terms with Our Ancient Spiritual Heritage

G. J. Wiese

ACW Press
Phoenix, Arizona 85013

Scripture quotations are taken from the Holy Bible, New International Version®. Copyright © 1973, 1978, 1984 by the International Bible Society. Used by permission of Zondervan Publishing House. The "NIV" and "New International Version" trademarks are registered in the United States Patent and Trademark Office by International Bible Society.

Verses marked NKJV are taken from the New King James Version, Copyright © 1979, 1980, 1982 by Thomas Nelson, Inc., Publishers. Used by permission.

Spiritual Reality: Coming to Terms with Our Ancient Spiritual Heritage
Copyright ©2001 G.J. Wiese
All rights reserved

Cover Design by Alpha Advertising
Interior design by Pine Hill Graphics

Packaged by ACW Press
5501 N. 7th Ave., #502
Phoenix, Arizona 85013
www.acwpress.com
The views expressed or implied in this work do not necessarily reflect those of ACW Press. Ultimate design, content, and editorial accuracy of this work is the responsibility of the author(s).

Library of Congress Cataloging-in-Publication Data

Wiese. G. J.
   Spiritual reality: coming to terms with our ancient
spiritual heritage / G.J. Wiese.
   p. cm.
   Includes bibliographical references.
   ISBN 1-892525-63-1

   1. Foundations of Christian faith. 2. Christian life. 3. Christianity and culture. 4. Spiritual direction. I. Title.

BV4501.3.W54 2001   248.4
                          QBI01-701273

All rights reserved. No part of this book may be reproduced, stored in a retrieval system, or transmitted in any form or by any means–electronic, mechanical, photocopying, recording, or otherwise–without prior permission in writing from the copyright holder except as provided by USA copyright law.

Printed in the United States of America.

Contents

Introduction to an Ancient Spiritual Heritage . . . 7
A Brief Historical Overview of Old Testament Interpretation
Considerations for Interpretation
Basic Approaches to Old Testament Interpretation

Chapter 1 Spiritual Realities Behind Creation 17
Acknowledging Spiritual Realities
Spiritual Origin of Creation
Spiritual Mission of Creation
Spiritual Order of Creation
Spiritual Equipment of Creation
Spiritual Essence of the Creation of Humanity

Chapter 2 Emergence of an Unholy Spiritual Reality 45
Target: Eden's Kingdom of Priests
Lucifer the Legalist
Commencing a Perverted Mission

Chapter 3 The Spiritual Reality of Enmity 65
Eden becomes a Courtroom
The Verdict
City of Man vs. City of God

Chapter 4 The Spiritual Reality of a Desecrated World 83
Desecration through Unholy Bonds
The Reality of a World Submerged
Noahic Covenant: The Divine-Warrior and His War-Bow
Tracing our Spiritual Heritage in the Archive of Nations

Chapter 5   Coming to Terms with Satan's
                 Cosmic Mountain 115
                 Dispersion of the Nations at the Tower of Babel
                 Satan's Cosmic Mountain
                 Simulated Cosmic Mountain-Structures of the Ancient
                    Near East
                 Tongues of Judgment, Tongues of Fire

Chapter 6   The Spiritual Reality of Contemporary
                 Canaanite Culture 143
                 Yahweh's War
                 Canaanite Mythology
                 The Dichotomy of Satan: Prince Baal of Earth and
                    Queen of Heaven

Chapter 7   The Spiritual Reality of the Anti-Kingdom 169
                 The Babylon Harlot
                 Infiltration of the Anti-Kingdom
                 Destructive Fruit
                 The Abomination of Desolation

Chapter 8   Our Hope and Final Destination:
                 The Realization of Mount Zion 197
                 The True Cosmic Mountain of Yahweh
                 The Goal of Mount Sinai: Mount Zion
                 Integrating Sinai with the Davidic Tradition
                 Characteristics of Yahweh's Cosmic Mount Zion
                 Taking Up the Cultural Mandate

Appendix A Canaanite Ritual System and
                 Its Scriptural Prohibition Chart 235

Appendix B Twisted Parallels of Satanic-Canaanite
                 Mythology Chart 237

Introduction to an Ancient Spiritual Heritage

Out of a song of praise, the Psalmist declares that God has "given me the *heritage* of those who fear your name" (Psa.61:5b). Everyone has a family heritage. The Irish man from Boston, the Hispanic mother living in Miami, and the Vietnamese teenager in south central L.A. all possess a heritage both rich and complex. Dusting off our ancient family records, we find that to know our family heritage is to understand ourselves. To grasp the past is to take hold of the present and prepare for the future. Our progeny sustains us with a sense of security and cognizance, but it can also surprise us with the reality of destiny.

The Body of Christ must discover their spiritual heritage in the ancient records of the Old Testament. It reveals our heritage in the family of God. The saints of old speak directly into our hearts as if they are spiritual grandparents to us. Their lives aren't just interesting. We are somehow connected. We are part of a greater family of faith encompassing our past, present, and future. We are part of a greater plan – an ancient sovereign plan. Within the Old Testament we will find the spiritual heritage of the faithful sojourners from Eden to the New Jerusalem.

The study of our spiritual heritage brings God's approval and provides an extensive reservoir from which the Holy Spirit can draw. Through research and prayerful meditation, the Holy Spirit behaves like a pen and writes a thesis on our hearts concerning who we are, where we come from, and what we will become (2 Cor.3:3). God's divine fountain pen transforms the inspired written word into living epistles read and known by all.

Yet without the Holy Ghost-writer, the ancient Scriptures are like huge stacks of family lineages in a dusty old room in the basement corner of a library. As we begin to understand our spiritual heritage in the family of God, we will grasp our place in God's sovereign plan.

Just how significant can an Old Testament heritage be to those of us who live in an age of unparalleled technological development? Can such an old document be relevant to a corporate executive, a suburban mother of three children, and a department store clerk? Maybe biblical scholars can handle the complexities of interpreting the ancient Hebrew text, but can we? Yes, but pursuing our spiritual heritage in the Old Testament will require that we set down some guidelines to keep us true to sound exegesis and a biblical hermeneutical framework.

A Brief Historical Overview of Old Testament Interpretation

After the reign of Solomon (mid eighth century B.C.), the prophets of Yahweh clearly took a prominent role over and above a corrupt priesthood in matters of interpreting God's law. They convey judgment and restoration, yet the essence of their message is nothing beyond the message of the Pentateuch. They simply expound on revealed truth. For example, the prophets viewed breaking covenant with Yahweh to mean spiritual prostitution with false gods (cf. Jer.2:20-25; 3:1-9; Ezek.16:15-43; Hos.4:10-5:4). Were the prophets over-spiritualizing Moses' inspired text? No, these prophets were able to understand the clear historical meaning of the word and its spiritual significance for their contemporaries. The Old Testament prophets frequently announce that the people of God "had eyes to see" but could not see; they had "ears to hear" but they could not hear (Jer.5:21; cf.6:10; Ezek.12:2). By the time of Christ, Jewish hermeneutics distinguishes between two senses of the biblical text: 1) the *peshat*, the plain historical meaning, and 2) the *remaz*, the hidden sense or the spiritual significance of the text to the wider body of Scripture.

But since the reformation, Old Testament hermeneutics has become more secularized and humanized by rationalization. With the development of historical criticism and its emphasis on the various parallels to Babylonian, Egyptian, Phoenician, and Arabic archaeological and mythological data, evidence is adduced against the originality and truth of Old Testament revelation to decipher its editorial pollution and access its preliterary format. So much of our biblical scholarship nurtures a relationship with an anthology of ancient literature, rather than a revelational encounter with God through the Holy Spirit. With the emergence of historical and literary criticism to center stage, we have alienated the Body of Christ once again from the Scripture—just like pre-Reformation days.

Considerations for Interpretation

Place ten Christians in a room and read any portion of the Old Testament text and one will hear a variety of opinions pertaining to its meaning. Anyone can make an assessment to determine what the intent of the author might have been; nevertheless, what is relevant is what *God intends to say to us through those inspired texts*. Many scholars affirm that the biblical "text cannot mean what it never meant" yet at the same time believe that yet a "second, or fuller meaning is possible."[1] Hagner states it this way:

> The New Testament writers looked for the meaning of the Old Testament as contained in its *sensus plenior* (full meaning). In so doing, they found varied correspondences, analogies, and suggestive similarities—some more substantial, some less substantial—but all based on the underlying presuppositions of the sovereignty of God in the affairs of history.[2]

---

1. Fee, Gordon and Stuart, Douglas. *How to Read the Bible for All Its Worth*, (Grand Rapids: Zondervan, 1993), p.26.
2. Donald Hagner, "The Old Testament in the New Testament," in *Interpreting the Word of God*, ed. Samuel Schultz and Morris Inch (Chicago: Moody, 1976), p.103.

Yet some will make the restriction that *sensus plenior* "is a function of inspiration, not illumination."[3] In other words, only the New Testament writers can legitimately find fuller meanings underlying redemptive history—not us.

Although the risk and apparent abuse involved in opening up the principle of *sensus plenior* to all believers is real, it is still necessary to affirm *sensus plenior* as a function of both inspiration and illumination. The serious student of the Bible can apply the inductive principle of the analogy of Scripture which carefully relates passages that reveal the same terminology, imagery, or comparable redemptive events, and recognize that Christ alone is the true interpreter of his word.

> We do not profess to get into the mind, psychology, or feelings of the author. We have no way of obtaining or controlling such data. Instead, we are interested only in the truth-intention of the author as expressed in the way he put together the individual words, phrases and sentences in a literary piece to form a meaning.[4]

Kaiser encourages us to ask: "Is the divine intention in the revealed word the same as the human authorial intent, or is it different?" If we hold that the biblical text must carry a hint of its own significance and inferences within itself, "rather than classifying this kind of inference as a direct expression of authorial intention, it seems best to consider it an example of 'consequent' or 'implicit' significances that the text of Scripture encourages us to find as a legitimate part of its total meaning."[5] This book is an attempt to move meaning a step further from what the original author intended to the fuller general truth-fulfillment within each sense or meaning. Again, anyone can take a shot at determining what the original intent of the

---

3. Fee and Stuart, pp.184-185.
4. Kaiser, Walter and Silva, Moises. *An Introduction to Biblical Hermeneutics*, (Grand Rapids: Zondervan, 1994), p.37.
5. Kaiser, pp.40-42.

author, but what is essentially relevant is what *God intends to say to us through those inspired texts.*

Ultimately, we must come to the conclusion that to attempt to adjust the tension between historical particularity (exegesis) and eternal relevance (hermeneutics) into an exact science or formula is not viable. Why not? Because God demands an intimate relationship with his people—one that thrives on communion and spiritual fellowship—not a formulation of some systematic approach to him. Those who learn to do valid research coupled with prayerful interaction and thoughtful meditation can indeed faithfully execute valid exegesis, sound hermeneutics, and a life of obedience to Christ.

Basic Approaches to Old Testament Interpretation

Traditionally, there are four approaches to studying the Old Testament. First, we may approach it primarily as a history book that concerns itself primarily with the nation of Israel. Our concentration is on understanding ancient historical facts, information about ancient cultures, dates, and archaeological evidence. This information is extremely important and we have an abundance of Bible dictionaries, commentaries, and handbooks to help our studies. Yet to focus solely on this approach, we may find ourselves barricaded in the confines of historical criticism. The meaning of the Old Testament is thereby reduced to only that which is objectively verifiable. To stay within the boundaries of its historical context is safe for scholars for it requires no interpretation, no application, and essentially no interaction with a personal God.

The Old Testament is a fascinating history book, but it is more than history. In fact, history begins long before Israel ever existed. In the beginning of creation, God creates humanity from one blood (Acts 17:26). After Adam makes a covenant with sin and death, evil inevitably accelerates and divine judgment ensues. God promises to break this treacherous cycle by "first show[ing] his concern by taking from the Gentiles a people for himself" (Acts 15:14). That Gentile is Abram, the father of our faith, who is picked out of the sea of humanity and thrust into the forefront of salvation history or *heilsgeschichte* (Gen.12:1,2). The Old Testament is a historical account, but its story is not for the sake of Israel alone. This would be divine favoritism. Israel's history is redemptive, that is, for the sake of all nations throughout the history of the world. This makes the Old Testament's historical facts relate to the rest of human history. Abraham inaugurates the Great Commission to fulfill the missionary task of bringing the saving knowledge of God to the rest of humanity (Gen.12:3; Deut.4:6-8). This makes ancient Israel very significant not only to the New Testament Church, but also to all the nations of the world.

Second, we may approach the Old Testament as a literary masterpiece. To handle the Bible as literature, we must use proper methods of interpreting various literary genres. Each literary form used in the Bible, whether it is narrative, poetry, or a vision, has rules of interpretation. We simply cannot interpret one of Ezekiel's visions as we would the Ten Commandments. They are different literary genres. Taking a literary approach is vital to proper interpretation and yet if taken to its extreme, we can become stuck in the technical analysis of the arrangement and wording of literary criticism and lose sight of any meaningful application.

The key to unlocking the Old Testament's literary rules is found in a basic understanding of its original language: Hebrew. The Hebrew language is full of parallelism, symbolism, and imagery. The artistic richness of this oriental language is accentuated even more by the fact that it is the inspired word of God. This bit of information sets the Bible apart from all other books. God breathes into this ancient Hebrew text words that are spirit and life—which leads us to depend on the Holy Spirit for illumination and again to interact with a personal God. Inspiration makes historical and literary truth matter.

Third, we may approach the Old Testament as a complex system of rules about religious behavior. Although guidelines to living a devout lifestyle are not laid out systematically, we can concentrate on character studies and obey the laws that seem relevant. If we attempt to relate this old system of beliefs to the gospel, we are faced with deciphering which stipulations still apply. Can we simply leave out what doesn't seem to fit into our New Testament doctrine? Can we throw out portions we don't like or which are odd and offensive to us? To embrace the totality of Scripture, we must not look on the Old Testament as a religious system, but as an older *covenant*, which implies yet again, an interactive relationship with God.

The Old Testament is not a religious system of dos and don'ts, but is actually the reestablishment of humanity's broken relationship with God. It uniquely expresses the life of faith in covenant terms. Human beings may pursue a system of religious rituals or seek idolatrous diversions, but our Creator demands intimate covenant relationship. The *Older Covenant* is not about religion, but about relationship with God. If we focus on it being the revelation of the one true God and seek to know him in his presence, then we will be transformed and our behavior will reflect our time with him.

Fourth, we may approach the Old Testament as an eschatological collection of typologies, symbols, and prophecies that anticipate fulfillment in the New Testament. With all the direct quotations and indirect allusions from the Old Testament, we can see how it foreshadows the spiritual realities in the New Covenant age. Some may simplify their approach to interpreting the Old Testament and say, "All is fulfilled. We need to focus on the New Testament because Jesus fulfills the Old." Others may approach the Old Testament in the opposite way. Obsessing over its eschatological pieces, some seek to decode hidden messages that only serve to tantalize creative minds with sensational predictions.

What does fulfillment imply? If the Old Testament is fulfilled, what does that mean today? In other words, even if we decode its eschatological message, how then do we relate to its fulfillment now? Throughout his earthly ministry, Jesus uses phrases that pertain to his personal fulfillment of the old Scriptures. So then we understand that the Old Testament is the progressive revelation of God through his Son, Jesus Christ. It is not *just* about fulfillment, but it is essentially about revealing the knowledge of God until the fullness of the Godhead is manifested in the coming of Christ. Yet fulfillment takes it a step further. By fulfillment Jesus means, "to make it happen" or "to make it reality." Eschatology then finds its inauguration in his first appearance on earth and its consummation in his Second Coming. Out of countless examples, one outstanding typological fulfillment is the Passover lamb. The little Old Testament ewe typologically becomes the Lamb of God who takes away the sin of the whole world, and we in Christ offer ourselves as living sacrifices to God. Fulfillment reaches into the realm of realization. This makes our pursuit of our spiritual heritage all the more relevant and exciting.

This book is an attempt to utilize and incorporate: 1) the historical background, 2) the literary genres, 3) the covenantal framework, 4) the eschatological fulfillment, and 5) the unfolding revelation of God to ultimately make our Old Testament spiritual heritage significant for today. Our desire is to fashion our hermeneutics to reflect Jesus' approach to the Old Testament. Our aim is to interact with the biblical text and the vast research that is available while personally conversing with our Creator. If we come to terms with spiritual reality, then our relationship with God will be deep, our spirituality will be authentic, and our ministry will have profound ramifications.

Using these hermeneutical principles, let us plunge into the depths of this ancient document and search for our rich spiritual heritage. It is critical to extensively investigate Genesis 1-11 for it not only discloses the complexities of our spiritual origin, but it also covers a minimum of two thousand years. The rest of the Old Testament covers yet another two thousand years. A profound awareness of the forefathers and mothers of our faith enhances our present spiritual experience. We are all on the same journey, from Eden to the land of promise. As believers, we too have escaped the bondage of the world, Satan's reign of terror that Egypt, Canaan, Assyria, and Babylon so vividly represent. Our redemption has come through the blood of the Passover lamb. When our enemies drive us to the brink of despair, God is faithful to take us through the waters of deliverance and to disable every worldly chariot that attempts to force us back into bondage.

As we join with the two on the way to Emmaus, Jesus expounds to us "all the [Old Testament] Scriptures concerning himself" and we, too, exclaim, "Were not our hearts burning within us while he talked with us…and opened the Scriptures to us?" (Lk.24:27-32). This is the aim of this book: to walk and talk with Christ as we read the Old Testament; to listen to his voice as he expounds on our spiritual origin and heritage and all the things concerning himself. Our hearts will burn as he opens up the spiritual reality behind this ancient inspired text and shares his own testimony. We will see that our testimony is really his testimony. Our Old Testament heritage is not only quintessential to Christian maturity and true spirituality, it is dynamically a revelation of Christ and therefore personally life-changing.

Chapter One

Spiritual Realities Behind Creation

The quest for our spiritual heritage originates in the initial construction of God's estate. Before human lineage came into existence, the Creator God laid out creation according to the pattern of his celestial blueprint. The plan is to create a universe that reflects his character and glory. Heaven and earth are designed not only to manifest his glory and reflect his invisible attributes (Psa.148; Rom.1:20), but they are God's dwelling place of rest (*manuhah* Isa.66:1; Psa.104). *Manuhah* signifies the lordship and enthronement of God over his universal sanctuary. Though carefully designed to house human beings and their animal friends, creation's primary purpose is to furnish a dwelling place, a habitation for God. As Creator he discloses himself "with measuring line in hand, defining the space, determining the dimensions according to specifications, setting the building on foundations and laying the cornerstone, enclosing the living areas by boundary-walls with their doors and bars (Job.38:4ff.)."[1] God builds his own house to dwell in. It is created by God and for God. Paul clarifies for us creation's ultimate purpose: "all things were created *by* [Christ] and *for* him... so that in everything he might have the supremacy" (Col.1:16, 18). This may send a jolt into our busy schedules, but the universe really does not revolve around us!

Evolution is built on the idea that everything is really about us, and its dogma assumes that the earth's age must reach into the billions. Evolution examines ancient fossils and uses radiometric-dating methods as proof of a very old earth. Yet the reliability of the carbon-14 method is certainly questionable. Any honest attempt to calculate the date of the earth solely on biblical genealogies points to a young earth. If we trace all the genealogies from Messiah back to Adam, the date of creation would be about 4000 BC. However, in patriarchal societies the grandfather often represents whole generations. So to include 10,000 to 30,000 years of generations to the biblical genealogies still leaves a very young earth. Scripture itself portrays the earth's age to coincide with the age of humanity (Lk.1:70; 11:50,51; Heb.9:26; Matt.13:35; Mk.10:6; Rom.1:20; Prov.8:29-31).

In an attempt to coincide with many geological findings, the Gap Theory promotes the idea that there was a gap of billions of years between Genesis 1:1 and 1:2. This widely held view relies heavily on the premise that God first created a perfect universe (v.1). Many Gap theorists claim that a pre-Adamic race with its own history and animal kingdom existed before chaos entered the scene. When Lucifer rebels (v.2a), God needs to begin the creation process again (v.3bc). This implies that sin and death existed before Adam. Scripture, however, testifies that death initially came into the world when Adam and Eve fell in the garden (Rom.5:12; 1 Cor.15:21). The biblical account does not seem to support a gap or an old earth.

Genesis 1:1 reads more like a newspaper headline: "Hear ye! Hear ye! Read all about it! In the beginning God creates the heavens and the earth!" So all inquiring minds want to know

---

1. Meredith Kline, *Kingdom Prologue*, Vol.1, (1985), p.42.

the exclusive report contained in the rest of the chapter. This ancient article centers on God who creates (*bara*) something out of nothing. Though God himself is uncreated with no beginning or end, he reveals himself to be both immanent and transcendent over his masterpiece. C.S. Lewis refutes pantheistic thinking by stating that God "could not show [himself] inside the universe—no more than the architect of a house could actually be a wall or staircase or fireplace in the house."[2] Just as furniture is designed with a particular function in mind, the sovereign Creator fashions the universe to fulfill its divine destiny.

God's universe can be objectively observed and scientifically verified, but it must also be discerned spiritually. Creation has a spiritual reality behind it. In order to comprehend Genesis 1 we must grasp the spiritual origin of creation, the spiritual mission of creation, the spiritual order of creation, the spiritual equipment within creation, and the spiritual essence of the creation of humanity.

Acknowledging Spiritual Realities

The original draft is a formless watery dispersion dwelling over static darkness. "Now the earth was formless and empty, darkness was over the surface of the deep, and the Spirit of God was hovering over the waters" (Gen.1:2). History as we know it begins with the Spirit of God hovering over the primeval chaotic waters. Is this merely a rough start for our beautiful world? Or does this demonstrate a spiritual reality behind the universe? Throughout the Bible, the chaotic sea (*yamm*) poetically illustrates the reality of a spiritual atmosphere that surrounds the earth (cf. Job 38:6-11; Psa.24:1,2; 74:10,13; Hab.3:8-15). This spiritual dimension, where only angels dwell, is apparently showing signs of trouble. Darkness has invaded. An uprising is beginning to emerge among the angelic network. Nevertheless, God proceeds with his plan.

Utilizing the whole trinity to begin constructing his resting place-project, God sends his Spirit to hover over the spiritual

---

2. Lewis, C.S. *Mere Christianity*, (New York: MacMillan, 1960) p. 33.

atmosphere and this provides the precise climate for God's pre-incarnate Son to speak forth a word (Jn.1:1-3). The universe then is "formed at God's command, so that what is seen was not made out of what was visible" (Heb.11:3). By stating that the perceptible three-dimensional world is originally created out of nothing, one must acknowledge an invisible spiritual reality behind creation. In an attempt to understand the mysteries of life, philosophers from Socrates to Descartes have debated, overlooked, and denied this intriguing element. But to acknowledge a spiritual dimension behind the universe does explain how Jesus calms a visibly threatening storm over the sea of Galilee by simply speaking to it (Lk.8:24). It explains why demons flee when Jesus verbally commands them to leave people (Mt.17:18).

Jesus understood how creation works. The things that we see—the storm itself and the tormented soul—are influenced by things that are not logical to our natural senses. It is certainly true that television weathermen point to wind and air pressures interacting in a frontal system, but Jesus sees a certain spiritual reality behind the storm facing his disciples. Psychologists may diagnose people as bi-polar or dissociated, but Jesus discerns a spiritual entity behind the tormented soul. From the beginning the omnipotent Creator desires to personally supervise the spiritual atmosphere that surrounds the earth. Because he creates this sphere to be a communication link between heaven and earth, he must deal with the dark insurgence that is intensifying among the angelic ranks.

Spiritual Origin of Creation

If from the beginning the Creator personally initiates creation's conception, then God is the origin, source, and beginning of creation. He faithfully executes his plan and imparts the spiritual unction for all things to exist. Being previous in everything, God sends his Spirit to hover over the spiritual atmosphere until there is a transformation from nothing to something. This incubation period produces a supernatural substance called faith (Heb.11:1). Faith-substance acts like evidence for the things hoped for in the spiritual dimension.

Though this faith-substance is evidence of expectation, it has yet to make its outward appearance. What makes the "virtual reality" of faith turn into actual reality? A spoken creative word from God: "Let there be," which releases the divine power to implement his will. A spoken word from God is really a "Christ-indwelt" word (*rhema* Jn.1:1-3). It is vocalized with the distinct purpose of transforming nothing into something that glorifies the Creator (Rom.10:17)—much like Jesus' stilling of the storm and his casting out of evil spirits.

When God initiates his plan for our lives, he begins with nothing. No vision, no purpose, no faith. He finds nothingness in our hearts. He deliberately chooses people who have nothing to give him (1 Cor.1:26-29). We may say in our hearts, "I want to have faith, but no matter how much I try, my positive thoughts and attempts to live a good life don't seem to produce faith in me." If striving to believe in something doesn't fulfill us, then what will catapult us from despair? Believing in someone. Biblical faith is not a cause—it is a relationship. True faith demands intimacy with God. Intimate contact with our Creator allows the substance of faith to take up residence in a vacant heart. Jesus asks, "When the Son of Man comes, will he find faith on the earth?" (Lk.18:8). No doubt he will find lots of work done, impressive performances, and an accumulation of things in our garages. But will he find faith—the kind of faith-substance that incubates in the spiritual realm and comes to fruition at his word? When God sends his Holy Spirit to hover over our hearts, he speaks his word, imparts saving faith, and transforms our nothingness into something that glorifies our Creator.

Faith-substance anchors our hearts with a pledge from heaven. God wants to make the unchanging nature of his purpose very clear, so that when he speaks, it is guaranteed to accomplish his will for it is impossible for God to lie (Isa.55:8-11; Heb.6:17,18). What a relief this is to weary souls who incessantly conjure up explanations for living. To speak meaningless repetitions to some distant deity is like barking out orders to a complete stranger on a street corner. There is no response without relationship. We simply cannot expect to receive anything from someone we don't really know. Genuine faith offers freedom and purpose, while its two counterfeits, positivism and witchcraft, entrap their adherents in a ruinous web of performance, presumption, and disillusionment.

From our initial faith-encounter with God through Christ (the living Word), we continue to look to Jesus who authors, imparts, grows, and completes our faith (Heb.12:2). All day long, every day, believers are invited to the heavenly board meetings to hear the Creator's agenda and receive enablement to carry out kingdom operations. Because God first loved and chose us, we humbly come to him in simple obedience with nothing but love in our hearts. During these divine appointments in the heavenly boardroom, the Holy Spirit hovers over us and imparts mountain-moving faith.

Spiritual Mission of Creation

Even before sin enters the world through the fall of humanity, we find the spiritual reality of creation's sanctifying mission. If creation is made by God and set apart for his Son, then any sign of revolt must be dealt with immediately. In a bold and notably prophetic gesture, God makes a distinction between darkness and light in the spiritual dimension. "And God said, 'Let there be light,' and there was light. God saw that the light was good, and he separated the light from the darkness" (Gen.1:3,4). God does not remove the darkness completely, he merely contrasts it from the light. He carefully draws a line between light and darkness. There is no gray zone in the spiritual realm. In a profoundly prophetic sense, both spheres will coexist until the consummation of all things (Rev.21:25; 22:5). One is either within the boundary of light or within the confines of darkness.

Ironically, throughout history this coexistence actually propels sanctification and is illustrated in the parable of the wheat and tares.

> The kingdom of heaven is like a man who sowed good seed in his field. But while everyone was sleeping, his enemy came and sowed weeds [tares] among

the wheat, and went away. But when the wheat sprouted and formed heads, then the weeds also appeared…The servants asked him, "Do you want us to go and pull them up?" "No," he answered, "because while you are pulling the weeds, you may root up the wheat with them. Let both grow together until the harvest." Matthew 13:24-30

The tares are *zizanias*. They are botanically very close to wheat when they are sown. This makes it extremely difficult to distinguish both plants when they are young. As the wheat and tares grow, their roots become entangled. It is not until the wheat grain matures and is fruitful that tares are exposed. Jesus explains that the spiritual coexistence of light with darkness will continue until the end. God appoints the angelic reapers to separate the tares because they saw the source of defection first hand.

Tares from the enemy cannot be distinguished until the wheat grain matures. Our level of maturity in the Lord determines the extent of our spiritual discernment of tares. The temptation in our discovery of potential tares among the wheat is to boot them out of our lives. But Jesus tells his servants, "No, lest while you gather up the tares you also uproot the wheat with them." This may surprise us but it is destructive to the wheat if the tares of darkness are prematurely eliminated. We must believe that God has a very good purpose for entangling our roots. Tares of darkness actually reinforce the roots of the wheat making them stronger than if left alone. Clashing with evil strengthens the righteous.

Unfortunately as human history unfolds, people love the dark side and hate the truth of God's light. But God mercifully calls us out of darkness into his enduring light and enables us to live in truth "so that it may be seen plainly that what [we have] done has been done through God" (1 Pet.2:9; Jn.3:21,22). Some might appear to be irretrievable from the darkness, but Paul exhorts us to "judge nothing before the appointed time; wait till the Lord comes. He will bring to light what is hidden in darkness and will expose the motives of men's hearts" (1 Cor.4:5).

Nevertheless, a distinction will always be made as to whether one is a child of light or a child of darkness (1 Thess.5:4,5).

All spiritual maneuvers behind creation have one mission: to carry out the business of sanctification. To sanctify something means to set it apart for God. Sanctification is a process that disconnects light from darkness so that creation may be free to embrace truth. The Holy Spirit is in the business of not only exposing the hidden works of darkness, but also convincing us to love truth and holiness.

From the text in Genesis, there's no suggestion relative to the consistency of this light. But the light of day one must be different from the physical, natural light emanating from the luminaries of day four. Henry Morris describes Genesis 1:3 this way: "The Word of God brings light! The Father is the source of all things (verse 1), the Spirit is the energizer of all things (verse 2), the Word is the revealer of all things (verse 3)."[3] So given the context, we understand that the light of God's word exposes the true nature of spiritual darkness. If this is part of sanctification's mission, then the consequence of sanctification is that "everyone who wants to live a godly life in Christ Jesus will be persecuted" (2 Tim.3:12). Why? Because those who are sanctified are like a lighted city situated on a hill. Lights of a city expose the hidden alleys of darkness. Although they coexist throughout history, God is in the business of distinguishing between wheat and tares, sheep and goats, light and darkness. Light must expose everything in the spiritual realm, fulfilling its sanctifying mission.

Spiritual Order of Creation

Through the next two days of creation, the sovereign Creator meticulously builds his habitation in a very orderly fashion. He separates and sanctifies, separates and sanctifies.

> And God said, "Let there be an expanse between the waters to separate water from water." So God made the

---

3. Morris, Henry. *The Genesis Record*, (Grand Rapids: Baker Book, 1982) p. 55, (cf. 2 Cor.4:6; Jn.1:1,14; 8:12; 1 Jn.1:5).

expanse and separated the water under the expanse from the water above it. And it was so. God called the expanse "sky." And there was evening, and there was morning—the second day. And God said, "Let the water under the sky be gathered to one place, and let dry ground appear." And it was so. Genesis 1:6-9

The Lord divides the higher and lower waters with a firmament or what we simply call "sky." The lower water sustains life on earth, while the higher water furnishes a protective canopy over the earth. The lower water gathers to form one extensive water mass, making the original expanse of ground cover over one large continent. The overhead canopy protects the earth until the windows of heaven are opened and the higher water is unleashed in the flood (Gen.7:11). This causes the dry land to break up into its present arrangement of many continents.

A person's work is often an extension of his or her personality. So, too, the handiwork of the Creator and his craftsmanship is characteristic of his being. The first three days reveal that all spiritual operations are done in respectful, orderly fashion (cf. 1 Cor.14:40). When God is on the move, there is peace and stability (v.33).

Set according to a divine Daytimer, history runs its purposeful course as predetermined before the foundation of the world. Kingdom business starts in heaven's throne room and from there God manages the affairs of creation by appointing a time for everything. The sovereignty of God comforts and bring assurance that God uses all things to fulfill his purpose. Solomon later catches a glimpse of the agenda and sees that the divine timetable manages and safeguards life on earth (Eccl.3:1-8). God promises to make all things beautiful in its time because everything has a definite purpose (v.11a). "I know that everything God does will endure forever; nothing can be added to it and nothing taken from it. God does it so that men will revere him" (v.14). The creative Potter holds all things in his hands and molds them progressively into something beautiful that will stand forever as a testimony to his loving character and awesome plan.

Although life can appear chaotic and accidental in the narrow-angle lens of everyday living, when we look through the wide-angle lens of hindsight, we find both good and evil circumstances woven into a splendid tapestry of what makes us who we are today. Monet's magnificent *Water Lilies* is exceptionally brilliant. Viewed from afar, the simple pond looks so vivid. But close to the canvas, the massive painting seems like a haphazard conglomeration of brush strokes. Close-ups of impressionist paintings can look like kindergarten artwork, for the artist appears to have erratically placed clumps of paint on the canvas. So also, appreciation of life's grandeur does not come when our faces are inches away from the moment, inspecting and dissecting each situation that arises. It comes later, sometimes years later, when in hindsight we are awed by the spiritual reality "that in all things God works for the good of those who love him, who have been called according to his purpose" (Rom.8:28).

Set apart unto the God of order, believers enjoy clarity in thought, purpose, and conscience. Under the lordship of God, we can understand that life has an eternal spiritual reality behind it. Living in God's kingdom nurtures vision and strategic planning as we seek to fulfill his plans and purposes. Separation from darkness bolsters holy living and, as living stones, we are molded, sharpened, and polished until we become "like that of a very precious jewel, like a jasper, clear as crystal" (Rev.21:11). Sanctification brings separation and order to life while association with darkness entangles us with irrational thinking, confusion, frustration, and despair.

Spiritual Equipment within Creation

The earth brought forth the herb that bear seed and "trees on the land that bear fruit with seed in it" (Gen.1:11,12). Just as Adam and Eve are created as full-grown adults, so are the plants and trees. The world is created full-grown, not in seed form. So to answer the age-old question—yes, the chicken came before the egg. The Creator Lord acts like a farmer who sows the Spirit-illuminated word into the earth. His creative command issues forth to mobilize creation as a fully developed, operating greenhouse.

Spiritual Realities Behind Creation

The spiritual reality behind creation is that everything has a God-given, built-in ability to function. Everything has the potential to yield a harvest: some a hundred-fold, some sixty, some thirty. The heavenly Farmer plants seeds of potential—loaded with purpose—in the hearts of his people. Tragically some seeds are devoured, some wither from the scorch of tribulation, while still others are choked out by worldly thorns. The parable of the Sower dramatically illustrates the personal spiritual empowerment behind all kingdom operations (Matt.13:1-23).

In the parable of the talents, Jesus likens God to "a man going on a journey, who called his servants and entrusted his property to them. To one he gave five talents of money, to another two talents, and to another one talent, to each according to his ability" (Matt.25:14,15). The indictment at the end of the parable is upon the one who hid his talent because, as he put it, "Master…I knew that you are a hard man, harvesting where you have not sown and gathering where you have not scattered seed" (v. 24). Is he right about God?

God is not "a hard man," but he is a smart "businessman" who makes his investments through his "employees." The opera singer is given the awe-inspiring gift of melody. The gourmet chef knows just the right ingredients to mix together. Anyone can take a few singing lessons or read a cookbook, but only a few are especially gifted in these areas. This is divine enablement. The three people in the parable receive investments that are designed to prosper through their God-given abilities. God is not a hard man, but in a way he is a heavenly businessman of sorts, who invests in people's abilities.

The heavenly businessman also expects to reap and gather where he has not sown seed. Is this fair? Well, God must hold a very high view of his workers. The opera singer doesn't just sing in the shower. She sings to bless an auditorium full of people. The gourmet chef doesn't eat the whole meal himself. He shares his carte du jour with a table full of guests. Heaven's investment is given to bless and profit others. It is obvious that the disastrous end of the buried talent is like a chef preparing a delectable feast and then throwing it into the garbage disposal. God is not a "hard" God. He wisely invests in his servants, each according to their abilities for a bountiful exchange of blessings. The wise Farmer plants his people in all areas of the earth's soil. These unique seedlings are carefully planted and systematically plowed by the God of the harvest.

> When a farmer plows for planting, does he plow continually? Does he keep on breaking up and harrowing the soil? When he has leveled the surface, does he not sow caraway and scatter cummin? Does he not plant wheat in its place, barley in its plot, and spelt in its field? …Caraway is not threshed with a sledge, nor is a cartwheel rolled over cummin; caraway is beaten out with a rod, and cummin with a stick. Grain must be ground to make bread; so one does not go on threshing it forever. Though he drives the wheels of his threshing cart over it, his horses do not grind it. All this also comes from the Lord Almighty, wonderful in counsel and magnificent in wisdom. Isaiah 28:24-29

Isaiah pictures the judicious Farmer as one who carefully distributes his seed and plants them with a particular project in mind. His disciplinary plowing is appropriate to the seed planted. The heavenly Plowman plants us in a particular place in his field, then uniquely prepares us to produce a harvest of fruit. Harvest comes by plowing, breaking, and crushing discriminatorily according to his overall plan.

The spiritual equipment within creation regulates sowing and reaping. How spiritual tools function is described by the significant phrase, "according to their kind," which occurs ten times in Genesis 1 (vv.11, 12, 21, 24, 25). Each department in creation produces a product that reflects itself. Golden retrievers produce golden retrievers; apple seeds grow into apple trees. Whether or not parents want to admit this, their children do bear quite a resemblance to them. They are supposed to! So also spiritual equipping or multiplying may occur through discipleship.

Spiritual multiplication involves loving others so much that we share with them not only the gospel but our whole lives as well (1 Thess.2:8). Students learn from their teachers, daughters discover life's possibilities from their mothers, and young athletes observe Olympic champions. Built inside each person is the equipment to bear fruit, but this enablement is not an end in itself. God commissions us to pass on to others what we have been freely given by him. It is just another spiritual reality behind creation.

Barnabus disciples Paul, who disciples Timothy and Titus, who disciple the elders of their churches, who then disciple the younger members of their congregations. Paul affectionately refers to those he disciples as sons in the faith (Tit.1:4a). Discipleship takes on images of a heartfelt father-son bond. Paul sounds like the businessman in the parable of the talents when he says: "The reason I left you in Crete was that you might straighten out what was left unfinished and appoint elders in every town, as I directed you" (Tit.1:5). Paul invests much of himself into the life of young Titus, but he wants all of the Cretans to understand the necessity of multiplying our spiritual equipment. The older women are to "train the younger women to love their husbands and children, to be self-controlled and pure, to be busy at home, to be kind, and to be subject to their husbands," while the older men are to "encourage the young men to be self-controlled. In everything set them an example by doing what is good" (Tit.2:2-7). By imparting their lives to one another, they multiply their fruitfulness through discipleship.

Jesus' Great Commission to "go" rests on having been given all authority over heaven and earth. He sends us to the nations to "make disciples...teaching them to obey everything I have commanded"(Matt.28:18-20). Emphasis is usually on the "go" but missionaries will readily agree that simply getting to the nations is easy. Real work is toiling in discipleship and laboring to impart your life to others. Only those truths written on our hearts by the Holy Spirit can be imparted to others. All other shared information will be entertaining at best. Discipleship fulfills the second clause of the Great Commission and passes on our spiritual equipment to others in God's creation.

The fourth day produces two generators of light for the earth.

> God said, "Let there be lights in the expanse of the sky to separate the day from the night, and let them serve as signs to mark the seasons and days and years, and let them be lights in the expanse of the sky to give light on the earth." And it was so. God made two great lights—the greater light to govern the day and the lesser light to govern the night. Genesis 1:14-16b

These rulers govern the day and the night and have an incredible influence on the inhabitants of the earth. "The sun knows when to go down. You bring darkness, it becomes night, and all the beasts of the forest…roar for their prey and seek their food from God. The sun rises, and…they return and lie down in their dens. Then man goes out to his work, to his labor until evening" (Psa.104:19-23). The sun determines the work shifts of both man and beast. What a marvelous portrayal of the spiritual reality behind kingdom administration!

God bestows leadership qualities to those who are called to serve as gifts to the saints (1 Tim.3:1-13). They supervise ministry work shifts. These ministry-gifts to the Body of Christ are appointed by God to facilitate ministry-work for believers (1 Pet.5:1-4). Leadership ministry-gifts are personal trainers who encourage the Body to exercise and build strong spiritual muscles. Kingdom business is teamwork and God has called certain people to coach the team to victory. They rally the Body of Christ together and encourage every part to share in kingdom work. This causes the Body to support, grow, and build itself up in love (Eph.4:16). When people are placed in positions of delegated authority according to God's call, believers are free to "roar for their prey and seek their food from God." Delegated authority is like sending in the plays from the sidelines. The ministerial coaches release the gifts and callings of God's people (2 Tim.2:1-26).

Unfortunately, authority can be abused. Just as the sun knows its going down, people in God's kingdom must humbly remain within their ministerial boundaries. Overt control and spiritually manipulative words and gestures push some to step over the lines of their calling, damaging those who earnestly desire (sometimes naively) to serve God. "Distorted pictures of God and self, difficulty trusting those in authority, problems understanding and accepting grace are just some of the struggles shared" by those who have felt the impact of over-regulated authority.[4] The Bible cites many kings, priests, prophets, and the religious leaders of Jesus' day as abusers of authority. Nations, families, and churches have struggled under their twisted regimes.

Authority can also be undermined. This is evident in the cases of Korah, Miriam and Aaron, and of course, Lucifer. All these met up with a God who defends those whom he appoints to run his kingdom business. The present age is characterized by lawlessness and it is apparent in the Church. Throwing off any restraint, refusing to submit to anyone, some abandon any accountability in order to follow their own spirituality and build their own ministry. We must resist the temptation to join with the spirit of lawlessness in the world. The spirit of lawlessness is diabolically setting the stage for the son of lawlessness to dictate. Authority will increasingly be undermined until all worldly authority topples and lawlessness rules.

Jesus addresses this potentially explosive area by nonchalantly asking his disciples: "What were you arguing about on the road?" (Mk.9:33). Embarrassed by their heated debate over who is the greatest disciple of all time, they keep silent and do not respond to him (v.34). Insisting that "I am the best disciple" implies "I hear from God more than all of you" and so of course, "my great ideas are better than your suggestions." By insisting that our ideas for the youth program are better than the youth pastor's plan of action, we are really saying that we are the greatest. What

---

4. Johnson, David, VanVonderen, Jeff. *The Subtle Power of Spiritual Abuse*, (Minneapolis: Bethany, 1991), p.40.

is Jesus' response to this? "If anyone wants to be first, he must be the very last, and the servant of all" (Mk.9:35). The purpose for creation's spiritual equipment is to serve.

Jesus then takes into his arms a living example of a great servant—a little child. Being a parent, some days I would beg to differ! What makes children the best examples of servitude in God's kingdom? Children are born into boundaries. Drs. Cloud and Townsend offer invaluable insight.

> From an early age, children need to be able to accept the limits of parents, siblings, and friends. They need to know that others don't always want to play with them, that others may not want to watch the same TV shows they want, and that others may want to eat dinner at a different restaurant then they do. They need to know that the world doesn't revolve around them. This is important for a couple of reasons. First, the ability to learn to accept limits teaches us to take responsibility for ourselves...A second, and more important, reason... Heeding others' boundaries helps children to love.[5]

Boundaries mold us into respectful, responsible, and loving people. This is Jesus' definition of the greatest servant in the kingdom of God. Children display a servant's heart when they obey the boundaries set by their parents.

If the sun does not set, beasts of the forest cannot capture their prey and eat. If the sun does not rise, man cannot work and enjoy the fruits of his labor nor provide for his family. How utterly interdependent all God's workers are in their appointed realm of ministry! There is a definite spiritual reality behind discipleship and ministerial fruitfulness within creation's operations.

---

5. Cloud, Henry, Townsend, John. *Boundaries: When to Say YES, When to Say NO To Take Control of Your Life*, (Grand Rapids: Zondervan, 1992), pp. 182-183.

Spiritual Essence of the Creation of Humanity

Then God said, "Let the water teem with living creatures" (Gen.1:20). During days five and six the earth is ready to be inhabited by living creatures, first by fish, fowls, and animals, and then by humans. Francis Schaeffer relates a common discussion among his students:

> Often in a discussion someone will say, "Didn't God, then, if He is personal and if He loves, need an object for His love? Didn't He *have* to create? And therefore, isn't the universe just as necessary to Him as He is to the universe?" But the answer is, No. He did not have to create something face-to-face with Himself in order to love, because there already was the Trinity. God could create by a free act of His will because before creation there was the Father who loved the Son… God had someone face-to-face with Himself in the three Persons of the Trinity.[6]

Before and throughout the creation process, God the Father delights in his Son and the Son rejoices always before his Father (Prov.8:30). There is no need within the trinity. There is no compulsion to create anything. There is only fullness of joy. So why create animals and human beings? God so delights in his Son that he naturally desires more just like him (Prov.8:31). There is no lack of love within the eternal Godhead; the Father God simply desires to extend his family.

Michaelangelo's magnificent painting on the ceiling of the Sistine Chapel is probably more of a depiction of God in the likeness of man than vice versa. If God is Spirit (Jn.4:24a) and there is none like him, then there is nothing to which we can compare him. So what does it mean to be created in his image? Three facets of his reflection in us appear to be involved: 1) God is love and we are created to love and be loved, 2) God is just

---

6. Schaeffer, Francis. *The Complete Works of Francis Schaeffer, Vol.2*, (Westchester: Crossway, 1982), pp.15-16.

and we are created with a conscience, and 3) God is sovereign and we are created to reign with him.

1. Created to Love and Be Loved

The word "living" (*nephesh*) means "soul" and occurs for the first time when describing the animal kingdom, including the "great sea monsters" (*tannin* great dragons), or what we now call dinosaurs, of the past (Gen.1:20, 24). This means that animals have consciousness, but plant life does not. We place framed pictures of Sam the dog and Buddy the cat on our office desk—not of our favorite plants. Why? Because animals are created with *nephesh*; they are living souls. What sets humanity apart from the animal kingdom is that God breathes into humanity's *nephesh* the "breath of life" (Gen.2:7). We are creation's masterpiece because we are created in God's image: spirit, soul, and body.

We have the capacity to love and receive love. We must relate. It is a part of our makeup. We are born to relate spiritually, emotionally, and physically. *Nephesh* uses many verbs to indicate that the soul is created to need something. The spiritual reality of *nephesh* is that we have had this special yearning device placed inside of us. Is this a setup? It appears so. The soul has a built-in a sense of longing. It yearns to love and be loved, to connect and be intertwined with God and other human beings. We are created to love.

Every soul longs for love's constant reassurance and devotion in covenant relationships. Proverbs 19:22 informs us that everyone desires *hesed*. The intensity of this Hebrew word may be lost in its English translation to "loving kindness" or "steadfast love," but *hesed* reflects heartfelt commitment. It is best understood as intense loyalty and affectionate devotion. If all desire *hesed*, then all share in the profound longing to give and receive unfailing love. This proverb tells me that I am like everyone else in this world. *Hesed* is forever crying out for fellowship that is pure, genuine, and unconditional. It's the kind of love that "sticks closer than a brother" (Prov.18:24). Having never seen God, we can manifest his abiding presence by expressing love in our relationships with one another. "If we love one another, God lives in us and his love is made complete in us... God is love. Whoever lives in love lives [abides] in God, and God in him" (1 Jn.4:12-16). We no longer relate to people "from a worldly point of view" [according to the flesh], but we see them all through the eyes of Christ (2 Cor.5:16).

By behaving like God in our relationships, we enjoy the plentiful adventures that commitment brings to our life. Yet with the abundance of material blessings at our disposal, many people commit their lives to things instead of people. Regardless of how much we might love our television, or our Saturday morning golf game, we simply can't develop an intimate relationship with our favorite talk show host or a steel golf club. Made in God's image, we possess the innate need to seek and commit to real, "live" people—and a real, living God.

Hesed extends affection and commitment to those precarious friends and neighbors around us. To love with *hesed* is risky, sometimes heart-wrenching and quite bothersome at times because it requires a vulnerable surrender of our deepest wants, needs, and desperate struggles. *Hesed* extracts a bit of consternation and wringing of sweaty hands. We feel vulnerable to the frustrating reality of careless conversations and hurtful deeds, but building walls of isolation simply runs contrary to our nature. "An unfriendly man [who isolates himself] pursues selfish ends [seeks his own desire]; He rages against all wise judgment" (Prov.18:1). Intentionally disconnecting is essentially selfish. Isolation may seem to protect its victims, but it will leave them stripped of their image-bearing capabilities. Though *hesed* only intensifies the intrinsic craving for unfailing love, we will always have the desire for *hesed* permanently installed in our soul. *Hesed* is the hidden spiritual reality that drives our *nephesh*—soul.

Without intimacy, success becomes the barometer of our fulfillment. The spirit-filled *nephesh* safeguards us from the tyranny of a performance-oriented life. If not for the soul, busy servants could easy become robotic by the flurry of activity at both home and work. The soul rescues us by unleashing emotions such as sadness, joy, sympathy, and elation. Without the soul, we cannot jump for joy or fall to our knees in intercession. We are easily tempted to gauge our ministry on numbers, prosperity, and recognition, but this is merely a diversionary tactic of the dark side. Overlooking the devoted handful coming to our Bible study, we are depressed that the imaginary crowd somewhere out there does not show up. When numbers are valued over people, the soul kicks in and protects us from such estrangement. Kingdom business is family business. The soul continually reminds us of the kind of spiritual realities in which we are involved. The reality of being created with a living soul breaks down the invisible alarm system when others invade our space. Our spirit-filled *nephesh* constantly alerts us to our incompleteness as individuals and lures us into interdependence.

We groan for intimacy with one another, but yearn more emphatically for *hesed* with our Creator. "O God, you are my God...my soul thirsts for you, my body longs for you, in a dry and weary land where there is no water...Because your love [*hesed*] is better than life, my lips will glorify you...My soul will be satisfied" (Psa.63:1, 3, 5a). Again in Psalm 42:1, 2, "As the deer pants for streams of water, so my soul pants for you, O God. My soul thirsts for God, for the living God." The human soul may go to great lengths to bury the desire for *hesed* under a variety of defense mechanisms. When self-protection kicks into high gear, it's a sure indication that there is a past hurt in dire need of healing. *Hesed* offers the hardened, hurting heart an opportunity to be made whole through the love and prayers of other fellow sojourners. Surely, this is hard evidence for having received a soul. It is one of the spiritual realities that lie behind our existence as part of God's creation. The yearning, thirsty soul will be established, not as an employee of the divine CEO, but as a child of the Creator. Our soul demands nothing less.

2. Created with a Conscience

As image-bearers of a just Creator, we are given a conscience. People are created with a sense of right and wrong. C.S. Lewis describes this truth so succinctly.

> There is one thing, and only one, in the whole universe which we know more about than we could learn from external observation. That one thing is Man. We do not merely observe men, we are men. In this case we have, so to speak, inside information; we are in the know. And because of that, we know that men find themselves under a moral law, which they did not make, and cannot quite forget even when they try, and which they know they ought to obey.[7]

Lewis's moral law is really describing the conscience. The conscience makes us sit in judgment as to the rightness or wrongness of our deeds and attitudes. Acting as an internal judge and jury, the conscience hands down its verdict on everything. It is the conscience that pulls for the good guys and cheers when the bad guys are caught. Agitation wells up inside as we watch a plot thicken. When justice finally prevails at the end of the movie, our conscience breathes a sigh of relief.

Paul proves that everyone has been given a conscience that reflects a just God. He refers specifically to the Gentiles who are not taught the values contained in the law of God. Astonishingly, they "do by nature things required by the law...[and] show that the requirements of the law are written on their hearts, their consciences also bearing witness, and their thoughts now accusing, now even defending them" (Rom.2:14, 15). Paul verifies the powerful spiritual reality of our having been given a conscience that reflects heaven's justice.

Originally made to be our inner balance of justice, the conscience is now blurred by sin. Our ability to make proper judgments causes us to fall prey to the dark side (1 Tim.4:1, 2). The world turns upside down and inside out. Right is wrong and wrong is right. Good is called evil and evil is good. Sin leaves us squinting to see through our foggy conscience, but we can't see well enough to make accurate conclusions about anything. Without a clean, clear conscience, our judgments are faulty because sin pollutes our ability to discern right from wrong.

---

7. Lewis, C.S. p.33.

Yet even if it is blurry, the conscience can still bother us. Instead of repenting, however, the blurry conscience acts like an undercover cop, spotting criminal activity in everyone—everyone, that is, except for our own selves (Rom.2:1). We can easily point out other people's weaknesses because those same weaknesses are splattered all over our own conscience. We are all too familiar with it and eventually, our heart will undergo microscopic treatment on the same issue. We notice the specks of dust in someone else's eye, but we are oblivious to the big board in our eye (Matt.7:1, 2). Our issues have been lodged in us so long, even back to many previous generations, that we don't even know anything is there. The key to our deliverance is the question Jesus asks: "Why do you look at the speck of sawdust in your brother's eye and pay no attention to the plank in your own eye?" (v.3). Why do we look at the specks? Because our conscience is pointing them out. The conscience is God's awakening mechanism to expose the spiritual covert operations firmly attached to our personality. Only repentance, forgiveness, and renunciation remove sin and clean the conscience. A clear conscience is sensitive and free to lovingly minister in the delicate removal of someone else's sawdust (v.5).

Believers can readily embrace the benefits of a clean conscience before God. The cleansing power of the blood of Jesus clears and renews our thinking. A purified conscience enables us to draw near to God, boldly coming to his throne of grace, "with a sincere heart in full assurance of faith, having our hearts sprinkled to cleanse us from a guilty conscience" (Heb.10:22; cf. Heb.9:9-14; 10:1-4). Holding a sincere heart and a clean conscience, we genuinely "consider how we may spur one another on toward love and good deeds" (Heb.10:24).

3. *Created to Reign with God*

God reigns supreme. On the sixth day, however, he does make a risky spiritual transaction. He decides to delegate the administrative responsibilities of the earth to his newly created spirit-filled team. They are to be vassal-kings under the King. Created in his image, people are born to rule the earth

(Gen.1:28). We are created with the built-in desire to achieve, overcome, and attain proficiency, even to a high level of expertise. What drives one to succeed in business or to be the best husband or wife possible? What pushes us to strive to improve our tennis game or outmaneuver our teenage son in a go-cart race and teasingly gloat over our insignificant victories? There may be other reasons, but the inner drive to achieve and master things is part of being made in the image of a sovereign God. Just attend a committee meeting and it's obvious that every person has his or her own distinct opinion. Whose idea will win over all others? After attending countless meetings, we walk away from them thinking how we would have run it. We may be pretentious but it might, however, merely confirm that we are created to rule because we are made in the image of a sovereign God.

Adam is born to rule. He assigns names to all the animals in the garden. He is the manager-king under the King. Adam is created to achieve mastery over all circumstances arising from managing the earth. Under the lordship of God, Adam is to fasten his will on every predicament he faces and line it up with God's purposes. Man's dominion is not propelled by his desires or needs. It is based solely on the will of the King of kings.

There are a couple of prerequisites to properly using our God-given dominion. First, when appropriating authority, people are to be led and empowered by the Holy Spirit (Jn.14:12,16). By walking in the presence of the Spirit of God, Adam and Eve can make good decisions and fulfill their responsibilities to God, to one another, and to creation. Managerial or delegated authority still requires instructions from heaven and total dependence on God. So we are to be guided through prayer when exercising dominion. To come to God with our "grocery list" prayer, checking off each item, and ordering God to bag our requests and scurry to the trunk of our cars, is not exactly Spirit-led prayer! The Holy Spirit wants to help us pray in accordance with God's will (Rom.8:26,27). Waiting on the Lord and leaning on the Holy Spirit to lead us in prayer is of utmost importance in managing the earth.

Second, our "dominion guidebook" is the Word of God. Solomon has a dream where God promises to give him anything he wants. His remarkable request is for "a discerning heart to govern your people and to distinguish between right and wrong" and God commends him for it (1 Kgs.3:9). The Hebrew word for "discerning heart" implies receiving a "hearing heart." It is one that is able to hear and understand the voice of God. It is one thing to hear God's word but another to understand it, and quite another thing to respond in obedience to it. In Solomon's prayer, he beautifully points out that to reign with God as managers of the earth is to fill the earth with God's glory (Psa.72:1,2,8,19). Eventually, the whole earth will be filled with God's glory when dominion reaches its goal and the "kingdom of the world has become the kingdom of our Lord and of his Christ and he will reign forever and ever" (Rev.11:15b).

Elohim creates "Adam" male and female (Gen.1:26,27). *Elohim* is the plural form of El (the generic term for "god" or "God, the all-powerful") and so represents the plurality of persons in the trinity. We see this same plurality in the makeup of humanity (spirit-soul-body) and in the dynamics of the spiritual bond between God-man-woman. He makes them according to his kind so that they reflect his image. Created with a God-centered image, "Adam" is appointed to the position of joint-rulership. God designs the male and female together as "Adam" to fully express his image. One gender by itself cannot completely display the entire image of God. God purposely ordains the male-female relationship to be the sole reflection of his image on the earth. This explains why it's not good for the man to be alone. It isn't good for the woman to be alone either. God provides for man a helper who is suitable to assist in the job assignment.

Adam welcomes Eve as a soul mate and helpmate to share in the job assignment: to rule the earth as kings and priests unto God. Through interrelationships of joint rulership, cooperating in ministry and marriage, "Adam" carries out the purposes of God in the unity of the Spirit (cf. Eph.4:3). Simple maybe, but not easy. The plan releases men and women to fulfill God's will together. As joint-heirs with Christ, men and women together can display God's image in marriage and church leadership (Eph.5:21-6:9; 1 Cor.11:3,11; 12:28). All are valuable and equal in worth, for "there is neither Jew nor Greek, slave nor free, male nor female, for you are all one in Christ Jesus" and made in the image of God (Gal.3:28). This unique partnership implies neither inequality nor inferiority, but rather humble aptitude and respectful appreciation—one that is strikingly similar to Christ's relationship with God.

The family unit is designed to be a little church—a sanctuary where parents nurture, encourage, and teach their children to develop their gifts from God. Developing their spiritual gifts as they mature prepares children to flourish in their spiritual gifts as adults. When we see that to "submit to one another out of reverence for Christ" begins a section on Paul's teaching on the practical outworking of mutual submission in marriage, family life, and in the work situation (Eph.5:21-6:9), we can understand that mutual submission creates a healthy spiritual heritage. It really has nothing to do with battling over who wears the pants in the house. Truly, kingdom business begins in the home when parents reign in partnership as joint heirs in ministry and family life.

The spiritual reality of Eden shows no division between the sacred and the secular. The kingdom is the sanctuary of God and his king-priests supervise Eden's theocracy. It is the realm where God is King, where all activity is performed in his name. The creation of a vassal-kingdom of priests reveals the very heartbeat of God. Vassal-kings personally interact with the King and enjoy the honorable position of carrying out heaven's command. God's desire for intimacy with his king-priest managers never diminishes throughout history. Moses attests to God's desire for a kingdom of priests for the nation of Israel (Ex.19:5,6), and then Peter maintains God's continued aspirations to build his kingdom of priests in the Church, the Israel of God (1 Pet.2:5,9; cf. Rev.1:6; 5:10). God's original plan of operations has stayed its course, never changing directions or strategies, just like the character of its King.

God elevates Adam and Eve to a status that exceeds the rest of creation (Psa.8:5). Can they handle such a high level of managerial responsibility? Many people shrink back from advancement and responsibility, while others rise to the occasion—especially when the pressure is on. God commands Adam and Eve to have dominion, but he doesn't twist their arms. God gives them the choice to be either active or passive in their new position as co-managers of the whole earth.

The bird, fish, and animal kingdoms are not likely threatened by humanity's position. God already appointed rulers over the air, water, and land respectively. If anyone is uneasy about Adam's new position, it will most likely come from the darkness that surfaced on day one. One angel in particular is calculating a devious plan to test Adam and Eve. He wants to see if they are worthy of their image-bearing status of vassal-kings under the King. Unfortunately at the tree of the knowledge of good and evil, Adam and Eve fail miserably in all three areas of bearing God's image. Instead of standing secure in their identity from God, they lose all sense of identity.

To fully bear the image of God is to participate in the "image of God"—the judicial function of glory (discernment and dominion, cf. Gen.9:6) and to reflect the "likeness of God"—the ethical characteristics of glory (the transformation of character and the act of investiture, cf. 2 Cor.3:7-18; 4:4-6; also Gal.3:27; Eph.4:24; Col.3:10; Rom.13:14; 2 Pet.1:4, 16ff.). Nevertheless, in the fall, humanity becomes destitute of the glory of God (Rom.3:23) yet still maintains its judicial office as image-bearers of God (Gen.9:6; Ja.3:9). Sinful humanity loses its "likeness" to their Creator-God as the ethical dimension of glory is completely lost and is replaced by wickedness and shame.

Francis Schaeffer aptly describes our predicament since the fall:

> In his own naturalistic theories, with the uniformity of cause and effect in a closed system, with an evolutionary concept of a mechanical, chance parade from

the atom to man, man has lost his unique identity. As he looks out upon the world, as he faces the machine, he cannot tell himself from what he faces. He cannot distinguish himself from other things.[8]

Unable to "distinguish himself from other things," people scramble to find their self-identities in their careers, hobbies, ministries, finances, and even as fathers and husbands, mothers and wives. Many are searching to find themselves—anywhere outside of God himself. We handed over our relationships, our conscience, and our dominion to a jealous angel. Now helplessly captive to the law of sin and death, humanity drops their identity into the hands of a traitor.

---

8. Schaeffer, Francis. *Genesis in Space and Time*, (Downers Grove: InterVarsity, 1975), p.31.

Chapter Two

Emergence of an Unholy Spiritual Reality

A birthright belongs to the firstborn son. It is a legal term relegating the father's business to the firstborn son as an inheritance.[1] The birthright places responsibility on the firstborn son as head and caretaker of the family. It gives him the privilege of exercising jurisdiction over the father's estate. To comprehend our spiritual birthright as children in the family of God, we begin with the firstborn Son of God and the inheritance he received from his Father.

> He is the image of the invisible God, the firstborn over all creation. For by him all things were created: things in heaven and on earth, visible and invisible, whether thrones or powers or rulers or authorities;

---

1. Deuteronomy 21:15-17 sets forth the law of birthright. One example of this law is found in 2 Chronicles 21:3, while we see that Elijah applies the spirit of this law with Elisha in 2 Kings 2:9.

all things were created by him and for him. He is before all things, and in him all things hold together. Colossians 1:15-17

Being God's only Son, Jesus is appointed heir of all things and inherits all of creation (Heb.1:2, 6). He alone is entitled to it because it is his birthright. His two responsibilities are 1) to be head and caretaker of the family of God and 2) to exercise dominion over the Father's estate. He is head over the Church and head over all creation. This description of Christ as the head is not just a title of reverential esteem. Elohim's designation of Christ as head points directly to his functional position of authority within the trinity.[2]

Eden, the "garden in the east," is Adam's estate (Gen.2:8). Although no one can verify the exact location of Eden, we do know that a river flowed from it and that it separated into four headwaters, two of which are situated in ancient Mesopotamia, now the modern day country of Iraq (Gen.2:10-14). If the river of paradise is the source of the four rivers, it is likely that the path of the Fertile Crescent leads us straight to the promised land. This would explain why that particular spot is offered to Abraham as his inheritance. It is probably Eden.[3]

With such noble appointments over God's majestic estate, the darkness rumbles: "Is there a loophole in all these legal appointments?"

Target: Eden's Kingdom of Priests

If I leave my house in your charge while away on vacation, and I say, "Please take care of my cats and be sure to stay on

---

2. Theologically speaking, there are three "persons" in the Godhead. This can bring confusion to our understanding of his essence for we know that "God is Spirit" (Jn.4:24); he is not a human being or person. It is better to conceive of God as a personal, intimate God who is the embodiment of one substance and made up of three subsistances: Father, Son, and Holy Spirit, of which the whole indivisible essence of God belongs equally to each of the three (cf. Col.1:9; 2:9; Eph.3:19).
3. Cf. Magnus Ottosson, *"Eden and the Land of Promise,"* Supplement to Vetus Testamentum, Vol. 40, 1988, pp.177-188.

your guard!"—I am implying two things. I have two hungry cats that demand a lot of attention and I am alerting you about intruders in the neighborhood. While in the garden, God warns Adam about a tricky prowler who is going to try to steal, kill, and destroy everything. Since the first day of creation, an ominous, jealous angel has plotted to trick God's king-priests into making an unholy alliance with him.

As a kingdom of priests, believers are directed to fulfill two specific assignments: 1) to cultivate the garden and 2) to guard it against intrusion (Gen.2:15). The word "to tend" (*abad*) means "to cultivate, take care of, to work at." Just cultivating a backyard garden requires hard work and devotion, but this assignment extends far beyond pulling a few weeds. The meaning of *abad* is stated in a command: "Be fruitful and increase in number; fill the earth and subdue it" (Gen.1:28). To take care of the garden is to be fruitful, to increase, and to subdue. This is not just a mandate to fill the garden with children. Nor is it merely a solicitation to productivity. To be fruitful means to celebrate life! We are not survivors, merely existing day to day. We are created to develop and mature, to celebrate life in the presence of God. There is nothing better "than to be happy and do good…that everyone may eat and drink, and find satisfaction in all his toil—this is the gift of God" (Eccl.3:12,13). We delight in fulfilling our God-ordained mission and marvel in our reflection of his image—it is God's gift to us.

In addition to cultivating the garden, Adam and Eve are given a second assignment. "To keep" implies the imperative "to guard" (*shamar*). It is a warning about an immanent intruder. They are to defend the Edenic garden against any intrusion that is hostile to God and his kingdom purposes. God's appointed vassal-managers are to celebrate life, to bask in the warmth of his love, revel in his goodness—and defend the birthright, inheritance, and heritage that the Lord has given to them.

There are many trees in Eden, yet God points out just two trees planted in the heart of Eden (Gen.2:9). Why is the tree of the knowledge of good and evil even in this wondrous garden? Is God a prankster who wants to put Adam and Eve in jeopardy of losing their estate? No, the tree is an opportunity for them to display their devotion to their Creator and to present their true identity as king-priests made in the image of God. Times of testing prove the genuineness of our faith, which is "of greater worth than gold, which perishes even though refined by fire—may be proved genuine and may result in praise, glory and honor when Jesus Christ is revealed" (1 Pet.1:7). Trials subject God's king-priests to direct solicitations meant to provoke them to judge between good and evil—to choose life or death.

The reverberating factor in every trial originates in the paradigm testing tree. The same question is posed to every priest of Elohim: "Will you believe in God's character, trusting what he says is true, and serve him just because you love him?" Our other option is to dispute God's integrity, view him with suspicion, and serve him on the contingency of receiving certain benefits from him. The tree of testing is God's attempt to prove something about us, while at the same time, it is the dark side's attempt to swindle something from us.

The testing tree poses the opportunity for God's kings to rise to their place as image-bearers of the King. They are people of relationship; they're a team. Eve needs Adam to be her helper as much as he needs her. At the testing tree, they falter in their relationship with God and with each other. Instead of joining together in unity, their relationship crumbles under maleficent accusations.

They are people with a built-in conscience. The tree of the knowledge of good and evil is the place where their keen conscience can emerge. Trusting solely on God's word, Adam and Eve can confidently judge the matter at hand, for their conscience equips them to discern good from evil. To come to the tree of the knowledge of good and evil is to come to the tree as God's appointed judge. They have the capacity to know the difference between good and evil, so they are well able to discern the matter and choose the appropriate response. Unfortunately, Eve becomes deceived and fails to distinguish between good and evil. Adam is not deceived. He just plain rebels against his conscience and chooses evil (1 Tim.2:14).

They are people who have been given dominion. Adam and Eve are joint-heirs, co-laborers in the administration of God's kingdom. They manage the earth in joint rulership and are able to defend it against any hostile takeover.

> In the probation tree man found himself face to face with the claims of absolute lordship. Restricting man in the exercise of his royal authority and privileges, the probationary commandment compelled him to acknowledge that his own kingship was that of vassal-king, that the world was his only in stewardship...It appears...that the name of the tree pointed not so much to something man would acquire as to something he must do. It referred not to knowledge of a certain kind that he might gain, but to knowledge in action, knowledge engaged in pronouncing judgment.[4]

As kings, they have the authority and the equipment to maintain their territory. It is the intruder who is brought to this tree to be judged by God's kings. He doesn't belong in Eden. He is brought there to be judged and cast out. But at the testing tree, Adam and Eve relinquish their God-given authority and become slaves to a diabolical regime. The intruder takes advantage of Adam and Eve's failure to reflect God in all three areas: in their relationships, in their conscience, and in their dominion.

Why does God point out the bad tree? "You are free to eat from any tree in the garden; but you must not eat from the tree of the knowledge of good and evil, for when you eat of it you will surely die" (Gen.2:16). Eden displays a heavenly Father's concern. Why not say, "Hey, Adam! Eat the tree of life and live forever." It's like looking at a bowl of apples and noticing the badly bruised one. As a parent, I would say to my boys, "Go ahead and pick any of these apples, but be sure not to take that one." I'm not a dictator who makes every decision for them, but

---

4. Kline, pp.160, 162.

neither am I indifferent to their choices. If I pick out their apples for them, they miss out on a simple pleasure in life. I am also sending a subtle message, "I don't think you are responsible enough. I'll pick it out for you. You're unable to make the right choice." A simple bowl of apples can encourage responsibility and confidence or breed insecurity and rejection in the heart of a child.

Our heavenly Father desires his children to choose for themselves whom they will serve. Will we serve God? Or someone else? He wants Adam and Eve to boldly proclaim, "As for me and my household, we will serve the Lord" (Josh.24:15). In principle, the tree of the knowledge of good and evil is set before us every day. "See, I set before you today life and prosperity, death and destruction…blessings and curses. Now choose life, so that you and your children may live" (Deut.30:15, 19bc). Our choices can bring life and blessing or poison us against the richness of true spirituality. The testing tree is Adam and Eve's opportunity to choose life—and rebuke the intruder.

What would have happened if they chose to partake of the tree of life? Eden would likely have entered an eschatological transformation and eternity would have been heralded. Unfortunately, tasting the poisoned fruit from the tree of the knowledge of good and evil banishes Adam and Eve from the eternal tree of life. Devoid of conscience, selfish in their relationships, and abusive to their environment, humanity could annihilate themselves and creation by biting into the eternal tree of life. So guardianship of the garden and the tree of life is transferred from Adam to the cherubim holding their flaming swords (Gen.3:24). The tree of life remains a restricted area until God's cherubim are finally relieved of their duties when the door to paradise is opened once again by the second Adam (Rev.2:7). When the eternal state is consummated, the tree of life is found residing in the middle of the river of life that proceeds from the throne of God (Rev.22:1,2). It stands as a prophetic symbol of the Lord's faithfulness to a faithless people.

Heaven's admonition is crystal clear: "You will surely die" (Gen.2:17c). Death delays consummation and threatens to permeate everything, particularly Adam's relationship with God. To "surely die" means more than physical death. It is the demise of relationships, the decay of their identities, and the doom of the whole world. Adam and Eve are suddenly in danger of eating something that poisons them. Sin and death threatens to penetrate every area of life.

The garden seems so peaceful—so perfect for Adam and Eve. Why all this talk about death and dying? Isn't it a bit ridiculous to be on guard—in Eden? Who would sabotage the garden? God is acting like one of those overprotective fathers. The plant and animal kingdoms are well cared for. The monkeys and tigers have no reason to undermine Adam's dominion. Who in the world feels threatened by the divine order?

Apparently someone within the angelic ranks becomes a green-eyed monster. Who is man, anyway? And why does God make them higher in position than angels in the divine economy? Angels were created before human beings even existed. They sang together and shouted for joy while they watched the magnificent Creator fasten the foundations of the world and lay its cornerstone (Job 38:7). God creates his angels as spirits; they are his ministers of flaming fire (Psa.104:4). Man is part dust, for heaven's sake! What an insult to angels everywhere! If anyone should be given authority to rule the world, shouldn't it be the best angel? Because of man's honored place as king-priests to God, a jealous angel sets in motion his diabolical plan to pervert God's beautiful creation into a treacherous prison for man and beast. He wants the estate. But legally, he has no grounds to usurp Adam's birthright and inheritance. He must find a legal loophole.

Lucifer the Legalist

To fully understand the fall of man, we must examine the original order in heaven. We see God—the Father, Son, and Holy Spirit—reigning over all. He creates an angelic organization to help mankind fulfill their destiny as king-priests. In God's administration, angels play a particularly important role. They are the *UPS* of kingdom business. They act as messengers sent out from the heavenly boardroom to either relay or carry out assignments for men. "Are not all angels ministering spirits sent to serve those who will inherit salvation?" (Heb.1:14). Their jobs coincide with their rank. The original angelic alliance operates under an appointed hierarchical structure. "For by him all things were created: things in heaven and on earth, visible and invisible, whether thrones or powers or rulers or authorities; all things were created by him and for him" (Col.1:16). In this passage these angelic beings are described in their original state, while the rest of the passages in the New Testament infer that these beings represent evil's counterfeit organization.

God entrusts certain angels to leadership positions as members of his heavenly court. Some scholars believe that seven specific angels are given special assignments before the Lord (Rev.8:2). Three archangels are mentioned by name in Scripture: Michael, Gabriel, and Lucifer. The other four are found outside the Bible, in both the scrolls of Qumran and the Apocrypha: Raphael, Sariel, Uriel, and Jeremiel. Biblical passages surrounding the first three archangels suggest that Michael is the valiant "Commander of Military Affairs," Gabriel is the honorable "Speaker-of-God's-House," and as we look at Ezekiel 28, Lucifer may be viewed as the "Chief Magistrate."[5] It is not until after the fall that God stations the remaining two faithful cherubim, Michael and Gabriel, to guard the tree of life with their flaming swords (Gen.3:24).

---

5. The irregular literary style of Ezekiel 28:11-19 makes it difficult to classify as prose or poetry. However, Ezekiel's portrayal of the king of Tyre in Edenic imagery marks the passage as poetry and therefore gives ground for typological interpretation. "During the second temple period, the view developed that Ezek.28 was based on a tradition of an angelic "fall," closely associated with the "fall" of humanity. Since the time of Origen many conservative Christians in particular have equated the king of Tyre with Lucifer… Accordingly, Ezekiel's prophecy is thought to recount the circumstances of the original fall of Satan, who had previously been one of the cherubim attending the throne of God. But those who interpret the oracle historically reject this approach" (Daniel Block, *The Book of Ezekiel, Chapters 25-48, NICOT*, Grand Rapids: Eerdmans, 1998, p.118).

It is Lucifer who is the mastermind behind the darkness of day one. Only Lucifer becomes disgruntled and jealous. Why Lucifer? He is described as "the model of perfection," or better translated, "the seal of perfection" (Ezek.28:12b). In the ancient Near East, seals are mainly used to signify authority or authenticity of letters or documents (1 Kgs.21:8; Esth.3:12; 8:8-10; Jer.32:11-14; Neh.9:38; 10:1). Apparently, Lucifer perfectly executes every legal technicality when it comes to approaching the Creator. Both Job and Ezekiel portray Lucifer-turned-Satan as originally being deputized with full legal authority and flawlessly crafted to hold legal status—even after the fall of man. He continues to legalistically carry out his perverted ministry of misery based on the technicalities of sin. Job describes this deranged luciferic Leviathan as becoming unstoppable because he layers seals and shields onto his battered victims (Job 41, especially v.15).

The legalist is "full of wisdom and perfect in beauty" (Ezek.28:12b) and while still in Eden, the astute magistrate of justice is colorfully adorned with every precious gemstone imaginable (v.13). These gems seem to be worn as some kind of priestly robe. It is no coincidence that later, the garments worn by the high priest during the Mosaic era fit a similar description (Ex.28:17-20; 39:10-13). What is the meaning of the imagery of wearing gemstones? Stone imagery is closely connected to covenant-witness. "Stones appear as witnesses… A covenant is made, a sacrificial meal is eaten, and stones serve as witnesses (Gen.31:44-54). Archaeologists have uncovered several circles of stones (some with eyes or hands on them) almost certainly representing witnesses to covenants or other religious rites."[6] These precious gemstones worn by legal priestly-executors symbolize their legal authority to approach the throne of God based on corporate loyalty to covenant obligations. This makes sense if we view Lucifer as heaven's top legal consultant.[7]

---

6. Ryken, Leland, Wilhoit, James, and Longman, Tremper. *Dictionary of Biblical Imagery*, (Downers Grove: InterVarsity Press, 1998), p.815.

7. Walter Eichrodt states that "Originally, indeed, *hassatan* designates an angel of Yahweh entrusted with a particular task. He is the Public Prosecutor or District Attorney, who brings men's guilt to God's remembrance," (Old Testament Theology, Philadelphia: Westminster, 1975, p.205)

Although Ezekiel 28:13,14 is difficult to translate in both the Hebrew Masoretic Text (MT) and the Greek Septuagint (LXX), we can speculate as to Lucifer's original position in the heavenlies. Ezekiel 28:13c uses three Hebrew words, which poses difficulties in translation: 1) *melaket* which could mean "workmanship, business, craftsmanship", 2) *tuppeka* which is ambiguous, but may derive from *yapa*, "beauty" or *tapap*, "to beat" explaining the translation "your tabrets," and 3) *neqabeka* which is also uncertain, but may derive from *naqab*, "to pierce" thus alluding to "hammer" or possibly "chisel." Even though these Hebrew words make Lucifer's original job description obscure, we must not lose sight of Ezekiel's highlighted imagery. He portrays Lucifer as a beautiful attorney general whose job is to oversee interaction with the sovereign Creator.

Before the fall, there is no element of sin and rebellion. It is therefore logical that Lucifer would be "anointed as a guardian cherub" who is set to watch over any legal (or later, illegal) approach to worship God (Ezek.28:14a). This is clearly seen when Satan later approaches God to spitefully analyze Job's character and his devotion to God (Job 1,2). He is the "accuser of our brothers, who accuses them before our God day and night" (Rev.12:10; cf. Zech.3:1-3). Lucifer's original position in the heavenly court clearly explains the legalistic tendency of Satan and his demons to promptly enter doors opened to them and to stubbornly resist ground given to them through man's sinful actions. Only through the shed blood of Christ and the forgiveness of sin is the legalistic accuser hurled down from his evil podium (Rev.12:10). In Christ's New Covenant, prior perverse covenants are broken, our relationship with God is reestablished, and Satan's technical accusations against us hold no weight in God's court of law. The guilty are set free in Christ.

Lucifer's description, "the anointed guardian cherub," actually alludes to the meaning of his name: "son of the morning." Like the aurora of the morning, Lucifer brilliantly coordinates the rallying of the heavenly host to God like the sun dawns radiantly across the horizon. His legal-priestly position enables the hosts of heaven to light up the universe as they approach the

Creator. God anoints him for the monumental task of shielding or supervising everyone, in heaven and on earth, in their covenantal interaction with God. But Lucifer has another plan and the strategy is simple: seduce humanity into breaking covenant relations with God, offer them perverse contracts with evil—so that he can be a legal shield to separate them from their Creator.

"Every precious stone adorned you…Your heart became proud on account of your beauty, and you corrupted your wisdom because of your splendor" (Ezek.28:13,17ab). This reveals the root cause of Lucifer's descent. It is his self-image. Lucifer emerges as the mastermind behind distorted concepts of self-esteem. He reasons that he is the ideal angel, the beautiful model of perfection, and everyone should recognize him as such. So Lucifer sets out to realize his full potential and extend his sphere of influence. For the sake of his splendor he must be the center of the universe. He alone deserves this position. Michael and Gabriel, who are his peers, are evidently milquetoast in comparison. They don't hold a candle to his brilliance, let alone those dusty creatures, Adam and Eve. Lucifer thinks so highly of himself that he resolves to make this positive confession in his heart:

> I will ascend to heaven; I will raise my throne above the stars of God;
> I will sit enthroned on the mount of assembly, on the utmost heights of the sacred mountain.
> I will ascend above the tops of the clouds; I will make myself like the Most High.
> Isaiah 14:13,14

Rebellion is the fruit of Lucifer's arrogant heart.

Commencing a Perverted Mission

The nature of pride finds its source in self-misrepresentation. The heart defrauds itself when it aspires to exalt itself beyond its true condition. In order to exalt self, one must be convinced that one has no deficiencies, no needs, and no limitations. The heart persuades itself that it is completely self-sufficient. The proud really believe they are exceptional—special, above all the rest. Elitism leads the proud right into the arena of competition. "By pride comes only contention," and out to prove their extraordinary distinction, the proud are constantly trying to verify themselves as superiors (Prov.13:10a, NKJV).

Competition can't just be good old-fashioned fun for the proud. To win or to lose, being the best dressed or worst dressed takes on monumental meaning. An incident of competition at its worst, is the story of two aspiring American Olympic ice skaters. One became tangled in a plot to put the competition out of commission. Pride led a gifted athlete into a downward spiral of delusion. The proud are so consumed with themselves that they become irrational. After observing many prideful people Solomon quips: "Pride goes before destruction, a haughty spirit before a fall" (Prov.16:18). The road of pride may wind around many curves of deception, but the final destination is always self-destruction.

With his headquarters situated on the holy mountain of God, Lucifer walks back and forth on the carpet of fiery stones that line his office. He was perfect until the iniquity of pride swells into a violent attitude (Ezek.28:14,15). Therefore, God fires him from his position as Chief Magistrate and casts him out of the mountain of God (v.16). But before Lucifer leaves office, he defiles his sanctuaries by persuading one-third of his fellow angelic workers to join with him in his revolt (v.18; cf. Rev.12:4). Prior to Lucifer's uprising, the angels are classified according to their task in God's kingdom (Col.1:16) and even after insurrection, there remains a distinction between lesser and higher, more powerful demons. Paul's use of certain Greek words place demons in ranks, beginning with the lowest rank, "rulers" or "principalities" (*archai*), then "authorities" (over a certain sphere or designated jurisdiction), then "powers (*kosmokrator*) of this dark world" (spirit beings who control parts of the world system), and then the highest listed authority over all demonic ranks, "spiritual forces of evil in the heavenly realms" (Eph.6:12). Their range of influence appears to encompass individual oppression and full demonization to generational bondage, and to a greater degree, influencing the spheres of government officials and the affairs of entire nations. But Lucifer has exchanged his anointed beauty and honorable position to forever be a horror to the nations (Ezek.28:14-18).

Pride easily raises its ugly head. Enjoying the afterglow of a successful ministry crusade, the seventy followers of Christ return to him saying, "Lord, even the demons submit to us in your name" (Lk.10:17). Their testimony smells a little prideful, so Jesus responds, "I saw Satan fall like lightning from heaven" (v.18). Pride caused Satan to be fired from his post—so fast it made the other angels' heads spin. God kicked Lucifer out of his heavenly headquarters like lightning crashes down out of the sky. Jesus is warning the seventy of the dangers of pride. Having received authority over all the power of the enemy, they are to maintain a grateful, humble heart (vv.19,20). Arrogance my "feel good" but it leads one unknowingly down Lucifer's path.

Convinced of his own deception, Lucifer must occupy the throne of God. He devises an evil strategy to confiscate what rightly belongs to humanity. Lucifer incorporates his plan to rule the world so that he may capture the recognition he thinks he so eminently deserves. The cunning angel has been waiting since day one to set his hideous game plan in motion in the garden. When Lucifer appears in Eden, every precious stone adorns him; he is the seal of perfection, full of wisdom and perfect in beauty until iniquity came to its full fruition (Ezek.28:12,13).

Lucifer begins his strategy by bartering with Eve at the tree of the knowledge of good and evil. Lucifer is a slick lawyer who desires to cut a deal. He proposes the sinister business transaction. "Through your widespread trade you were filled with violence, and you sinned. So I drove you in disgrace from the mount of God, and I expelled you, O guardian cherub…By your many sins and dishonest trade you have desecrated your sanctuaries" (Ezek.28:16, 18). Lucifer offers to trade places with

Adam and Eve. He must have thought, "I'll get to be king over the world and they'll think they can be gods. Ha!" The swindle cost him his heavenly job, and God hurls Lucifer like a lightning bolt, straight out of heaven—but Lucifer's tail drew a third of the angels along with him (Rev.12:4, 9). Lucifer "trades places" with Adam and becomes the god of this world, but Adam and Eve are duped. They didn't achieve godhood. This is no trade! They are swindled out of their mission in life, they lose their estate, and they are left completely bankrupt.

Lucifer must now implement his perverse mission: 1) to deceive the world into making legal alliances with evil, and 2) to desecrate any signs of rebuilding a resting place, a sanctuary of God. This two-fold mission has one goal in mind: to set up his apostate, antichrist kingdom. History proves that Lucifer is not altering his intentions. He mercilessly assaults the image-bearers. Let's look at his diabolical two-fold mission more closely.

In the garden, Lucifer appears in the form of a serpent, not as an angel. Revelation 12:9 and 20:2 confirm that it is Satan who is "that ancient serpent" who appears here in Eden. Out of all the animals of the garden, why does Lucifer choose to appear in reptilian form? Why not a spider, or lion, or a tyrannosaurus rex? The serpent is "more crafty than any of the wild animals the Lord God had made" (Gen.3:1). Lucifer finds in the serpent just the right character features necessary to project his own character. "Crafty" means to be skillful or ingenious. Remember, Lucifer is not only perfect in beauty, but also full of wisdom (Ezek.28:12). The serpent is the closest in character to him out of all the creatures in the garden. Animals are commonly linked to personalities: "She is as graceful as a swan," or "Our leader is as bold as a lion." Even Jesus considers serpents to be wily and shrewd (Matt.10:16).

The serpent's wisdom, nonetheless, is shaded with dark tones. In Psalm 58:3-4, David compares the serpent's poisonous venom to the deadly effects of lying: "Even from birth the wicked go astray; from the womb they are wayward and speak lies. Their venom is like the venom of a snake, like that of a cobra that has stopped its ears." The serpent is a liar.

The deadly serpent that fastened onto Paul's arm on the island of Malta typologically reflects the New Covenantal appropriation of authority over evil.

> The islanders showed us unusual kindness. They built a fire and welcomed us all because it was raining and cold. Paul gathered a pile of brushwood and, as he put it on the fire, a viper, driven out by the heat, fastened itself on his hand. When the islanders saw the snake hanging from his hand, they said to each other, "This man must be a murderer; for though he escaped from the sea, justice has not allowed him to live." But Paul shook the snake off into the fire and suffered no ill effects. Acts 28:2-5

Paul shook off the viper's attack and flung him into the fire. His response to the serpent is the way that Adam and Eve are to judge and convict Lucifer as the intruder at the testing tree. They are to rebuke the lying intruder with truth.

Lucifer's first move is to go for the woman. Why Eve? Why not Adam? Teachings that stereotype women as being inferior to men infer that the serpent takes advantage of Eve because she is the "weaker" sex. This is a misguided interpretation of 1 Peter 3:7 where Peter admonishes husbands to "be considerate as you live with your wives, and treat them with respect as the weaker partner and as heirs with you of the gracious gift of life." The Greek word for partner is *skeuei*, which indicates a jar or dish that is made for a particular purpose (i.e. pickle jars, soup bowls, water basins, and pots for stew). Each vessel has its own mission in daily life. Paul picks up this same principle, but uses a different analogy. Instead of using the phrase "weaker partners-jars," he calls them "weaker parts."

> Those parts of the body that seem to be weaker are indispensable, and the parts that we think are less honorable we treat with special honor. And the parts that are unpresentable are treated with special modesty, while our presentable parts need no special

treatment. But God has combined the members of the body and has given greater honor to the parts that lacked it, so that there should be no division in the body, but that its parts should have equal concern for each other. 1 Corinthians 12:22-25

In this age of political correctness, nobody wants to be called weak or less honorable or unpresentable. Yet God refers to the weaker vessels as necessary parts of the body. It is on the "less honorable, the unpresentable parts" that we are to bestow greater honor.

The term "weaker partners-parts" has nothing to do with physical limitations, emotional instability, or inferior status. The inference to weakness is really a matter of visibility and recognition. A vessel is weak because it is covered, or in Paul's words, because of its need for modesty. In other words, these parts of the body are not as visible as other more prominent ministries (1 Cor.12:27-31). Weaker vessels are not inferior vessels. They are the unassuming, unknown servants of God. Jesus tells his disciples about invisible vessels that perform their charitable deeds without blowing a trumpet. They actually pray to God without anybody knowing about it—and they fast without receiving the admiration of other people (Matt.6:1-18). Weaker members are not often recognized because most of them are probably involved in behind-the-scenes ministries of the church. Many in the Body of Christ are really unsung heroes. Peter encourages the more visible ministers to honor the weaker members, for without them, they cannot function as a body (1 Pet.3:7).

So why did the serpent go for Eve? Eve is the ticket to Adam's heart. The serpent says to Eve, "Did God really say, 'You must not eat from any tree in the garden'?" Eve replies, "We may eat fruit from the trees in the garden, but God did say, 'You must not eat from the tree that is in the middle of the garden, and you must not touch it, or you will die'" (Gen.3:1b-3). The serpent cunningly twists the word of God, but Eve gives it a further twist. Unabashedly, Lucifer aims straight for the tree meant to judge him. Oh, the audacity of freely twisting the word of God into evidence to lay charges against God himself. Lucifer is trespassing and should be on the defense. Instead, he proceeds arrogantly on the attack. Can Eve properly interpret God's word? Quoting only half of God's stipulation, the serpent begins to lie through his teeth. James Sire brings insight into the matter of Scripture twisting.

> The Bible has long been a book that commands attention. If you can employ it in the service of your own cause, you can gain for your cause a certain credibility…When Scripture is quoted, especially at the beginning of an argument which turns out to promote a cult doctrine or point of view, it may be that it is being used primarily as a hook to grasp the attention of readers or listeners. "The Bible says" gets the attention, but what follows the quotation may be far from traditional Christian teaching and far from the intention of the Bible itself.[8]

Lucifer's hook is to quote the word of God, but he prefaces it with a suspicious interrogation of the implications of God's character. Like a slick lawyer, he casts reasonable doubt over God's integrity and therefore undermines God's authority. Implicit in his suspicions is the inference that Eve hasn't really grasped the meaning of God's word. He is right.

Unable to quote Scripture word for word, Eve adds a peculiar clause: "You must not touch it." Maybe in her conversations with Adam, they said something like: "Let's not go near that tree—let's not even touch it!" Whatever made Eve come up with this odd increment, the important thing is she made an addition to the word of the Lord. Confusion enters the scene when we add or subtract from the truth. The Hindu leader, Maharishi Mahesh Yogi, adds this to the words of Jesus, "Christ said, 'Be still and know that I am God.' Be still and know that you are God

---

8. Sire, James W. *Scripture Twisting, 20 Ways the Cults Misread the Bible*, (Downers Grove: InterVarsity, 1980), pp.41-42.

and when you know that you are God you will begin to live Godhood, and living Godhood there is no reason to suffer."[9] Sounds like Maharishi has sat under the teachings of the serpent himself. By adding to the word of God, Eve was already confused. Unfortunately, confusion ultimately leads to deception.

Eve heard the word of the Lord, but it never took root in her heart. A seed of truth is sown in her heart, but she did "not understand it, [so then] the evil one comes and snatches away what was sown" (Matt.13:19). Or maybe she heard the word and received it with joy, but since she has "no root…lasts only a short time. When trouble or persecution comes because of the word, [she] quickly falls away" (vv.20,21). Eve probably did not take the time to meditate and pray through this word from God, so it never became a revelation to her. To hear and humbly accept the word planted in her would have saved her from deception (Ja.1:21,22). God's word to Eve never got implanted in her heart.

Confused and on the defensive, Eve falls right into the hands of Lucifer. "'You will not surely die,' the serpent said to the woman. 'For God knows that when you eat of it your eyes will be opened, and you will be like God, knowing good and evil'" (Gen.3:4,5). All of Lucifer's four points *are* lies. The truth is: 1) they will die (Eph.2:1), 2) their eyes will be made blind (2 Cor.4:3,4), 3) they will be most unlike God, being alienated from the life of God (Eph.2:2,3; 1 Pet.4:3), and 4) their conscience will be so darkened they will have trouble discerning good from evil (Rom.1:21c,22; Isa.5:20,21). Jesus did not mince words when describing Satan: "He was a murderer from the beginning, not holding to the truth, for there is no truth in him. When he lies, he speaks in his native language, for he is a liar and the father of lies" (Jn.8:44). Eve takes hold of the scriptural hook and is bamboozled with falsehood.

Suddenly Eve contemplates the feasibility of a vigilant, jealous God who is reluctant to share his privileged position with others. Eve ponders the apparent concern of the serpent. She wonders, "Is this so-called 'forbidden tree' our ticket to reaching

---

9. Yogi, Maharishi Mahesh. *Meditations of Maharishi Mahesh Yogi*, (New York: Bantam, 1968), p.178.

our full potential? How selfish of God to limit us! Is God really a cruel tyrannical liar? Maybe the serpent has come to liberate us from God's oppression and enable us to assert our rights." Sounds like Eve is converting to Lucifer's corrupt doctrine. Lucifer commissions her to be his first missionary: "When the woman saw that the fruit of the tree was good for food and pleasing to the eye, and also desirable for gaining wisdom, she took some and ate it. She also gave some to her husband, who was with her, and he ate it" (Gen.3:6).

> Eve perceives in the fruit certain commendable assets...It is nutritious. It is not unhealthy nor cancer producing. It is not "junk food"...Eve was not only a primeval nutritionist, she also was aesthetically inclined. She appreciates beauty. Finally the tree helps her education. She is concerned to become a wiser and more educated person. What could be better than taking care of her body, choosing something pleasurable and beautiful, becoming wiser and more educated, and moreover, at the same time? Is God against food, beauty and education?[10]

Obviously, the answer is no. God desires us to be good stewards of our bodies. It is the temple of the Holy Spirit. He also wants us to enjoy his beautiful creation and grow in wisdom and knowledge. The issue is not whether Adam and Eve will become like God. This is the serpent's greatest lie. The issue is will they love God and serve him, or will they narcissistically love themselves and serve the serpent. Eve's problem is that she uses the commendable assets of the testing tree to justify her desire to find fulfillment outside of her Creator.

Eve rejects the lordship of God and believes in the greatest hoax in the history of the world. She is duped into believing that converting to the serpent's new religion will bring about the realization of her godhood. To the college crowd in the taverns,

---

10. Spencer, Aida Besancon. *Beyond the Curse, Women Called to Ministry*, (Nashville: Thomas Nelson, 1985), pp.32-33.

parties are fun at the beginning. When entering his thirties, the party animal is now called "the alcoholic." Not much fun for his family, he has become enslaved to his drink. So also the tree of the knowledge of good and evil might appear like sparkling wine swirling around in its glass, but it leaves the biting aftertaste of the serpent. Eve doesn't realize that the serpent's theology means imprisonment, not freedom to reach her full potential. It means bondage to sin and death, not liberation to godhood. The serpent lied to her.

Eve swallows Lucifer's lie—hook, line and sinker. She truly believes in the serpent's lie. As Lucifer's first convert, she becomes his first proselytizer. She doesn't have to look very far. Adam was with her all along (Gen.3:6c). He watches the whole ordeal and idly stands by. Is Adam duped along with his wife? "Adam was not the one deceived; it was the woman who was deceived" and literally fell into transgression (1 Tim.2:14). Adam sees through the whole escapade. He should have stood up and run to rescue his wife by saying, "It is written...!" and rebuked the intruder. Adam knows what is going down and still chooses to join the serpent's religion. Why? Why would Adam convert to a religion that he knew to be false? Why would any husband join his wife's church even though he didn't believe in its doctrine? The answer, of course, is that Adam loves Eve. He loves her more than God.

Evil did not originate in God, but it came through the free will of a fallen angel. It was supposed to have been Lucifer's judgment day. But it became the day that Adam and Eve lost their place as joint rulers over the world and traded their kingly position for slavery. Instead of ruling and reigning over creation, the world became a hostile place for human beings. Lucifer's perverse mission has been inaugurated. He founded his religion on deception and will soon gather a huge following. Some will refuse to join his regime so Lucifer will persecute them and attempt to set up his abomination of desolation in their midst. The story of history is how Lucifer, now renamed as Satan, the adversary of God, attempts to set up his apostate antichrist kingdom in opposition to the kingdom of God.

Chapter Three

The Spiritual Reality of Enmity

Adam and Eve "heard the sound (*ruach*) of the Lord God as he was walking in the garden in the cool (*ruach*) of the day" (Gen.3:8). Within this verse the various meanings of *ruach* (voice, spirit, breath, wind) come into play. God is not being described as taking a leisurely stroll in the garden. On the contrary, the connotation is that God has come down into the garden "in the spirit of the day"—as in a day of visitation or judgment. This begins a series of supernatural interventions by the Lord known throughout the Old Testament as "the day of the Lord." It is a day where God "visits" the earth with judgment. In the garden, the Creator-Lord steps into his chambers as the heavenly judge and with his verdict draws a line to divide two emerging cities.

Eden Becomes a Courtroom

By partaking of the tree of the knowledge of good and evil, the eyes of Adam and Eve "were opened, and they realized they were naked" (Gen.3:7). This idiom illustrates their shame. When sin enters the heart, the conscience automatically feels a sense of guilt. Instead of being conscious of God's presence and enjoying the sweetness of fellowship, they are now shamed by the legalist. Suddenly disconnected from God, Adam and Eve sense a loss of identity. Separated from their Creator, they feel awkward; humanity cannot comprehend who they really are without relating somehow to something. They embark on the futile pursuit to find themselves apart from God, seeking to find meaning in anything but him.

Adam and Eve agree to regroup and start up a new business venture. They try their hand at custom tailoring made from the finest fig leaves. Adam prefers the basic green and brown leaves, while Eve has difficulty deciding. Where did they purchase the new line of fig apparel? From the tree they just ate from—the tree of the knowledge of good and evil. They stitch up and put on their new religious uniform and openly affirm their affiliation with the serpent's cult. This causes a dilemma to rise in the hearts of Adam and Eve. Though their hearts harden in sin and rebellion, they are still made in God's image. The conscience maintains its role as catalyst for repentance. By sewing clothes for themselves, they admit their shame, declare their alliance with Lucifer, and disconnect themselves from each other. The Judge's verdict will accentuate the latter consequence.

The Lord calls out to Adam, "Where are you?" (Gen.3:9). God has not lost sight of them. He is giving Adam an opportunity to come out and fess up. Their eyes are "open" in the sense that in the moments after committing a sin, there is window of grace that God offers the guilty to give them time to repent. Adam dodges his guilty conscience and refuses to own his sin. He bases his defense on fear—fear of a severe and oppressive God. "I heard you in the garden, and I was afraid because I was naked; so I hid myself" (v. 10). The Lord gives him another chance to confess: "Who told you that you were naked?" (v. 11a). Someone must have immediately stepped in to accuse and shame them (Rev.12:10). This is God's way of appealing to Adam's conscience. In essence, the Lord is saying, "Who is it,

Adam, that made you feel ashamed? What did you do?" Then God takes the direct approach: "Have you eaten from the tree that I commanded you not to eat from?" (v. 11b). God is gracious to give Adam ample opportunities to come clean. Adam refuses, sidesteps the issue, and astonishingly, blames God for giving him a wife.

God turns to Eve. He is signaling that he is done listening to Adam's closing arguments. Adam's poor defense brings on his own verdict. The Lord gives the same opportunity for Eve to confess: "'What is this you have done?' And the woman said, 'The serpent deceived me, and I ate'" (Gen.3:13). At least she told the truth. She confessed! But confession is not repentance. People readily admit to struggling with sin. They often claim license to operate in sin by declaring it to be their weakness. Confession, therefore, precipitates repentance, but does not automatically usher in its cleansing power. So what qualifies as true repentance—and what evidence is there to ensure that it is genuine?

> Yet now I am happy, not because you were made sorry, but because your sorrow led you to repentance. For you became sorrowful as God intended and so were not harmed in any way by us. Godly sorrow brings repentance that leads to salvation and leaves no regret, but worldly sorrow brings death. See what this godly sorrow has produced in you: what earnestness, what eagerness to clear yourselves, what indignation, what alarm, what longing, what concern, what readiness to see justice done. At every point you have proved yourselves to be innocent in this matter. 2 Corinthians 7:9-11

God does not rejoice in our sorrow. He rejoices when sorrow leads to repentance. God desires Adam and Eve to experience godly sorrow that produces repentance to salvation. Eve has the sorrow of the world. She drowns in self-pity, like so many of her future followers, a casualty of victimization. Christians are easily caught in the dregs of the world's deadly sorrow. Warped confessions such as, "The devil made me do it," or "It's my parents' fault," are not really confessions at all. We act like Adam, blaming anyone but ourselves. Eve confesses her sin, but does not repent. Therefore it produces death.

The Verdict

The heavenly Judge announces the sentence of judgment on the mutinous threesome. Interpreting the verdict, it is vital to note that Genesis 3:14-19 is Hebrew poetry.[1] Hebrew poetry uses profoundly vivid imagery to convey deep truths from ordinary matter. Biblical poets masterfully employ figurative speech that often startles the reader, like a surrealist painting shocks its viewers the first time. Hebrew poetry is figurative, that is to say, its meaning is real, but not literal. The biblical poet paints pictures out of words. Parallelism is the other main feature of Hebrew poetry. The first line of thought parallels the second with a comparison or contrast of ideas. Keeping these factors in mind, let's examine the verdict from the fall.

God begins sentencing with the serpent. Lucifer receives the indictment of being cursed above all in the animal kingdom and is thrown down on his belly to eat dust (Gen.3:14). This is classic Hebrew poetry. Cursed above and beyond all the beasts emphasizes the immensity of the curse.[2] God throws Lucifer down to the earth so hard that he skids on his belly. Hebrew poetry comes alive in the deeper truths that lie behind the literal statements. Man is created out of dust and his body of flesh becomes food for Satan. God curses Satan, demotes him to the status of death angel, the destroyer and devourer of

---

1. Most Bibles will indent the lines or stanzas of Hebrew poetry so that the student of the Old Testament will have a clue whether a text is narrative or poetry. It is important to note that one-third of the Old Testament is written in Hebrew poetry. Rules for interpreting Hebrew poetry are based primarily on imagery and parallelism.
2. The phrase, "above all the livestock and all the wild animals" is poetic parallelism. "Livestock" and "wild animals" are figures of speech, namely synechdoche. A *synechdoche* is a word that represents the whole by a part, or a part by the whole. In other words, "livestock" and "wild animals" are parts that represent the whole of creation. Another example of *synechdoche* is "Give us this day our daily bread"—bread being the part that represents all needs.

man's dust-body. Lucifer, once the seal of perfection, and Chief Magistrate, is forever cursed as the angel of death. God is not locked into time and space. He is Spirit and he is eternal. In his foreknowledge, he knows the beginning and the end. By placing animosity between the godly line and the evil seed of the serpent, God is declaring spiritual war. The battle for souls is played out on the earth's turf. The seed of the serpent derive their nature from Satan and stand in opposition to God while building their City of Man. The obvious candidates of this evil line include Hitler, Stalin, Pol Pot, Mao Tse-tung, serial killers, and others who have committed horrific deeds. But then Jesus shocks most of us when he adds the Pharisees to the list. They are not mass murderers—they are religious leaders. Jesus points to them and says: "You belong to your father the devil, and you want to carry out your father's desire" (Jn.8:44). 1 John 3:8 is even more forceful, "He who does what is sinful is of the devil, because the devil has been sinning from the beginning."

The seed of the woman are the faithful believers in God. The righteous line serves the Lord and seeks to build his eternal city. God is their Father, therefore they are born of the Spirit, born from above (Jn.3:3-7). The seed of the serpent and the seed of the woman do not propagate biologically, but spiritually. The lines are being drawn. One is either in the kingdom of darkness or in the kingdom of light. There is no kingdom of gray.

Genesis 3:15 not only forms two corporate lines, it also the first messianic prophecy in the Bible. The individual seed of the serpent is Satan himself. The seed of the woman is Jesus Christ, the Messiah. The verb "to crush" or "to bruise" (*shuph*) occurs in only two other passages in the Old Testament. Job indicates the sense of crushing or bruising (Job 9:17), while the psalmist does not lend to either interpretation (Psa.139:11). It is best understood in light of both the Greek and Aramaic words "to strike" because they describe bites and stings. This aptly describes the effects of an attack from a serpent.

"The reason the Son of God appeared was to destroy the devil's work" (1 Jn.3:8c). Yet before Satan's figurative "head" is crushed, he first lashes out to sting the Messiah's "heel." All divinely initiated. God commands Satan to bruise Christ's figurative heel.[3] Why? "He was pierced for our transgressions, he was crushed for our iniquities…Yet it was the Lord's will to crush him…he will see his offspring [seed] and prolong his days…by his knowledge my righteous servant will justify many, and he will bear their iniquities" (Isa.53:5, 10,11). God's seed, Jesus Christ, endures the venom in his heel at Calvary on our behalf. The cross transforms into a weapon to crush or bruise Satan's authority as head of man. Ultimately, Satan will be thrown into the lake of fire along with his demonic hordes in the final judgment (Rev.20:10,15).

Christ is the head of all things and we are his Body (Eph.1:22,23). Seated in heavenly places with Christ, we are placed in a position that is far above all rule and authority, power, and dominion (Eph.1:21, 2:6). Satan is still slithering around trying to bite the heel of the Body of Christ, yet like Paul on the island of Malta, his bite is no longer life-threatening. Through Christ, we can throw off the viper's attacks. "Having disarmed the powers and authorities, he made a public spectacle of them, triumphing over them by the cross" (Col.2:15). Satan's sting ironically knocks him out of the ring. The cross enables the corporate seed of the woman to trample Satan under their feet (Rom.16:20). The enmity between the two seeds continues to be played out in history.

God does not curse Adam or Eve. He merely pronounces the devastating consequences of sin and death that will dramatically impact their lives and all future generations. To the woman, God says, "I will greatly multiply your sorrow and your conception; In pain you shall bring forth children; Your desire *shall be* for your husband, And he shall rule over you" (Gen.3:16, NKJV). God lists four consequences to her part in the fall.

---

3. Both "head" and "heel" in Genesis 3:15 are figures of speech called a *metonomy*. *Metonomy* occurs when there is a word that acts like a substitute for a suggestive word. "Head" suggests the destruction of all his power; "heel" suggests limited harm.

Because of the effects of sin, God announces that women will experience an increase in pain and sorrow—particularly in certain areas. Human history attests to the sorrows of women who have endured mental, emotional, physical, and spiritual abuse because of sinful man. The fall instigates the anguish and humiliation that women of every generation have undergone. Yet also, her capacity to conceive will increase, implying that Eve's ability to conceive was divinely regulated. A third area of increase for women is that there will be much sorrow in bringing forth children. This speaks of the sorrow of raising children now born with original sin. Little sinful hearts bent on rebellion generate much sorrow for mothers through the centuries.

Fourth, there will be enmity in marriage. The Hebrew text of Genesis 3:16 connotes an abnormal desire on the part of women to overflow and pass their husbands. Responding to the chaotic conditions that sin imparts into family life, women will strive to control the home, especially their husbands, to maintain order. It usually manifests in two ways: 1) by overt manipulation of men through feminist doctrine, or 2) by insisting that men take an apparent commanding role, which women then subtly manipulate. Either way, God's prophetic judgment predicts the awful frustration that occurs in marriages riddled by sin and selfishness. Tensions escalate not only because of women's desire to control, but because their husbands shall rule over them. Instead of cooperating as joint heirs in ministry and marriage, there is dominance, oppression, and manipulation by both spouses. All this may seem like a curse, but it's not. It is the aftermath of sin and death's fallout on women.

Adam is next. God turns to Adam and curses the ground. Only Satan and the ground are cursed! Adam's consequence is: "Through painful toil you will eat of it all the days of your life. It will produce thorns and thistles for you…By the sweat of your brow you will eat your food until you return to the ground" (Gen.3:17-19). Like God's prophecy to Eve and her daughters, Adam's role in the fall presents four consequences to men.

Under the curse, "The earth reels like a drunkard, it sways like a hut in the wind"—it is now an abnormal macrocosm

(Isa.24:20). Some of the astronomical effects of sin on the animal and plant kingdoms are disease, parasitism, decay, and death, so all of creation begins to groan: "We're cursed!" Meredith Kline describes the earth's rueful plight from the book of Isaiah.

> In the context of 24:4, what makes the earth groan is that it is obliged to become a grave, to cover over the human dead. But the relationship of that passage to 25:6-8, which has a redemptive focus on God's people, argues for a special (even if not exclusive) concern with the death of the righteous in the former. Pointing in the same direction is the explanation in 24:5 for the entrance of death and the resultant mourning of the earth: "The earth is profaned (*hanepa*) under its inhabitants." In view of the use of *hnp* elsewhere for polluting the ground by spilling innocent blood on it, it appears that the sin against God's covenant by reason of which the whole earth suffers defilement and mourns is hostility vented on the covenant faithful, resulting in their martyrdom.[4]

Suffering from the contamination of sin and death, the earth has been transmuted into a large tomb. God's beautiful creation was never meant to be a graveyard.

Man is displaced as king-priest over creation with no power to rule. Instead of reigning like a king, he finds himself toiling like a slave over cursed land. Man's first consequence is felt in a cursed, futile, work environment. In a cursed world, to be fruitful is no longer a blessing—it is drudgery. Solomon sums it up best, "What does a man get for all the toil and anxious striving with which he labors under the sun? All his days his work is pain and grief; even at night his mind does not rest" (Eccl.2:22,23). Rather than find fulfillment, the male species

---

4. Kline, Meredith. *"Death, Leviathan, and the Martyrs: Isaiah 24:1-27:1," A Tribute to Gleason Archer,* Kaiser and Youngblood editors, (Chicago: Moody, 1986).

will likely join Solomon's "mid-life crisis" support group and exclaim, "All is futile!"

Second, thorns and thistles will perforate and injure man while toiling in his vocation. Disharmony, strife, and a host of other prickly obstacles will hinder his dreams. Work-thorns take their toil on man's ability to provide for his family, all because of sin in the workplace. These thorns and thistles will result in the third consequence on man. Poetically illustrating the intensity of such turmoil, man is described as sweating it out. Working in a cursed world takes its toll on man's physical well being. Fourth, the inevitable result is the tragic return to dust. Physical death threatens to eventually triumph over all of man's efforts. Life becomes "a mist that appears for a little while and then vanishes" (Ja.4:14b). Man must now make his appointment with the one who promised him godhood—the death angel (Heb.9:27).

The divine Judge first classifies his verdict according to gender and orders distinct ramifications for each. The daughters of Eve bear the repercussions of sin in their relationships. The sons of Adam suffer primarily in their careers. Why is this? Losing their identity in God, human history is the continual search for meaning. Some teach that women will find their self-identity in being a wife and/or mother, while men will find their identity in their vocation. Such a pursuit is deluded. God knew that women would seek to establish their self-image in relationships and that men would try to "find themselves" in their work. Relationships, ministry, and work are all satisfying and fulfilling for men and women to some degree. But forming a self-image from a job or another person will leave us with a distorted image of ourselves. All malformations of our self-image are derived from connecting with something outside of God, the one whose image we are to reflect.

All these dire consequences lead to the relocation of Adam and Eve. Having sent them out of the garden, God equips his hired cherubim with flaming swords. He positions the new Edenic bouncers at the garden gate, protecting it from its former tenants. Driven from the presence of God, Adam and Eve sustain spiritual death. "Just as sin entered the world through one man, and death through sin, and in this way death came to all men, because all sinned"—it was through one man's offense that condemnation came for all men (Rom.5:12). "For just as through the disobedience of the one man the many were made sinners" and so the death producing venom of sin would reign over all life's experience on earth (Rom.5:18-21). Separated from God, sin and death quickly begin to permeate everything like a toxic infection poisoning every area of life.

God responds to evil by delaying its judgment. Why? Why not wipe the slate clean, kill that devil, and start all over with Dick and Jane? God postpones judgment to allow sin to expose its true character. Sin may cover itself for a time, seemingly left unpunished, but eventually it will demonstrate the awfulness of its own character. Simply put, if sinful human beings are left to themselves, they will eventually self-destruct. Astonishingly, though the odds of sin are against us, God is out to prove that some individuals will still humbly serve him, not for what they can get from him—but solely because they love him. Satan, on the other hand, is on a mission to prove God wrong.

The advent of Christ breaks the destructive effects of the fall. The New Covenant offers individuals and their families a break from the vicious cycles of sin that have plagued generation after generation. The Holy Spirit steadily reverses our twisted relationships and gently transforms our self-image into God's image. We slowly realize that we have been deceived, brainwashed to believe lie upon lie. Truth is setting us free. Ironically, "where sin increased, grace increased all the more...so also grace might reign through righteousness to bring eternal life through Jesus Christ our Lord" (Rom.5:20,21). In Christ, we regain our position as king-priests through the sanctifying work of the Holy Spirit. The Lord lavishes his enabling grace on us that we may bear his image once again.

Christ redeems our relationships and transforms our work into purposeful and fulfilling ministry. He reestablishes our self-identity in the Lord. We are known by our love for one another and for God. We can properly discern, for our conscience is clear of the debris of sin and guilt. Through Christ we reign victoriously over all circumstances in life. "Dear friends, now we are children of God, and what we will be has not yet been known. But we know that when he appears, we shall be like him, for we shall see him as he is" (1 Jn.3:2). Christ has removed the crown of thorns from man's head, bearing it shamelessly himself at Calvary. He thereby repositions man to his original place as God's king-priests on the earth.

Once the verdict is set, Adam comes to terms with his sin. He turns to his wife and names her Eve, "because she would become the mother of all the living" (Gen.3:20). Quite an astonishing choice considering that Eve has not yet become pregnant. This implies that Adam is taking hold of the messianic promise to deliver them *through her seed*. Because the wages of sin is death and because God is also a God of justice, death is the appropriate response (Rom.6:23). True justice is summed up in the phrase, "Take life for life, eye for eye, tooth for tooth, hand for hand, foot for foot, burn for burn, wound for wound, bruise for bruise" (Ex.21:24). The punishment must be equal to the crime. Yet in his love and mercy, God chooses to atone or cover their sin. He provides a substitute to die in their stead and graciously provides them with a new uniform made from an animal skin (Gen.3:21; cf. Lev.17:11). It is highly probable that God uses the skin of a young lamb to cover Adam and Eve, signifying his atonement for their sin.

City of Man vs. City of God

Surviving a rocky honeymoon, Adam and Eve bear two sons, Cain and Abel. From these two brothers the adventurous tale of two cities begins. There is the apostate, antichrist City of Man, and there is the heavenly, holy City of God. Augustine wrote in his classic, *City of God*, that there are:

> Two kinds of society, which, according to our Scriptures, we have rightly called the two cities. One city is that of men who live according to the flesh. The other is of men who live to the spirit…The one

City began with the love of God; the other had its beginnings in the love of self...What we see, then, is that two societies have issued from two kinds of love. Worldly society has flowered from a selfish love which dared to despise even God, whereas the communion of saints is rooted in a love of God...In the city of the world both the rulers...and the people they dominate are dominated by the lust for domination; whereas in the City of God all citizens serve one another in charity.[5]

Both groups of citizens construct their own cities. The City of Man is built by the seed of the serpent, while the City of God is built by the seed of the woman.

Cain is the founder of the City of Man. What kind of man is Cain? "Cain worked the soil. In the course of time Cain brought some of the fruits of the soil as an offering to the Lord" (Gen.4:2,3). Offering a sacrifice to God originates with God himself after Adam breaks the Edenic covenant and makes a covenant with sin and death instead (Gen.3:21; cf. Jer.33:20-26; Hos.6:7). Simply put, the sacrifice symbolizes the substitution of an innocent for the guilty covenant-breaker. It is based on the justice of God. Because of covenantal violations—or because there are "wages" or consequences to sin—death is required. God provides the rite of sacrifice as a merciful substitution for sinful humanity and so the biblical basis for whole idea of sacrificial death is covenantal in its core meaning.

Complications arise when God refuses Cain's offering. Is Cain in the wrong profession? Or did he offer the wrong kind of offering? It is neither of these things. God explains why: "If you *do what is right*, will you not be accepted?" (v. 7, emphasis added). Cain's offering is unacceptable to God because of his ungodly lifestyle. His offering is hypocritical and meaningless. Jude enlightens us to Cain's true character when he describes people who have gone the way of Cain (Jude 11).

---

5. Augustine. *City of God*, (New York: Doubleday, 1958), pp. 295, 310, 321.

These men are blemishes at your love feasts, eating with you without the slightest qualm—shepherds who feed only themselves. They are clouds without rain, blown along by the wind; autumn trees, without fruit and uprooted—twice dead. They are wild waves of the sea, foaming up their shame; wandering stars, for whom blackest darkness has been reserved forever...These men are grumblers and faultfinders; they follow their own evil desires; they boast about themselves and flatter others for their own advantage. Jude 13, 16

Cain serves only himself. He is a rebel who walks according to his own selfishness. God sees through Cain's pretense of virtue and calls him on it. "But if you do not do what is right, sin is crouching at your door; it desires to have you, but you must master it" (Gen.4:7). Sin "crouches" (*robes*) at the door of Cain's heart, ready to pounce. *Robes* is cognate to the Akkadian term used to describe a type of demon. In order for the seed of the serpent to enter Cain, he must receive permission. This of course reiterates Satan's legalistic procedures and also confirms that the seed line is spiritually transferred—as opposed to a biological transference. Cain's rebellion determines his destiny within the kingdom of darkness. Demonic spirits cannot attack unless one opens a door to allow legal entrance. Now exposed, Cain opens the door of his heart to the serpent and becomes angry.

His brother Abel, a keeper of sheep, intensifies the situation by offering his best: the fattest of the firstlings of his flock to the Lord, who readily receives it. Is it because Abel works in the right profession? Or did he offer the appropriate gift? Again, it is neither of these reasons. "By faith Abel offered to God a better sacrifice than Cain did. By faith he was commended as a righteous man, when God spoke well of his offerings" (Heb.11:4). His offering matches up with his heart and his righteous lifestyle. Abel worships God at work, at home, at play, and now at church with his gift. The enmity between Cain, the ungodly seed of the serpent, and Abel, the righteous seed of the woman, surfaces over spiritual matters of the heart. Persecution will soon follow.

The seed of the serpent furiously builds the bustling City of Man, while the seed of the woman humbly pursues the peaceful City of God. Living a godly lifestyle, the righteous build the brilliant, glorious City of God, its light exposing Cain's dark city streets. Cain builds his city on the foundation of unrighteousness, rebellion, and selfishness. Sin and deception lie at the entrance door of every building constructed in the City of Man. The prophetic judgment of enmity begins to enfold itself in the antagonism displayed by the two brothers.

Satan's mission is to set up his antichrist kingdom. Righteous Abel is in the way, so he begins to persecute Abel, even to the point of murder. Abel is the first martyr of our spiritual heritage. 1 John 3:10-12 explains:

> This is how we know who the children of God are and who the children of the devil are: Anyone who does not do what is right is not a child of God; nor is anyone who does not love his brother. This is the message you heard from the beginning: We should love one another. Do not be like Cain, who belonged to the evil one and murdered his brother. And why did he murder him? Because his own actions were evil and his brother's were righteous.

Cain was of the wicked one, or in other words, he was of the seed of the serpent. The righteous seed will endure the devil's persecution, even in death, for the righteous have the last word. Even after his death Abel's blood cries out from the ground (Gen.4:10). As citizens of the heavenly City of God, the blood of all martyrs throughout history cry out, "How long, Sovereign Lord, holy and true, until you judge the inhabitants of the earth and avenge our blood?" (Rev.6:10). It is the cry for justice.

God's way of dealing with brutal persecution may be contrary to our reasoning, but vengeance is not ours to take. "Do not take revenge, my friends, but leave room for God's wrath, for it is written: 'It is mine to avenge; I will repay,' says the Lord" (Rom.12:19). We need to leave room, or more literally understood, "to get out of the way" of God's wrath. By taking matters into our own hands, we are getting in God's way. He promises to repay; he must repay because he is a God of justice. We get out of God's way and employ our most effective weapon, the dreaded burning coals of goodness, bombarding those who mistreat us (Rom.12:20,21). If we respond to evil with evil, we concede to the mission statement of the devil. Ironically, goodness is the only thing that overcomes evil. While expending goodness on the undeserving, Christ's blood "speaks a better word than the blood of Abel" (Heb.12:24). Abel's blood cries out for vengeance. The redeemed are covered under Christ's blood, which speaks forth love, grace, and forgiveness.

The curse on the seed of the serpent befalls Cain, "You will be a restless wanderer on the earth" (Gen.4:12). Every generation follows the way of Cain by living a life of alienation. Separated from God and one another, the citizens of the City of Man cry out the same hopelessness of Cain, "My punishment is more than I can bear!" (Gen.4:13). When difficult situations arise, the citizens of the God-less world find themselves all alone. It's this sense of loneliness that drives them to despair. Unable to connect, they become crippled by paralyzing fear and disappointment.

> Fearful of the outside world, he builds walls of protection. These walls can be high and thick, difficult to break through. Inside is an insecure individual, alienated from society...Seeking entertainment to fill his emptiness, reality is lost. Life becomes a vicarious experience within an entertainment world. Perhaps he wants to take hold of life, but fear keeps him from becoming involved. He chooses the painless way of non-commitment. Isolation can reach the point that one takes on a survival mode of living for the moment, clutching, grasping, and clinging to anything

and everything that indulges the soul and satisfies the flesh. Life then loses all purpose and meaning.[6]

Alienation is summed up in the words of Cain, "Am I my brother's keeper?" Cain is rejecting genuine fellowship. "Man has replaced all natural desire for community and union by a choice to live alone. He chooses to live without his brother, and in doing so he chooses to live for himself only. Man thinks this arrangement will solve all his problems."[7] This arrangement is really the source of all the problems that plague the City of Man. Created in God's image as creatures of relationship, man must connect with something. If not with God or his fellow man, he will connect with anything that appears to befriend him. Alienation offers an escape route into idolatrous addictions. These addictions manifest themselves in a variety of expressions. Addictive friends soothe man's soul only temporarily. Over the process of time, they inevitably mutate into enemies bent on destroying his soul.

Many walk the path of Cain by rejecting fellowship and yet at the same time their desperate isolation leads many to cry out: "My punishment is more than I can bear!" (Gen.4:13). The Lord in his infinite mercy set a sign for Cain and his spiritual descendents to protect them from overzealous reprisal (Matt.13:28-30; Rom.2:1-11). Cain's "mark" is better understood as a sign (*oth* uses the prefix "for" not "in"). This implies that it is *for protection*, as opposed to some physical mark *inside* of Cain. God's merciful sign guarantees that final judgment for all must wait until the Second Coming of Christ (cf. 2 Pet.3:9; Rev.20:11-15). Common grace extends to Cain and to future generations.

Cain settles in the land of Nod, which means "wandering." For lost souls, the whole earth becomes the land of Nod. Cain exemplifies the aimless existence of the citizens of the City of Man. They live only for themselves. The dynasty of Cain builds

---

6. Thompson, Carroll. *Alienation: Dealing with the Basic Problem of Man*, pp.12-13.
7. Thompson, *Alienation*, p. 25.

its first city and names it after his son, Enoch. Cain pursues the making of great memorials to himself. By naming cities and streets after himself, man feels a sense of immortality and ownership over the earth. In reality, the opposite is true. Man is deceived into thinking he is still a god—ruler of his world. But in fact the earth has become his prison. Immorality, perversion, and injustice mark the inception of the antichrist City of Man. Its surprisingly impressive cultural achievements are paraded to overshadow its dark secrets (Gen.4:16-24).

The incongruity between the two cities is obvious. The founding fathers of the City of God, Seth and his son Enosh, are men who called on the name of the Lord (Gen.4:26). The righteous seed enjoys the sweet life of contentment in God's presence. As citizens of the City of God, the righteous delight in a simple life of intimacy, walking daily with their God (Gen.5:22-24). They are now sojourners and strangers in the world of Nod, but they eagerly wait for the unveiling of "the city with foundations, whose architect and builder is God" (Heb.11:10). They refuse to settle in the land of Nod. "Instead, they were longing for a better country—a heavenly one. Therefore God is not ashamed to be called their God, for he has prepared a city for them" (Heb.11:16). It is called the City of God, the New Jerusalem.

Chapter Four

The Spiritual Reality of a Desecrated World

One particular night while walking with my neighbor, my son decides to ride his bike along with us. Becoming very impatient, he rides past us to "the little beaver bridge," as we affectionately call it. The beaver bridge stands near a murky marsh. Being quite the explorer, my son stops at the bridge to seek whatever slimy creature he can get his hands on. A couple of steps into the swamp, he drops suddenly into the greenish quagmire all the way up to his chin. He becomes one of the scary creatures he was looking for. I'll never forget the fear and disgust on his face. He had never before felt the terror and nausea of being submerged in muck.

Noah lives in a world submerged in filth. Sin has escalated and lawlessness rules the earth. Morality has reached an all-time low. It's during this time that Scripture divides human history into two eras (2 Pet.3:6,7). The first era is the prediluvian world that perishes in the flood and the second era is the postdiluvian world that continues to exist today. When the prediluvian earth is submerged in the muck of wickedness, the floodwater of judgment acts as God's cleansing agent. This cataclysmic event serves as a paradigm for the present world, otherwise known as the last days.

The spiritual reality of enmity between the seed of the serpent and the seed of the woman is systematically laid out in the genealogies of Cain and Seth. As the godless City of Man begins to develop, evil accelerates. As it does we can see that Satan's plan remains the same throughout history. Satan aims to delude man and convert him to his diabolical religion and to harass and desecrate the righteous. Satan's sinister strategy emerges as he attempts to desecrate the City of God by seducing them into perversion and thereby losing their treasured intimacy with their Creator. Since being kicked out of the garden, the seed of the woman must learn to walk with God in the midst of a hostile world.

Desecration through Unholy Bonds

In the context of the previous two chapters, Genesis 6 is a continuation of the story of the descendants of Cain and Seth. Unclean spirits convince Noah's generation that sexual perversion is apropos. Seth's descendants are not only deceived, they are also desecrated to the point of being demonically inhabited by unclean spirits. Such a devilish intrusion completely resists the witness of God's Spirit. God pronounces the futility of striving with man and sets his timer to 120 years when the world that then existed will perish in a flood. This reveals the mercy and long-suffering of God who does not desire that "any should perish but that all should come to repentance" (2 Pet.3:9). Sadly, most of humanity rejects such mercy. They openly align themselves with a demonic network designed to accelerate wickedness on the earth.

> When men began to increase in number on the earth and daughters were born to them, the sons of God saw that the daughters of men were beautiful, and

married any of them they chose. Then the Lord said, "My Spirit will not contend with man forever, for he is mortal; his days will be a hundred and twenty years." The Nephilim were on the earth in those days—and also afterward—when the sons of God went to the daughters of men and had children by them. They were heroes [*gibborim*] of old, men of renown. Genesis 6:1-4

To comprehend the degenerate days of Noah, we must first secure an understanding of the expressions "the sons of God" and "the daughters of men." The description, "sons of God" (*bene elohim*), most likely refers to fallen angels. This appears to be consistent with other uses of this phrase in the Old Testament (cf. Job 1:6; 2:1; 38:7; Psa.29:1; 89:7). This view was taken by the early Church fathers, but during medieval times, the Roman Catholic Church interpreted these verses as some kind of illegal marriage between the line of Seth (sons of God) and the line of Cain (daughters of men). The Jewish view holds that the sons of God are dynastic rulers who marry commoners. Both the Catholic and Jewish views fail to explain the nephilim and the immensity of evil that overtakes the whole world through the offspring of their union with human women.

Apparently, there are fallen angels who followed Lucifer's mutiny and then there are certain other fallen angels who "did not keep their positions of authority but abandoned their own home" during the time of Noah (Jude 6). These fallen angels have forsaken their original posts as overseers of the nations (cf. Deut.32:7-9; Psa.82:2-7; 106:37; Dan.10:12,13). According to Jewish tradition, they are known as "the Watchers"—apparently positioned to watch over territories that correspond to the seventy nations of Genesis 10 (cf. Dan.4:13,17,23).

Even though angels are placed in a subservient role, they do have autonomous willpower and full voluntary resolution. Angels of God do not marry other angels, nor do they marry human beings (Matt.22:30). If in the time of Noah, some of these fallen angels left their proper domain to seek sexual experiences with women, two questions surface: 1) Can demons have sexual relations with humans? and 2) If they can, are they able to procreate and produce some kind of hybrid demon-persons? Admittedly, these answers are hard to verify, but a handful of scriptures address these issues. It is probable that fallen angels can observe humans (especially women) and be sexually aroused (cf. Gen.6:2; 1 Cor.11:10). The story of Sodom and Gomorrah affirms that *people* can lust for sexual intercourse with angels (Gen.19). The most telling verses come from Jude 6-7: fallen "angels (demons) who did not keep their position of authority, but abandoned their own home...*gave themselves up to sexual immorality* and *perversion [going after strange (human) flesh]*" (cf. NKJV emphasis mine). Jude makes it clear that demons can have unnatural sexual intercourse with human beings.

Whether or not demons can procreate impinges on our view of the sanctity of life. If we hold the view that life simply results from the union of sperm and egg (human or demonic), then the offspring is a product either made in man's own image—or they are designed to reflect a demonic image. If we believe that God is the author of all life, then human beings and fallen angels (of which Satan is one) have the propensity to have sexual relations, but not the ability to procreate.

If demons cannot breed, then how can we explain their diabolical covenant with "wives"? In order to understand this passage, we must understand the perversity of Satanism.

Demons target people to make occult contracts or what we have referred to previously as perverse covenants. This is Satanism. Kurt Koch explains:

> A conscious subscribing of oneself to the devil...will result in a terrible form of demonic subjection and oppression. Formal contracts with the devil of this nature take place much more frequently than one would care to think, but fear prevents many people from confessing what they have done. The motive behind this surrendering of one's life and soul to

Satan is usually the desire to have some special wish fulfilled...devilish contracts are frequently fulfilled and curses against others often succeed—except when uttered against genuine Christians.[1]

Demon spirits seek to propagate through "formal contracts" or "fear bonds." Perverse ritual covenants are ratified through a person's participation in unimaginable demonically induced acts of torture and eroticism. Let us look at the intensity of fear bonds in contemporary Satanism to further our understanding of Noah's day.

> Take, for instance, the way a Satanist community gathers to celebrate a child's birthday. Birthdays are often major ritual days. Involvement is intense. Men participate actively even when the birthday being celebrated is not their child's...[they] use intense sexual activity to bond...Satanists are looking for power and control, but not just control over children. Where control is important, fear bonds are the family dynamic. [They]...rely on fear bonds because fear gets quick results. Since occultists are intent on controlling spirits, fear bonds become their spiritual dynamic. Satanists extend their fear bonds to the spirit world as a way to do business with evil spirits...The means of controlling spirits in occult rituals is peculiar. Consider eating feces or causing the death of an animal in a way calculated to be painful. Why should doing painful things control the actions of spirit beings? This ritual behavior resembles family dynamics. Children impress their parents, and later their friends, by what they do. It amounts to gaining power by obtaining approval from the person [or demon] in power.[2]

---

1. Koch, Kurt. *Occult Bondage and Deliverance*, (Grand Rapids: Kregel, 1976), pp.138-139.
2. Wilder, E. James. *The Red Dragon Cast Down, A Redemptive Approach to the Occult and Satanism*, (Grand Rapids: Chosen Books, 1999), pp.132-134

Demonic pride comes to its fullest expression as these lustful spirits seek to dominate not just individuals, but multiple generations of families involved in the chaotic mire of Satanism. The issue at hand is a devious onslaught to secure individual conversion to spiritual darkness, thus controlling multi-family structures and ultimately all worldly systems to pave the way for the antichrist.

Satan's diabolical kingdom is built on perverse sexual rituals that "seal" a person's allegiance to the devil. Demon-possessed men commit their perverse sexual ritual-covenants with the daughters of men, thereby establishing Satan's layered sealing system (Job 41:15). The demon-possessed men, after having satanic ritual intercourse with a considerable number of women generate nephilim (Gen.6:4).

The meaning of *nephilim* is uncertain, but one thing is clear—nephilim is plural. Unfortunately, most translations mislead their readers by describing nephilim as "giants." Some scholars attempt to relate nephilim etymologically using *napal* or the noun *nepel* ("untimely birth" or "miscarriage"). Such implication might lead us to consider nephilim as hybrid monstrosities. Another likely reconstruction is to relate nephilim to the root *nepal* ("mighty ones") or *nephal* ("fallen ones").

Whatever one's definition of nephilim might be, we must consider the fragmentation of the mind and soul that occurs in multiple generations of satanic ritual abuse. Because of continual ritual abuse, the shattered human base to which these demonic power sources attach themselves may prove to be the spiritual network or "web" that generates a plurality of "nephilim" on the earth (see the chart on the following page).

The offspring that are conceived in satanic rituals are dedicated to Satan; they are described as "heroes of old, men of renown" (Gen.6:4). Again, the translation "heroes of old" is misleading. The word used is *gibborim*, which simply means "warriors." Yet the spiritual network of nephilim-gibborim is not an ordinary army, they are aggressive warriors for Satan. They arrogantly stand in opposition to God and belligerently persecute the righteous with demonic assignments (cf. Job 15:25; 39:6;

```
┌─────────────┬─────────────┬─────────────┐
│  Sons of    │  >>Target>> │  Daughters  │
│  God-       │  (Gen.6:2)  │  of Men     │
│  Demons     │             │             │
└─────────────┴─────────────┴─────────────┘
```

```
┌───────────────────────────────────────────┐
│   Participation in Multi-Generational     │
│      Occult Covenant Rituals (Gen.6:4b)   │
└───────────────────────────────────────────┘
```

```
┌─────────────────────────────────────────────┐
│    Offspring Conceived in Occult Rituals    │
│         Are Dedicated to Satan              │
│ and Given "Gibborim" Assignment (Gen.6:4c)  │
└─────────────────────────────────────────────┘
```

```
┌─────────────────────────────────────────────┐
│       Result is "Nephilim" on the Earth     │
│                  (Gen.6:4a)                 │
└─────────────────────────────────────────────┘
```

Isa.42:13). The nephilim-gibborim combination is notorious for their vileness and public defiance. "Every intent of the thoughts of [their] heart was only evil continually" (Gen.6:5). This clearly describes a world full of people bent on destroying lives. Koch describes the torment of such nephilim influence:

> The person finds he can only entertain evil thoughts in his mind and ideas which are opposed to God. He is gripped with a passion for lying and impure thoughts... Inwardly he feels a compulsion to do things demanded of him by the devil. He is thus liable to suddenly rebel against God or blaspheme, or to have fits of fury and be defiant towards other people, exhibiting spite, enmity, excitability and violent behaviour. When angry, he curses himself and will curse and hate others who have offended him.[3]

This description fits Noah's generation. For people who are connected to the demonic-nephilim network, the intent of every thought is continually evil. This worldwide crisis submerges the

---

3. Koch, p.140.

earth in violence (Gen.6:11). Being completely overwhelmed by nephilim-gibborim, the world deserves such a catastrophic response from heaven.

Noah's generation is a prototype of the last generation before Christ's Second Coming. We are warned not to have hearts "weighed down with dissipation, drunkenness and the anxieties of life" (Lk.21:34). History's final generation of believers will be in the minority, just like Noah.

> As it was in the days of Noah, so it will be at the coming of the Son of Man. For in the days before the flood, people were eating and drinking, marrying and giving in marriage, up to the day Noah entered the ark; and they knew nothing about what would happen until the flood came and took them all away. That is how it will be at the coming of the Son of Man. Matthew 24:37-39

This might sound like every generation that has ever lived, but Noah's particular generation was so corrupted by demons, it had to perish.

Under the directives of the antichrist, the City of Man will be so intoxicated with the Babylon harlot system that it will become a "home for demons and a haunt for every evil spirit, a haunt for every unclean and detestable bird. For all the nations have drunk the maddening wine of her adulteries" (Rev.18:2b,3a). In the latter days, believers will face the same predicament as Noah. The whole earth will be diabolically enmeshed in a similar satanic nephilim-gibborim ritual abuse scenario. John tells us that Satan will use sorcery to deceive all nations and to usher in the end times apostate age of antichrist (Rev.18:23d).

A study of the Gadarene demoniac will prove helpful to our investigation of the time of Noah and the phenomenon of nephilim-possession (Mk.5:1-13). The Gadarene demoniac demonstrates eight distinct symptoms of demonic penetration:

1. There is occult involvement (the demoniac exhibits an abnormal obsession with death).
2. An unclean spirit demonizes the person (Jesus orders the evil spirit out of him).
3. There are violent manifestations or fits of rage (no one can bind the demoniac).
4. Life is characterized by perversion (the demoniac wanders with no clothes on; cf. Lk.8:27).
5. There is an exhibition of inordinate emotional instability (the demoniac is always crying out day and night).
6. There is an obvious demonstration of self-hatred displayed by self-destructive and suicidal tendencies (the demoniac cuts and bruises himself).
7. There is a fragmentation of disposition (the demoniac worships Jesus, yet screams that Christ "torments" him).
8. There is an extraordinary ability to tap into the spiritual realm (the demoniac is spiritually keen to discern who Jesus is in spite of his tormented condition).

This gives a clearer picture of Noah's generation and a poignant description of the last generation. As in the days of Noah, the whole earth will be infiltrated by demonic hordes. Satan's plan to infiltrate the righteous line begins with unleashing his army of nephilim-gibborim upon the earth. The various types of demonic manifestations that occur on the earth are according to the evil spirit's particular mission. For example, there are spirits of infirmity (Lk.13:11), familiar spirits (Lev.20:27; 2 Kgs.23:24), lying spirits (1 Kgs.22:22,23; 2 Chron.18:21,22), seducing spirits (1 Tim.4:1), foul spirits (Mk.9:25; Rev.18:2), and jealous spirits (Numb.5:14, 30) to name just a few. The most frequently mentioned are the unclean spirits, which are used 22 times in the New Testament. Believers are obviously not immune to the pitfalls of Satan's tactics. By succumbing to these lustful demons, the citizens of the City of God can easily fall into a multitude of horrendous sins. Satan's strategy is to unleash legions of unclean spirits in order to bombard the righteous with manifold temptations in order to make a shipwreck of their faith.

God's indictment against Noah's generation is a worldwide flood, but he will have a different response to the wickedness of the last generation. After Noah builds his altar, God promises, "Never again will I curse the ground because of man, even though every inclination of his heart is evil from childhood. And never again will I destroy all living creatures as I have done" (Gen.8:21). The curse in Genesis 7:21 refers to the curse of the flood and not the original curse on the earth after the fall of Adam and Eve. As long as the history of the earth remains, God will never allow its destruction (Gen.7:22). This is comforting in light of all the environmental issues and the danger of nuclear armaments that continue to threaten the world at large. God promises to never again cover the earth with the waters of judgment even though the last generation will degenerate to the same condition as Noah's. Judgment does not solve the recurring problem of human-demonic alliances—but grace does.

The Reality of a World Submerged

The word "grace" or "favor" occurs for the first time in the Bible when referring to Noah (Gen.6:8,9). "Noah found favor in the eyes of the Lord…[he] was a righteous man, blameless among the people of his time, and he walked with God." Noah and his family are the City of God's sole survivors. Building the ark takes 120 years for Noah to complete. It stands as a symbol of a nautical capsule of the City of God. What is up God's sleeve during these 120 years?

While Noah is busy constructing the ark, Peter tells us that the pre-incarnate Christ "went and preached to the spirits in prison who disobeyed long ago when God waited patiently in the days of Noah while the ark was being built. In it only a few people, eight in all, were saved through water" (1 Pet.3:19,20). It is highly improbable that verse 19 infers that Christ preached a salvation message to a deceased evil generation down in Hades. There is no scriptural evidence to support a second chance for salvation after death. The ark, being a type of Christ, appears to be the preaching tool to the spirits in "prison." To be spiritually imprisoned is merely a poetic way of describing the captive sinner, imprisoned in the dark confines of Satan's kingdom (cf. Isa.42:7; 61:1). The building of the ark itself is a testimony of salvation from the corruptness of the world and it symbolizes the mission and ministry of Christ.

Noah commits himself and his family into the ark kingdom and in so doing he renounces and condemns the world. Water baptism carries the same meaning. Participating in Christian water baptism, we enter Christ's spiritual ark and our conscience is washed clean (1 Pet.3:21,22). Submerged in water, we outwardly demonstrate our renunciation of any alliance with evil. Just like the damages of a present day flood, this rite symbolizes a world submerged under the filthy waters of sin and therefore under God's judgment. We emerge from the water in the "ark of Christ," free from condemnation and saved from the wrath to come. Renouncing our slavery to sin, selfishness, and occult involvement, we emerge as slaves of righteousness forever blessed with newness of life (Rom.6:3,4).

During Noah's generation our spiritual heritage is reduced to a mere remnant of just eight souls. By entering the ark, Noah becomes an heir to the righteousness that comes by faith (Heb.11:7). Noah heard the gospel preached to him as he constructed each of the three levels of the ark and thereby became a recipient of covenantal privileges.

When Noah is 600 years old "all the springs of the great deep burst forth, and the floodgates of the heavens were opened. And rain fell on the earth forty days and forty nights…Pairs of all creatures…entered the ark…Then the Lord shut him in" (Gen.7:11b,12, 15,16). Once we enter into the ark of the kingdom of light, God will shut us in, in the sense that his faithfulness will keep us throughout the storms of life. God's wondrous covenantal love brings great comfort. Remaining in the ark of Christ does not depend on our sincere, but feeble attempts to good works, but on the door of Christ who helps us ride through life's stormy upheavals until the end. Jesus says, "I am the door. If anyone enters by Me, he will be saved, and will go in and out and find pasture" (Jn.10:9, NKJV). Jesus is the entrance door into the ark of salvation; he is the door that seals and protects against the waves of filth that swirl around us and cover the world.

As the waters decrease, the ark rests on the mountains of Ararat located in modern-day Turkey. Before Noah sets foot out of the ark, he sends forth a raven, a flesh-eating scavenger, and a dove, a plant eater. By sending them together, Noah typologically illustrates the future new creational world order inaugurated by the death and resurrection of Christ. The raven may search for the old nature's carcass—but it is crucified with Christ. The dove snatches up an olive leaf, depicting the resurrection power of the Holy Spirit to re-create the believer into a new man (Rom.6:3-6). The deluge symbolizes the believer's baptism into Christ's death and subsequent emergence into newness of life.

Noahic Covenant:
The Divine-Warrior and His War-Bow

The covenant that God made with Noah is known as the covenant of preservation.[4] God clarifies who are the recipients of the Noahic Covenant: "I now establish my covenant with you and with your descendants after you and with every living creature that was with you" (Gen.9:9). God promises to make a covenant with Noah, his descendants, and all of creation. It is essential to grasp the universal implications of this covenant. It's not only an agreement between God and his people, it's a promise between the Creator and his whole creation. God has basically four covenant stipulations on his mind: 1) the renewal of the creational mandate of dominion, 2) the reinstitution of food regulations, 3) the establishment of human government to restrain the acceleration of evil, and 4) the divine-warrior's formal declaration of spiritual war.

1. Creational Mandate of Dominion

In line with the original plan of operations, God renews the creational mandate to be fruitful and increase, and fill the earth

---

4. For further explanation, see O. Palmer Robertson's *The Christ of the Covenants*, (Phillipsburg: Presbyterian and Reformed, 1980), pp.109-125.

The Spiritual Reality of a Desecrated World

(Gen.9:1). He reinstitutes the call to celebrate life in his presence. Again, it's not just a command—it's a blessing. God reassures Noah that his life is not endangered by another flood of judgment. By faith, Noah and his descendants are to regain their position as king-priests unto God. In addition to the creation mandate to be fruitful and multiply, God attaches an appendix: "The fear and dread of you will fall upon all the beasts of the earth...they are given into your hands" (v.2). Humanity is to go ahead and rule the world, but creation will act like his troubled codependent wife who trembles because of his abuse. Humans may sense their power over such a vulnerable earth and attempt to completely dominate it. The creational mandate is reinstated, but the spiritual reality is that frustration and the pandemonium of disharmony will highlight it.

2. Reinstitution of Food Regulation

The second stipulation of the Noahic Covenant is the ordinance of food regulation. "Every thing that lives and moves will be food for you. Just as I gave you the green plants, I now give you everything. But you must not eat meat that has its lifeblood still in it" (Gen.9:3,4). Of all the things to talk about after a universal flood, God is concerned about food regulation. Why? What relation do foods have with ruling the earth—or spirituality? The subject of food regulation is probably not very popular among those of us who live in a fat-free society that spends millions of dollars on weight loss programs and products. Rarely will we hear an inspiring message on biblical food regulations from the pulpit on Sunday mornings. Yet the Bible has much to say about food. It may seem odd, but it must be important to God because he addresses the food issue with both Adam and Noah.

Food is designed to nourish our bodies, but if we do not regulate our food intake, food can turn into an addictive substance to generate emotional satisfaction. For some, mealtimes are simply an enjoyable time of fellowship; for others, food soothes their heart and becomes their coping mechanism for stress. Food often transforms into a delectable emissary that anesthetizes hearts that are hurting. Problems arise when food is deregulated. When people have no regulations on food, it emerges as a viable golden calf (Phil.3:19). On the other hand, people may also fall for obsessive regulations on food—ones that restrict their diet to certain particular foods (Col.2:20-23). Such self-imposed regulations on food do not enhance spirituality nor curb lustful appetites. In these passages, Paul refutes compulsive-additions and obsessive-techniques, not biblical regulations on food.

What are the biblical regulations on food? The concept of food is founded on the principles of consecration and sacrifice. Food functions as an expression of dedicating our lives to God. It represents sanctification and sacrifice. This is naturally brought forth in the circle of life: the air, water, and plants are sacrificially consecrated for man and the animal kingdom. This explains the prayer of blessing on our meals. When we pray over our lunch, we sanctify it, we set it apart to the Lord because our body is the temple of the Holy Spirit (1 Tim.4:4-5). It is not what we eat that matters. We are free to eat and free to refrain from eating. What does matter is what place food has inside our heart (Rom.14:6-20; 1 Cor.8:8).

More important than this is the command to refrain from blood consumption (Gen.9:4). God's judgment on the world's participation in occult practice has just occurred. Those involved in satanism kill animals not to eat its meat for dinner, but to derive power from consuming, not only its flesh, but its blood and other internal organs. Their depravity includes human sacrifice and incestuous cannibalism (2 Kgs.12:3; 14:4; 15:4; 16:3,4; 21:3-6; 2 Chron.14:3; Lk.13:1). Through blood consumption, occult participants access the life of the slain (Lev.17:11). Demons that inhabit the sacrificial victim are transferred to the occultists. Demons then use and empower the participants to carry out their dirty assignments. Blood consumption transforms a human being into a destructive warrior (*gibborim*) for evil.

We know that food is to be sacrificially consecrated to the Lord and then eaten. The blood, however, is to be left on the altar as a symbol of his atonement for our sin. In order to reconcile his own justice and the deplorable condition of humanity (Rom.6:23), God requires a ransom to clear accounts (Matt.20:28; 1 Tim.2:6; Rev.5:9). So the only acceptable and just requirement is the substitutionary death of Jesus Christ. Without his death there is no justice; without the shedding of blood there is no remission of sin (Rom.3:25; 5:9; Eph.1:7; Heb.9:22; 1 Pet.1:19). Blood represents the life that comes from the death of the one slain (cf. Jn.6:53-58). Life is obtained only through Christ's death. In light of the New Covenant, we may read Leviticus 17:11 this way: "For the life of [Jesus Christ] is in [his] blood, and I have given it to you to make atonement for yourselves on the [cross]; it is [Christ's] blood that makes atonement for one's life" (Lev.17:11).

So to drink the blood of animals, or other human beings, is to mock the symbolism of atonement and consecrate oneself to demonic use and abuse. This explains why the Jerusalem council maintains its stand against participating in such heinous practices (Acts 15:20).

3. Establishment of Human Government

Although humanity has forfeited their ruling position to Satan, God extends his grace by establishing human government. Though all of us are personally responsible to administer justice according to the principles set down in God's word, God institutes human government to restrain the acceleration of the evil.

Before the deluge, the Lord sanctions no formal government. In fact, before the Noahic covenant, lawlessness rules the earth. The arbitrary tyranny of Lamech sums up pre-deluvian rulers: "I have killed a man for wounding me, a young man for injuring me. If Cain is avenged seven times, then Lamech seventy-seven times" (Gen.4:23b,24). With no restraints, everyone acts according to their self-interests. To prevent a recurrence of universal anarchy, the Lord establishes human government—one that is founded on justice: "For your lifeblood I will surely demand an accounting. I will demand an accounting from every animal. And from each man, too…Whoever sheds the blood of man, by man shall his blood be shed; for in the image of God has God made man" (Gen.9:5,6).

This is not vengeance. This is known as *lex talionis* (justice); it is the principle of giving "life for life, eye for eye, tooth for tooth, hand for hand, foot for foot, burn for burn, wound for wound, stripe for stripe" (Ex.21:23-25). Punishment is to be equal to the crime committed. Dealing biblically with crime focuses on retribution rather than penalization (Numb.35:31-34). According to God's judicial proceedings, money cannot pay for the taking of a human life.

So on one hand, God ordains the sanctity of life. People are image-bearers of God. When Cain murders his brother Abel, the Lord declares, "if anyone kills Cain, he will suffer vengeance seven times over" and God "put a mark on Cain so that no one who found him would kill him" (Gen.4:15). Remarkably, life is so sacred that even a murderer's life is treated with dignity. John Murray believes that even the life of a monstrous killer "is not to be wantonly or ruthlessly taken away. Crime is not to be punished by crime; the life of the murderer is not to be taken in the way of violence or thirst for blood after the pattern of the murderer's own crime."[5] By carrying out justice, "it does not follow that the execution of the evil which consists in punishment is *per se* sinful. If this were so then God Himself would commit sin in executing wrath, a blasphemous thought."[6]

On the other hand, God establishes justice through the agency of human government. In the New Testament, God institutes all authorities (Rom.13:1,2,4; 1 Pet.2:13,14). God is the source of all authority. When governing rulers plot against God and his purposes, God sits on his throne and laughs (Psa.2). Their plans will

---

5. Murray, John. *Principles of Conduct*, (Grand Rapids: Wm. Eerdmans, 1981), p.108. Murray goes on to explain what is the purpose for the institution of the cities of refuge. It is "not for the purpose of affording asylum for those guilty of murder. They were established so that the manslayer might flee thither until he could stand before the congregation for judgment; and the congregation was given well-defined criteria by which to distinguish between the manslayer who was a murderer and the manslayer who slew his neighbor unwittingly, without hatred or intent of harm" (p.113).
6. Murray, *Principles*, p.114.

not come to fruition, but God's plans will. His purposes are actually accomplished through both good and evil governments. Concerning the rulers of the earth, the Lord "has put it into their hearts to accomplish his purpose by agreeing to give the beast their power to rule, until God's words are fulfilled" (Rev.17:17)—thus making the spiritual reality behind human government to be a paradox of evil purpose and ultimate triumph.

God ordains the righteous, like David, Hezekiah, and Josiah to govern over his people, but he also appoints Cyrus ruler over Persia and Nebuchadnezzar over Babylon. Jesus himself is subject to the political and religious authorities. He pays taxes to Caesar and submits to the obnoxious questions of the high priest before his death. It follows that we, too, need not presume the place of avenger, but pray to gracefully respond with goodness (Rom.12:19-21). This stunning revelation affirms that goodness is the only thing that overcomes evil. If we are insubordinate and hateful, we are merely joining with the forces of lawlessness and evil. When the man of sin, the lawless one appears, will we be a deterrent or an assistant? By God's grace and the empowerment of the Holy Spirit, we can love our enemies and bless those who curse us, do good to those who hate us, and pray for those who use and abuse us (Matt.5:44). By the divine institution of human government, humanity is responsible to execute justice and protect the sanctity of life.

4. Declaration of Spiritual War and the Divine-Warrior's Assurance of Victory

The Noahic covenant not only preserves humanity from self-destruction, it also promises restoration in its sign of the rainbow. The Hebrew word that is translated "rainbow" (*qeset*) means "war-bow" (Gen.9:13). *Qeset* is primarily used as an instrument of war. The sign of the war-bow is God's pledge to preserve the earth—and to fight for it until the final day when earth unites with heaven. Signifying his covenant in the brilliant span of the war-bow, God connects heaven to the earth beneath. The war-bow signals to all the inhabitants of earth and heaven that *El-Gibbor*, the divine-warrior God, rides his

Spiritual Reality

vehicular chariot-cloud to reclaim creation from the clutches of evil (Psa.68:4; 104:3-4; Isa.19:1; Nah.1:2-8).

> The Lord is a warrior; the Lord is his name (Ex.15:3).

> The Lord will march out like a mighty man, like a warrior he will stir up his zeal; with a shout he will raise the battle cry and will triumph over his enemies (Isa.42:13).

> The Lord is with me like a mighty warrior; so my persecutors will stumble and not prevail. They will fail and be thoroughly disgraced; their dishonor will never be forgotten (Jer.20:11).

The messianic warrior disarms the powers and authorities at the cross (Col.2:15) and then ascends in his chariot-cloud to the Ancient of days "when the times will have reached their fulfillment—to bring all things in heaven and on earth together under one head, even Christ" (Eph.1:10). This cosmic victory and regathering is the initial fulfillment of the Noahic covenant. Jesus invites us to be an integral part of its implementation by instructing us to pray: "Your kingdom come, your will be done on earth as it is in heaven" (Matt.6:10). In effect, we are praying for God to gather all things, in heaven and on earth, together under the reign of his Son, Jesus Christ. In the book of Revelation, the rainbow is found around the throne of God and on the head of an angel (4:3; 10:1). Both signify the promise of the eternal state, the consummation of the new heavens and new earth—the fulfillment of the Noahic covenant.

If God has to annihilate the present universe, then Satan wins the final, great victory. Can Satan so corrupt the earth that God's only resort is to destroy it? All of "creation was subjected to frustration, not by its own choice, but by the will of the one who subjected it, in hope that the creation itself will be liberated from its bondage to decay and brought into the glorious freedom of the children of God" (Rom.8:20,21). Paul ties creation's redemption with the believer's resurrection at Christ's Second Coming. The present earth will be completely resurrected, not annihilated, because the Greek word "new" (*kainos*) means "renewed in nature or quality" (2 Pet.3:10-13; Rev.21:1), as opposed to the other Greek word for "new" (*neos*) meaning, "new in origin." The description of the elements of the earth "melting with fire" is to be interpreted figuratively in the sense that fire most often symbolizes the sanctifying process of purging and purifying.

> Peter speaks of the two world judgments: one by water, the Flood, in which the world "perished" but was obviously not annihilated; and one by fire, in which the world shall be burned up, but not necessarily annihilated.[7]

Affirming the resurrected-new earth doctrine, the psalmist declares, "In the beginning you laid the foundations of the earth, and the heavens are the work of your hands. They will perish, but you remain; they will all wear out like a garment. Like clothing you will change them and they will be discarded" (Psa.102:25,26).

Seeing a dazzling vision of the new heaven and earth, John describes it along with "the Holy City, the new Jerusalem, coming down out of heaven from God, prepared as a bride beautifully dressed for her husband" (Rev.21:1,2). The beautiful bride of Christ comes down with heaven, converges with the earth, and ushers in the new eternal state. Together, the universal Body of Christ will meet the Lord in the air for the purpose of escorting him to earth.

> The world into which we shall enter in the Parousia of Jesus Christ is therefore not another world; it is this world, this heaven, this earth; both, however, passed away and renewed. It is these forests, these fields, these cities, these streets, these people, that will

---

7. Erb, Paul. *The Alpha and the Omega*, (Scottdale: Herald Press, 1955), p. 119.

be the scene of redemption. At present they are battlefields, full of the strife and sorrow of the not yet accomplished consummation; then they will be fields of victory, fields of harvest, where out of seed that was sown with tears the everlasting sheaves will be reaped and brought home.[8]

As citizens of the City of God, we cannot throw off this present world as a total loss nor carelessly rejoice in its deterioration. God creates the earth and declares that all of it is good; Satan swindles the world from humanity and attempts to transform it into something very evil. God is in the business of redemption, restoration, renewal, and resurrection.

After the earth is submerged under water and the flood begins to subside, the aftermath is devastating. What are Noah and his family going to do? Where do they even begin? It's a brand new world, but everything is soaked and the stench of filth lingers. Choices are made that have had a direct bearing on your spiritual heritage and mine.

Tracing Our Spiritual Heritage in the Archive of the Nations

Frankly, most of us would rather skip quickly over the genealogies of Scripture, but they are critical to the study of our spiritual family tree. Our spiritual heritage begins with Adam and Eve and extends for many generations, but the human race is pruned down to one family after the devastation of the flood. From Noah's three sons, we can trace the biological and spiritual origin of three distinct people groups (Gen.10). Herein lies the root and formation of humanity's ancient spiritual heritage.

The three streams of nations are not three races as some might conclude. Paul nullifies any notion of dividing human beings into races: "From one man [God] made every nation of men, that they should inhabit the whole earth; and he determined

---

8. Thurneysen, Edward. *Eternal Hope*, translated by Harold Knight, (London: Lutterworth, 1954), p.204.

the times set for them and the exact place where they should live. God did this so that men would seek him and perhaps reach out for him and find him, though he is not far from each one of us" (Acts 17:26,27). The different characteristics that exist today have not evolved but present the various combinations of pre-existing genetic data. The Bible does not use the word "race," nor does it acknowledge such a concept. All people are created in God's image. They are from one blood. Each person is divinely placed in a particular country of the world with a unique destiny to fulfill. God is patient with all of us "not wanting anyone to perish, but everyone to come to repentance" and reach out to find him in their designated place in history (2 Pet.3:9).

Evolution's idea that each generation is in the process of evolving into a better species can be contrasted to Scripture's presentation of humans uniquely created in God's image. To illustrate the biblical view of the human race, we can liken God to a colossal puzzle that is made up of billions of pieces. Each person born into the world, whether past, present, or future, represents one piece of that puzzle. Just as no one puzzle piece is the same and each piece can only fit into its particular place, so individuals are created to reflect God's image in their unique puzzle-piece personality. Jesus Christ has broken down the prejudicial walls of separation and has linked us all together in his love. God creates one race. It is called the human race. Examining the spiritual archive of the nations in Genesis 9-10, our family tree looks like a kaleidoscopic representation of God's image manifested in blended skin colors.

"The sons of Noah who came out of the ark were Shem, Ham, and Japheth. (Ham was the father of Canaan.)…and from them came the people who were scattered over the earth" (Gen.9:18,19). One can only imagine how traumatic it was for Noah's family to step out of the ark. After all, the rest of humanity has just been obliterated. Evidently this was way too much for Noah to handle. After planting a vineyard, he gets drunk and passes out naked in his tent. This humiliating experience exposes the seed of the serpent. The evil seed apparently creeps into the ark and is about to move sinuously into Noah's tent.

Noah is outwardly exposed while one of his sons is inwardly exposed. Apparently, Ham has secretly been in league with Satan's army. He is a traitor bent on encroaching and ultimately desecrating God's people. "Ham, the father of Canaan, *saw* his father's nakedness and *told* his two brothers outside" (Gen.9:22, emphasis mine). The Hebrew word "saw" (*ra'a*) is in the hiphil form of the verb, which means, "to look at intently, inspect, to make to feel or know or enjoy." Evidently Ham looked upon his father with some kind of homosexual lust and acted upon it (cf. Lev.18:6-19 which uses the phrase "to uncover his nakedness" as a euphemism for sexual sin). More precisely, one might conclude that Ham was bisexual because of his family relations with a wife and subsequent children.

Satan seizes the opportunity to take advantage of a righteous father who had succumbed to drunkenness and attempts to use Ham to break apart the only family left on the earth. He particularly wants to devastate Noah. Ham sexually violates his father and is obnoxiously disdainful of his perversity. He immediately boasts of his transgression to his brothers. When Noah awoke from his drunken stupor, "Noah *knew* what his *younger* son had *done to him*" (Gen.9:24, NKJV, emphasis mine), thus implying that something physically visible was "done to him." The perversity of Ham explains the harshness of the curse. God's indictment on such a devastating scene is merely the continuation of the curse on the serpent's seed and his blessing on the righteous' seed.

The three streams of nations are not three races; they each reflect a certain spiritual lineage. Within these three brothers, we find the root and formation of humanity's ancient spiritual heritage (Gen.9:25-10:32). Bloodlines guarantee neither salvation nor damnation, but they do transfer a particular spiritual lineage to each successive generation (Ex.20:4). Before we look into the progressive curse on the seed of the serpent through the spiritual lineage of Ham's youngest son, Canaan, let us first analyze the spiritual lineage represented in Ham's other two brothers, Shem and Japheth.

1. The Blessing of Shem

"Blessed be the Lord, the God of Shem! May Canaan be the slave of Shem" (Gen.9:26). Using the genealogy of Shem in Genesis 10:21-31 with 1 Chronicles 1:17-27, Shem's descendants can be traced all the way to Abraham. They constitute the righteous seed that believe in the only true God. It is critical to understand that the blessing of Shem is based on spiritual conversion, not on ethnic heritage (cf. Matt.3:9,10). The blessing of God rests on the godly line of believers within the descendants of Shem. "A man is not a Jew if he is only one outwardly," one who is born into the line of Shem, but "a man is a Jew if he is one inwardly; and circumcision is circumcision of the heart, by the Spirit" (Rom.2:28,29). Believers are the righteous remnant who by the power of the Lord's sustaining grace remain faithful to him (Rom.11:5). So not all who are descended from Israel are the true Israel; it is not through biological heritage that one is a child of God, but it is the children of promise who are Abraham's offspring (Rom.9:6b, 8).

There is no room in Christianity for ethnic elitism. To do so is to promote the superiority of one people group over another. The Lord is impartial (Rom.2:11). Yet Paul asks, "What advantage, then, is there in being a Jew?...Much in every way! First of all, they have been entrusted with the very words of God" (Rom.3:1,2). Nevertheless, some have not believed the oracles of God in Christ. So are Christians better than they are? "Not at all! We have already made the charge that Jews and Greeks alike are all under sin...so that every mouth may be silenced and the whole world held accountable to God" (Rom.3:9,19b). Paul then asks: "Where, then, is the boasting? It is excluded...Is God the God of Jews only? Is he not the God of Gentiles too? Yes, of Gentiles too, since there is only one God, who will justify the circumcised by faith and the uncircumcised through that same faith" (Rom.3:27,29,30). Faith is the key to receiving the blessing of Shem.

What is the blessing of Shem? God announces that Canaan will be Shem's servant. The very enemy of the righteous is destined to be the catalyst for blessing. Shem-Israel is to possess their promised land by subjugating the Canaanites and thereby making their enemies their servant-footstool (Psa.110:1; Matt.22:44). Instead of running away from our enemies, we are to fight the good fight of faith and dispossess the enemy. In so doing, the blessing of Shem becomes a reality. Every evil weapon that forms against the righteous will actually serve to benefit the righteous conqueror. "Shem would not be prevented from transmitting God's spiritual blessings to mankind through future opposition by Canaan…for indeed Canaan would be his 'servant,' helping him to accomplish it."[9] What Satan means for evil, God turns into good. Our enemies actually help us accomplish God's will.

"Shem" means "name." Shem carries out Seth's noble pursuit of calling on the name of the Lord. Shem is the image-bearer of God's name in the earth. Genesis 10:21-30 reveals some fascinating truths about the descendants of Shem. Through Elam, the Semites travel to Media-Persia. Asshur's descendants begin to build the Assyrian empire (Nimrod eventually invades Assyria and establishes Ninevah as his capital). This suggests that the lines of Shem and Ham cohabit in the land of Mesopotamia. Through Aram, came the Syrians who established the Aramaic language which is later used in parts of Daniel and Ezra and is commonly spoken during Jesus' earthly ministry. The Semites also make their way to Arabia through Joktan and the thirteen Arabian princes.

Joktan's brother, Peleg, is the predecessor of Abraham (Lk.3:34,35). Peleg means "divided." The earth is divided during the generation of Peleg (Gen.10:25) and this may infer that this division is caused by the scattering of the people at the tower of Babel. Shem's genealogy branches out through the Middle East and into the Arabian Peninsula. What is important to remember is that not all Shem-Israel is the true Israel of God. Faith is the key to receiving the blessings of Shem.

---

9. Morris, p.242.

2. The Blessing of Japheth

Noah's son, Japheth, receives a prophetic three-fold blessing of enlargement, inclusion, and authority. "May God extend the territory of Japheth; may Japheth live in the tents of Shem, and may Canaan be his slave" (Gen.9:27). The blessing of Japheth begins with enlargement, or better translated, "to break wide open." The Hebrew word "expand" (*yapht*) is in the hiphil future tense form of the verb which denotes the idea of making something open in order to be enlarged.

There is a paradoxical twist to Japheth's blessing. Japheth needs to be enlarged in order to fit into the tents of Shem. Japheth's heart must be spiritually enlarged. His heart must break wide open for him to enjoy the blessings of Shem's tent. Japheth's blessing falls on the descendants whose hearts are open to the God of Shem. The open-hearted Japheth-Gentiles change citizenship and transfer out of the apostate kingdom, City of Man, into the heavenly country, the City of God.

> Remember that formerly you who are Gentiles by birth...that at that time you were separate from Christ, excluded from citizenship in Israel and foreigners to the covenants of the promise, without hope and without God in the world. But now in Christ Jesus you who once were far away have been brought near through the blood of Christ. For he himself is our peace, who has made the two one and has destroyed the barrier, the dividing wall of hostility...to create in himself one new man out of two...Consequently, you are no longer foreigners and aliens, but fellow citizens with God's people and members of God's household...In him the whole building is joined together and rises to become a holy temple in the Lord...being built together to become a dwelling in which God lives by his Spirit. Ephesians 2:11-12,14-15,19,22

The Japheth-Gentile believers are engrafted branches of God's family tree. Paul says to them: "You will say then, 'Branches were broken off so that I could be grafted in.' Granted. But they were broken off because of unbelief, and you stand by faith" (Rom.11:19,20). Again, the basis for inclusion into the blessing of Shem's tents is faith in God, not family bloodlines.

Japhethite believers will take up residence in Shem-Israel's tents and construct a worldwide revival tent meeting.

> Sing, O barren woman, you who never bore a child; burst into song, shout for joy, you who were never in labor; because more are the children of the desolate woman than of her who has a husband…Enlarge the place of your tent, stretch your tent curtains wide, do not hold back; lengthen your cords, strengthen your stakes. For you will spread out to the right and to the left; your descendants will dispossess the nations and settle in their desolate cities. Isaiah 54:1-3

Isaiah expands Shem-Israel's tents to include the Japheth-Gentiles. This is the fulfillment of the Great Commission, the "whosoever-will" gospel message that goes out to all nations. Japheth's heart is enlarged and the stakes of Shem-Israel's tent open wide to include them. Joined to the covenant community of faith, Japhethite believers encounter Canaan as their enemy. In spite of this, God's promise to Japheth is to bring them under the same blessing of Shem and make Canaan serve him, too (Gen.9:27c).

The descendants of Japheth must experience the supernatural enlargement of their hearts to be included in the tents of Shem-Israel—but not all of Japheth is grafted into Shem's olive tree. Japheth's spiritual descendants are also "wide open" to following the dark side. Their open-mindedness leaves them susceptible to deception. So the spiritual heritage of the Japhethite lineage is open to be persuaded by truth or seduced into falsehood.

The seven descendants of Japheth are the progenitors of the European, Russian, and Indian cultures (Gen.10:2-5). The line of Gomer migrates up to Germany and into the Celtic regions, as well as Wales and Great Britain. Magog, Tubal, and Meshech travel to the Black Sea region and north to the Baltic States and modern Russia. Javan's line goes into Spain, Greece, and various parts of Asia Minor. The descendants of Madai head eastward to Persia and into India. Japheth's youngest son, Tiras, is probably the line that founded Italy.

3. *The Curse on Canaan*

The curse on the seed of the serpent continues: "Cursed be Canaan! The lowest of slaves will he be to his brothers" (Gen.9:25). Apparently, the curse of the serpent falls only on the youngest son, Canaan, not on all four sons of Ham (Gen.10:6). Unless any of the wives who entered the ark are descendants of Cain, we can assume that Cain's lineage perishes in the flood. More important than following the biological seed of Cain is to discern the diabolical spiritual seed of the serpent as it enters Ham and transfers only to Canaan. Noah discerns this evil transference and the text itself also lends to this conclusion by twice emphasizing "Ham, the father of Canaan" (Gen.9:18, 22). From the context we can assume that this phrase implies more than lineage; it signifies the transference of the spiritual seed of the serpent from parent to child (cf. Ex.20:5). The seed of the serpent thrives on generational curses.

Let's leave the spiritual seed of the serpent momentarily and look at the first three sons of Ham: Cush, Mizraim, and Put. All of Cush's descendants migrate to Ethiopia and south into Africa, except for one son, Nimrod. Nimrod did not follow his brothers into Africa, but joined forces with his uncle Canaan to eventually develop a kingdom in Shinar (Gen.11:2). Then "from that land he went to Assyria, where he built Ninevah" (Gen.10:10,11). Mizraim's line travel to Egypt and northern Africa, while Put goes beyond Egypt into Libya and further into western Africa. Mizarim's youngest son, Casluhim, also chooses to remain with his uncle Canaan, and from Casluhim come the

Philistines (Gen.10:14). The curse of the serpent did not fall on these lines, but only on Canaan. So it is fair to include the descendants of Cush, Mizraim, and Put in the same category as the "whosoever-will" Japhethites.

Amazingly, the delineation of Canaan's borders is the very perimeter of the promised land (Gen.10:15-20). This correlates with God's ironic use of his enemies. They are God's servants who paradoxically propel the purposes of God on the earth. Most of Canaan's descendants reside from Sidon and Phoenicia to the north and south toward Jerusalem and the Dead Sea. The Sinites are also descendants of Canaan and are the only people group who migrate east into China and Mongolia (cf. Gen.10:17).[10]

As stated earlier, the curse on Canaan is merely a continuation of the curse on the seed of the serpent. Such a discussion leads to the doctrine of predestination, which John Calvin refers as *decretum horrible* (the dreadful decree). The doctrine of predestination addresses two areas: election and reprobation. Louis Berkhof helps to clarify the mystery of God's predeterminate council.

> The fact that God favors some and passes by others, does not warrant the charge that He is guilty of injustice. We can speak of injustice only when one party has a claim on another. If God owed the forgiveness of sin and eternal life to all men, it would be an injustice if He saved only a limited number of them. But the sinner has absolutely no right or claim on the blessings which flow from divine election. As a matter of fact he has forfeited these blessings. Not only have we no right to call God to account for electing some and passing others by, but we must

---

10. Henry Morris states, "It is significant that the Chinese people have always been identified by the prefix 'Sino-' (e.g., Sino-Japanese War; Sinology, the study of Chinese history). The name 'Sin' is frequently encountered in Chinese names in the form 'Siang' or its equivalent." (*The Genesis Record*, p.256).

The Spiritual Reality of a Desecrated World

admit that He would have been perfectly just, if He had not saved any.[11]

Many of us may be uncomfortable with the concept of predestination, but we must trust in God's character and his sovereign plan. Jesus actually thanks God, the Father, because God has hidden the gospel truths "from the wise and learned, and revealed them to little children" as it seemed good to him (Matt.11:25,26). Christ acknowledges the mysterious wisdom of predestination as a doctrine based on good reasons sufficient to God alone. If all men are sinners, then election is a merciful and sovereign act of God. Reprobation is an act of justice. It responds to sin with judgment.

Paul expounds on this hard doctrine of predestination with the potter and clay analogy (Rom.9:18-24), while Peter addresses reprobation by stating, "They stumble [over Christ] because they disobey the message—which is also what they were destined for" (1 Pet.2:8,9). Jude refers to "certain men whose condemnation was written long ago...godless men, who change the grace of our God into a license for immorality and deny Jesus Christ our only Sovereign and Lord" (v.4). Since the fall, God has predestined two distinct lines: the seed of the serpent and the seed of the woman. Though all have sinned and come short of the glory of God, inclusion into the tents of Shem-Israel is based on God's sovereign election. It is by grace through faith that one is made righteous before God (Eph.2:8). Inclusion into the covenant community of God is not merited on the basis of family bloodlines, but rather it is established in grace, mercy, and faith.

The seed of the serpent thrives in the line of Canaan. They represent those actively opposed to the kingdom of God. The Lord desires all to receive salvation, but in his predeterminate counsel he knew those who would believe in him and those who would love darkness. Canaan represents the

---

11. Berkhof, Louis. *Systematic Theology*, (Grand Rapids: Eerdmans, 1984), p.115.

souls who love darkness. However, just because one is born into the family of Canaan does not automatically ensure condemnation. The same principle applies to Canaan as it does to those born into the families of Shem and Japheth. Bloodlines guarantee neither salvation nor damnation, but they do transfer a particular spiritual lineage to each successive generation (Ex.20:4).

Prophetic Pronouncement	Generational Seed	Migration Spiritual	Lineage
Curse	Canaan	Canaan "the land of purple"	Slavery
Offered Inclusion	Japheth (Cush, Mizarim, Put)	Europe, Asia, Africa	"Open-minded" to be either: 1) persuaded to join with Shem-Israel 2) seduced into deception with Canaan
Blessing	Shem	Mesopotamia, Arabia	God's Name-bearers of Righteousness

Predestination to election or reprobation is not based on bloodlines. It is purely granted on the basis of God's divine intervention and therefore a matter of the heart. Who dwells within the tents of Shem-Israel? Only those who believe in the Lord as the only true God. Their bloodlines may come from the families of Shem, Japheth, or Ham. Likewise, not all of Shem's descendants or all of Japheth's or Ham's children will be saved. Canaan represents the spiritual seed of the serpent who throughout history opposes and persecutes those who dwell in the tents of Shem. To ensure the point that even the descendants of Canaan can receive salvation is the fact that one of

Jesus' twelve disciples is Simon, the Canaanite (Mk.3:18). This proves that just because one is born into a certain family in a particular country does not automatically warrant blessing or curse. God looks on the heart.

Chapter Five

Coming to Terms with Satan's Cosmic Mountain

Dispersion of the Nations at the Tower of Babel

A mutinous revolution burgeons from Nimrod, one of Ham's grandsons. Nimrod is described as "a mighty warrior on the earth...a mighty hunter [against] the Lord," which fits the meaning of his name: "let us rebel" (Gen.10:8,9). Throughout his extensive empire, Nimrod builds strategic centers: Babylon, Erech (Uruk), Akkad, and Calnah in Shinar and Ninevah in Assyria (vv.10,11), with the express purpose to persecute God's people. He aggressively harasses the righteous seed, because he is a mighty hunter of *souls*. Nimrod determines to organize the nations to build an explosive, apostate, antichrist kingdom by tapping into Satan's cosmic mountain. Just like in Noah's generation, Satan is once again attempting to usurp God's timetable and manipulate certain evil conditions to unveil his man of sin.

In Genesis 11, Satan ostensibly proposes unlimited power to humanity—if only they will unify themselves in allegiance to evil.

> Now the whole world had one language and a common speech. As men moved eastward, they found a plain in Shinar and settled there. Then they said to each other, "Come, let's make bricks and bake them thoroughly."...Then they said, "Come, let us build ourselves a city, with a tower that reaches to the heavens, so that we may make a name for ourselves and not be scattered over the face of the whole earth." Genesis 11:1-4

Nimrod's followers settle in the fertile region between the Tigris and Euphrates rivers in Shinar (later called Babylonia), which is situated in ancient Mesopotamia and in modern-day Iraq. The seed of the serpent conspires to build its City of Man to counterfeit the City of God. The kingdom of darkness has its own city built on Satan's spiritual mountain. Its people gather together not to seek God or truth, but to contact the heavens for empowerment in order to make a name for themselves. In this scheme, Satan reveals that he has no original thought; he simply devises a ruse to pervert and counterfeit every aspect of God's holy mountain-kingdom (Isa.2:2,3).

All who join in Babel's united search for spiritual enlightenment will end up on a twisted, arduous journey to self-destruction. Augustine's famous dictum that the heart is restless until it finds its rest in God rings forever true, but unfortunately, many restless hearts build their own tower of Babel instead of seeking the Creator. Nothing can discourage the soul's longing for spiritual realities, even in its darkened state. The fact that they are frightened by an invisible threat of being scattered abroad over the earth is evidence of the effects of sin on their relationships. Fallen human beings yearn for brotherly love and unity, yet sin has isolated them from God and one another. So Babel is humanity's frail attempt to rally some kind of spiritual camaraderie, no matter how shallow, to replace the unity which was lost back in the Garden of Eden. The infamous tower of Babel represents humanity's aspiration to transcend their sphere of self. Humanity desperately wants to tranquilize the tumultuous spiritual void in their heart. Nimrod proposes that Babel's tower can offer some kind of connection with spiritual forces. Humans yearn to get in touch with something beyond themselves—what New Agers call "cosmic otherness." The ziggurat is designed to reach heaven; it is a simulated mountain-structure whose top is in the spiritual heavenly realm. It is Nimrod's point of spiritual contact with the forces of the universe. Babel is "the gate of god"; it is the birthplace of organized occultism ("that which is hidden" or "something secret, dark, mysterious, and concealed"). It is Nimrod who first organizes the occult's hidden secrets of demonic power into a religion. All ancient religions are merely elaborate spin-offs from the same basic occult techniques formed here at Babel's artificial mountain. Nimrod gathers the people together to encounter the secret gateways to the occult. They discover some shrouded passageways by which they can access the pernicious spiritual world of demonic influence. These secret mysteries of harlot Babylon will eventually spread throughout the world (Rev.17,18).

Satan's Cosmic Mountain

Throughout ancient history in virtually every culture, mountains have been regarded as sacred sites. Surely mountains can simply be considered as part of creation's landscape, but they can also represent mystical sacred space. Temples or towers are built on mountains, hills, and mounds that represent platforms for human-divine encounters. These elevated monuments are considered to bring the people closer to their deity, often where the god issues his decrees. From Mount Olympus for the Greeks to Mount Zaphon for the Canaanites, the dwelling place of the gods is constantly portrayed as a battleground for conflicting forces.

Simulated mountain-structures of the ancient Near East such as the ziggurat, the pyramid, Mount Zaphon, and the high place must also be considered as sacred sites. By a careful examination of cosmic mountain imagery, we can affirm the belief that these artificial pinnacles present an opportunity for humanity to access and be accessed by spiritual forces of evil. If we peel off the façade of the fascinating phenomena that surrounds them, we will be able to see them as diabolical representations of the true cosmic mountain of Yahweh as presented in the Bible.[1]

It is assumed that once a particular deity maintained a stronghold over its territory or locality, the followers could readily access the god. In the ancient Near East, each deity was assigned his locality in relation to the order of the satanically inspired mythological pantheon. When a god took on cosmic dimensions, their corresponding temple(s) were "made to symbolize, or represent, the cosmic divine abode."[2] In a similar way, spiritual demonstrations, which varied according to the mythological beliefs, sought to utilize everyday items to project this cosmic connection in its ritual symbolism.

> Thus either by means of their form, or some inner mysterious quality, earthly objects were thought to be capable of becoming charged with supernatural power, and so of establishing a link with the persons and abodes of the gods. This kind of reasoning undoubtedly lies at the basis of the use of images, which could, on account of their shape or substance, become one with the god himself.[3]

This is why God commands the Israelites not to "bring a detestable thing into your house or you, like it, will be set apart for destruction. Utterly abhor and detest it, for it is set apart for destruction" (Deut.7:26).

---

1. Because the term "mythological" has certain connotations that imply falsehood, my preference is to use the term "cosmological" when referring to the profoundly rich spiritual truths found in biblical mountain imagery.
2. Clements, R.E. *God and Temple*, (Philadelphia: Fortress Press, 1965), pp.1-2.
3. Clements, p.2.

Such reflective symbolism does not stop at sacred mountains. Mountains, as well as rivers, temples, cities, and territories all appear have their counterpart in the extraterrestrial sphere.[4] When profane space is transformed into sacred space through repetitive sacrifice, the site is secured—that is, when the ritual repeats or re-actualizes a primordial act performed initially by a god, an ancestor, or a hero—the sacred space transcends to enter "sacred time."[5] This suspension or transcendence of time occurs at a sacred locality on specific occasions of "cosmic regeneration" or "universal germination."[6] Details of various cultural mythologies may vary, but the "myth is 'late' only as a formulation; but its content is archaic and refers to sacraments—that is, to acts which presuppose an absolute reality, a reality which is extrahuman"[7]—or better stated, demonic.

If each temple represents an abode for spiritual encounters, then the elasticity of its imagery seems to point to a cosmic world-mountain, "so that the god who was worshipped in a particular area… was venerated at the same time as the creator of the universe."[8] Eliade sums up the "architectonic symbolism of the Center" in archaic belief systems:

1. The Sacred Mountain—where heaven and earth meet—is situated at the center of the world.

---

4. Eliade, Mircea. *The Myth of the Eternal Return or, Cosmos and History*, (Princeton: Princeton University Press, 1974), pp.6,9-10.
5. Eliade, *The Myth of the Eternal Return*, pp.20-29. These rituals repeat the "act of the cosmogonic construction. The sacrifice performed at the building of a house, church, bridge, is simply the imitation, on the human plane, of the sacrifice performed *in illo tempore* to give birth to the world" (p.30). Eliade states that "an object or an act becomes real only insofar as it imitates or repeats an archetype. Thus, reality is acquired solely through repetition or participation…A sacrifice, for example, not only reproduces the initial sacrifice…it also takes place at that same primordial mythical moment…man is projected into the mythical epoch in which the archetypes were first revealed" (pp.34-35).
6. Eliade, pp.25,35.
7. Eliade, p.27.
8. Clements, pp.2-3. Clements points out that a "certain elasticity was present even in the idea of 'land' itself, which could be interpreted both as a particular local region, and as the entire cosmos…Such a width of meaning is found in the Hebrew 'eres' = 'land, world.'"

2. Every temple or palace—and, by extension, every sacred city or royal residence—is a Sacred Mountain, thus becoming a Center.
3. Being an *axis mundi*, the sacred city or temple is regarded as the meeting point of heaven, earth, and hell.[9]

Satan desires to build his sacred (albeit sacrilegious) cosmic mountain. It is a spiritual mountain made up of multiple temple-sites (localities secured by territorial demonic entities). This worldwide multiplex creates a universal spiritual *axis mundi*. "When the *mundus* is open it is as if the gates of the gloomy infernal gods were open."[10] Apparently, the sacred mountain represents not only the dwelling place of the god, but also represents the mysterious yet arduous quest for the sacred Center, the navel of the world, "the zone of absolute reality."[11] To enter this spiritual zone, however, is to encounter the depths of satanism.

Simulated Cosmic Mountain-Structures of the Ancient Near East

Sumerian ziggurats, Egyptian pyramids, and Canaanite high places all functioned as artificial or imitation mountains.[12] The esoteric function of these artificial mountain-structures seems to offer humanity a passageway to the center of the threefold axis of heaven, earth, and hell beneath. Can they create a

---

9. Eliade, *The Myth of the Eternal Return*, p.12. Eliade affirms the idea that "Hell, the center of the earth, and the 'gate' of the sky are, then, situated on the same axis, and it is along this axis that passage from one cosmic region to another was effected" (p.13).
10. Marcus Terentius Varro, cited by Macrobius, *Saturnalia*, I, 16, 18.
11. Eliade, p.17.
12. The link between the mountain motif, the tower, and the Babylonian ziggurat is suggested in at least two other biblical allusions. First, in Jer.51:25 Babylon is dubbed "destroying mountain," perhaps a reference to the ziggurat (cf. Robert Cohn, *The Shape of Sacred Space, Four Biblical Studies*, AARSR 23, Chico: Scholars Press, 1981, p.34). Second, E.J. Hamlin argues that the mountains and hills to be "threshed" and destroyed in Isa.41:14-16 are Mesopotamian ziggurats, particularly the one in the city of Babylon itself ('The Meaning of Mountains and Hills in Isa.41:14-16,' *JNES*, 13, 1954, pp.185-190).

spiritual "stargate" where human beings can enter a fourth or multidimensional experience? They must offer some kind of mystical experience otherwise participants in this phenomena would simply discard its esoteric symbolism. They are deceptive, simulated representations meant to counterfeit the true cosmic mountain of God as presented in the Bible.

1. Mesopotamian Ziggurat

A ziggurat is a purposefully constructed, staged tower. Temple ruins may have accumulated on various sites but their piled up ruins do not qualify them as ziggurats. It is only when the builders construct terraces or stages that one can designate the site as a ziggurat. The ziggurat of Ur-Nammu (Ur) with its seven terraces may correspond to either the colors of the world as stated by the Greek historian Herodotus or to the astrological planetary spheres.[13] The ziggurat of Marduk in Babylon is known as *E-temen-anki* ("the house of the foundation of heaven and earth"), a pyramid-like structure that according to the Akkadian *Enuma Elish* was built by the Anunnaki. Even the names of the other ziggurats appear to indicate a cosmological function that connects heaven and earth and the netherworld.

There are a wide variety of theories for interpreting the purpose of the ziggurat: a king's tomb or throne, an altar, a sacred dwelling place, an image of the whole cosmos, or even the place where the energies of the earth are concentrated.[14] If Clements is correct that the "great Ziggurats, or stage-towers, of

---

13. Eliade, *The Myth of the Eternal Return*, p.13 (cf. Gutmann, p.10). The ziggurat of Ur was built by king Ur-Nammmu around 2100 B.C. and still stands today. Archaeologists have found about thirty ziggurats in the Mesopotamian area. One of the most famous is the ziggurat of the White Temple (Uruk, late 3000's B.C.).
14. See Andre Parrot, *The Tower of Babel*, trans. by Edwin Hudson, Studies in Biblical Archaeology, No. 2 (London: SCM Press, Ltd., 1955), p.57, and H.G. Wales, *The Mountain of God: A Study in Early Kingship* (London: Bernard Quaritch, Ltd., 1953), pp.14-15. Although more than one interpretation may be represented in its rich imagery, the theory of it representing a tomb is probably a false analogy to Egypt's pyramids (cf. Richard J. Clifford, *The Cosmic Mountain in Canaan and the Old Testament*, Cambridge: Harvard University Press, 1972, pp.22-25).

Sumeria...were an attempt on the part of men to build artificial mountains which could then serve as divine dwelling-places," then the formation of the ziggurat structure began during the Sumerian era from which the Babylonians later inherited.[15]

The main players of Sumerian belief are Anu, the supreme god of heaven, Enlil, god of the sea, and Enki, the creator and god of magic, plus other gods who personify local elements and natural forces. Sumerians believe that the gods and goddesses rule over them, but ceremonial priests that represent these gods and goddesses facilitate complex rituals in an attempt to ascertain and fulfill the will of the gods. Priests rule from their ziggurat-temples made of sun-baked brick with an outside staircase leading to a shrine at the top. It is striking that the Sumerian belief system seems more like a code of regulations that requires complete servitude, rather than a description of pure worship of the gods. This is also revealed in the sacred ritual marriage between rulers and Inanna, the goddess of love and fertility. Such union promises to yield not only prosperity, but also the lofty demigod status.

The ziggurat was considered to be a "giant step-ladder by means of which a man may ascend...to approach nearer to the deity whom he seeks."[16]

> In whatever religious context you find them—the shamanist rite or initiation rite, mystical ecstasy or oniric vision, eschatological myth or heroic legend—ascents, the climbing of mountains or stairs, flights into the air, and so on, all these things always signify a transcending of the human and a penetration into higher cosmic levels...it is their *ascent* that sets them apart form the mass of ordinary and uninitiated souls... their contact with starry spaces makes them divine.[17]

---

15. Clements, p.3.
16. Parrot, p.64.
17. Eliade, Mircea. *Patterns in Comparative Religion*, (Cleveland: World Publishing, 1968), p.108.

To ascend this artificial mountain, from the lowest to the highest terrace, is to transcend the earthly sphere and approach a cosmic otherness—the Center of the celestial world. "Attaining the center is equivalent to a consecration, an initiation."[18] And thus, the point of communication within the threefold axis of heaven, earth, and hell creates a center where "a break-through can occur, a passing from one cosmic zone to another."[19]

When we come to the text in Genesis 11, the obvious question is: Is the tower (*migdal*) of Genesis 11 a religious ziggurat? There are four uses of *migdal* in the Old Testament: 1) a shepherd's watchtower (the tower of Edar, Gen.35:21), 2) a vineyard watchtower (Isa.5:2; cf. Matt.21:33), 3) a military tower for defense (Jerusalem's towers, 2 Chron.26:9-15; Psa.48:12; Song.4:4; Neh.3:1; 12:39; Jer.31:38; Zech.14:10), and 4) religious towers (the migdal of Penuel eventually destroyed Gideon, Jud.8:9, 17; the migdal of Shechem, Jud.9:46; and the migdal of Syene, Ezek.29:10; 30:6). Associated with the migdal at Shechem we find a Canaanite revival in the temple of El/Baal-Berith, a foreign deity at Shechem (Jud.9:4, 27, 46-49). When the people hear about the fate of Shechem they flee from the migdal to "the house (temple) of the covenant god (Baal-berith), evidently not for the purpose of defending themselves there, but to seek safety at the sanctuary of their god"—thus linking the temple of Shechem with its religious migdal.[20] Ezekiel's pronouncement of judgment on the migdal of Syene in Egypt must allude to its religious connotation with Pharaoh's claim to be the creator-god of the Nile River (29:10; 30:6).

The Hebrew term *migdal* is certainly used as a military tower, but in all probability it is likely to include the ziggurat-structure. Although the Hebrew text of Genesis 11 does not use the term ziggurat, *migdal* may be a derivative of the Hebrew term *gdl* (large), which etymologically parallels the Akkadian

---

18. Eliade, *The Myth of the Eternal Return*, p.18
19. Eliade, *Patterns in Comparative Religion*, p.111.
20. Keil C.F., Delitzsch F. *Commentary on the Old Testament*, vol. 2, (Grand Rapids: Eerdmans, 1985), p.370.

zaqaru (high). The context of Genesis 11 and the background of the narrative compel us to consider a nonmilitary function of migdal.

If one looks at God's response to the building of the migdal-tower structure, one can see that its construction is disturbing to the heavenly council (Gen.11:1-6). Why? If this tower is simply a military fortification or a shepherd's tower or a vineyard watchtower, then why does God respond so harshly? Unity has many commendable assets that strengthen any given work. So why does God deem this harmonious project so threatening? The Lord explains to his heavenly council that this particular kind of unity is horrific and completely intolerable. The migdal-tower is obviously not a military fortification to defend Babylon, but a spiritual lightning rod—a religious ziggurat.

Archaeological excavations confirm that these ancient ziggurats of Babylon have two sanctuaries: one at the top and one at the base. If the Babylonian ziggurats are patterned after the Sumerian migdal, then we can reasonably conclude that the ziggurat-migdal provides a spiral staircase for the Mesopotamian gods to descend to meet their ascending devotees. The ziggurat is designed to reach heaven, a tower whose top is in the heavens. The ziggurat is built to be a point of spiritual contact with the evil forces of the universe, to unify humans with the demonic, and to secure their allegiance to evil—knowingly or unknowingly worshipping the devil himself. Humanity is uniting themselves with demonic forces bent on executing Satan's diabolical plan to accelerate the fruition of the antichrist kingdom and thwart God's timetable.

The people who gather around the ziggurat seek not a relationship with the one true God, but the heavenly realm for personal empowerment. Babel's ziggurat-tower offers a connection with spiritual forces beyond human existence, thus opening the doors for demonic spirits to legally gain access to the mind and spirit of human beings. Occultism via the ziggurat promises power and control over people and events. It purports that one can tap into its forces to manipulate one's circumstances and transcend God's sovereign rule. Resisting subjection to God, people seek to affect reality—but their power, however, is merely a delusion. The ziggurat represents humanity's vain attempt to overthrow their appointed jurisdiction and empower themselves with forces bent on destroying not only the kingdom of God but humanity as well.

2. Egyptian Pyramid

Thirty-five major pyramids still stand along the Nile River. The famous Egyptian Step Pyramid is built for Zoser about 2650 B.C. at the site of the ancient city of Memphis, Saqqarah. It rises in a series of six giant steps. The three Pyramids of Giza (Cheops) are built for Khufu, Khafre, and Menkaure about 2600-2500 B.C. Each pyramid includes a large mortuary temple on the east side and a smaller valley temple near the Nile. There is also a long passageway that links the two temples. Inside the pyramid are two chambers: the king's burial chamber, the most sacred part of the pyramid, and the queen's chamber. The Egyptians believed that if a person's body could be preserved, the soul could live forever. So the Egyptians mummified their dead and laid them in large tombs where they would await their transport to the next world.

To determine the exact purpose for the building of the Egyptian pyramids is difficult and complex.[21] There appears to be three main theories: 1) the Orion theory, 2) the divine time-line theory, and 3) the traditional theory. A brief overview of each of these theories will prove helpful to our discussion on Satan's cosmic mountain imagery.

The Orion theory proposes that the three Pyramids of Giza are designed in perfect alignment with the three stars in the Orion Nebula. Apparently, the purpose for building these pyramids is not to provide a burial chamber, but rather, because the air shafts

---

21. There are many pyramids throughout the world such as: the Pyramid of Hellenikon (Argolis, Greece), the Chinese Pyramids (Qin Chuan), the Pyramids of Guimar (Canary Islands, Spain), the Mayan Pyramids (Palenque, Mexico), the Valley of the Pyramids (Chiclayo, Peru), and the Teotihuacan Pyramids (Teotihuacan, Mexico), but for this study we will focus solely on Egyptian pyramids.

inside the pyramid point directly to certain constellations they are built with some kind of astrological design. At the time the pyramid was built, the king's chamber pointed toward Orion and Polaris, while the shafts coming out of the queen's chamber pointed toward Sirius and Alpha Draconis. The assumption would be that the deceased king and queen would be sent towards these constellations and unite with the power of their gods.

The divine timeline theory proposes that Isaiah testifies that the Egyptian pyramid is in fact "an altar to the Lord in the midst of the land of Egypt, and a pillar at the border...and it will be for a sign and for a witness" (19:19,20). Proponents also cite Jeremiah 32:30 as another proof text that God is the instigator of these artificial mountains in that he will "set signs and wonders in the land of Egypt, even unto this day." This theory presents the idea that salvation history, or some kind of prophetic chronicle, is revealed in the pyramid's dimensions and internal arrangement. So this theory presents the pyramid as a witness to God and in line with the biblical account.[22]

Is the pyramid "an altar (*mizbeah*)" to the one true God, Yahweh? Is the pyramid "a pillar (*matstebah*)", "for a sign (*oth*) and for a witness (`*ed*)" to him? Would these descriptions: an altar (used 401 times in the Old Testament referring to a place of sacrifice), a pillar (a monument or memorial), a sign (a signal or distinguishing mark), and a witness (designating a testimony or evidence), be applied to the Egyptian pyramid? The divine timeline theory could probably make their case with all the descriptions, except for one—the altar. There appears to be no evidence that the pyramids were used in any way for sacrifices.

Problems abound in the divine timeline theory interpretation of the pyramid. First, would God use pagan structures built for deified pharaohs to proclaim his redemptive plan? God warned his people to tear down pagan altars and smash cultic pillars (Ex.34:13; Deut.7:5). Second, were not the Egyptian pharaohs

---

22. See G. Riffert, *Great Pyramid Proof of God*, (Merrimac: Destiny, 1960), J. Seiss, *The Great Pyramid: A Miracle in Stone*, (New York: Harper & Row, 1973), and W. Smith, *Miracle of the Ages, the Great Pyramid*, (Terrytown: Robert Collier, 1948).

engaged in the worship of a multitude of false gods? The whole Exodus event occurs not only as a miraculous deliverance of God's people, but also as an indictment against the idolatry of Egypt (Ex.7-12; Jer.43:13). Third, if the pyramids were built in alignment with the constellations, would God encourage such participation in astrology? The law and the prophets vehemently denounce any involvement in this and all forms of occultism (Deut.18:9-12). Fourth, was not Egyptian theology particularly steeped in the myth of Osiris and Isis? To use the pyramid to reflect the plan of salvation history is an attempt to syncretize the Osiris/Isis mythology with the true Messiah and his virgin birth, death, and resurrection. This interpretation pushes its Masonic-like prophecies beyond the realm of solid hermeneutics. It is ultimately an effort to discredit, confuse, and mythologize the truth of the substitutionary death and resurrection of the Lord Jesus Christ.

Some believe that Isaiah 19:19,20 and Jeremiah 32:30 signify a future Jewish presence in Egypt, either referring to the Jews who fled to Egypt after the Babylonian invasion (Jer.44:1) or to the Jewish high priest Onias IV, who receives permission from an Egyptian monarch to build a temple "like that in Jerusalem" in 160 B.C. (Josephus, Ant.XII.9, 7)—even though it was really more of a castle than a temple.[23] In the literary context of these prophecies it is best to interpret them eschatologically, thereby referring to native Egyptians who convert to Christianity and join in a worldwide ministry with other Gentile peoples on the highway of holiness (Isa.19:20-25).

> It was a victory on the part of the religion of Jehovah, that Egypt was covered with Jewish synagogues...even in the age before Christ. And Alexandria was the place where the law of Jehovah was translated into Greek, and thus made accessible to the heathen world...The importance of Alexandria and of the monasticism

---

23. H.C. Leupold, *Exposition of Isaiah*, vol. 1, (Grand Rapids: Baker Book, 1988), p.319, and Herbert M. Wolf, *Interpreting Isaiah, The Suffering and Glory of the Messiah*, (Grand Rapids: Zondervan, 1985), pp.124-125.

Spiritual Reality

and anachoretism of the peninsula of Sinai and also of Egypt, in connection with the history of the spread of Christianity, is very well known.[24]

Traditional Egyptology suggests that the pyramids were primarily elaborate burial chambers. Their architecture reflects the ancient Egyptian belief that their kings were gods, and that they built tombs, temples, and palaces as monuments to them. Even if one cannot decipher the exact purpose for the pyramids, it is important to note the development of Egyptian mythology. During the first Egyptian dynasty of Menes (3100 B.C.), Egyptian myth places Osiris, the fertility god, in a primeval holy mountain to bury him, and then elevates and enthrones him in the heavens with a reborn status. The ancient Egyptians believed that the pyramid held some kind of cosmic power to transport the soul of Osiris to Orion, where he would assimilate to a physical incarnation of god on earth. By participating in a ceremony, the new pharaoh is infused with Osiris' spirit. The pyramid is used to bring about the union of the new pharaoh at his coronation with the spirit of Osiris to become the form of Horus, a living embodiment of Osiris and Isis' divine son. Upon death he joins in the oneness of Osiris.

We can see that Egyptian mountain-imagery projects both burial mound and throne.[25] So it is reasonable to believe that the pyramids symbolize the "primeval earth which arose from the primeval ocean on the day of creation and was the source of all existence...Because the primeval hill was the source of all life, the burial mound represented a center of great potency."[26] Apparently this potency was symbolized in its triangular sides which "represented the rays of the sun which formed a ladder of light...the ramp or passageway...to heaven"[27]—not unlike the symbolism of the ziggurat.

---

24. Keil, C.F., Delitzsch, F. *Commentary on the Old Testament,* vol. 7, Isaiah, (Grand Rapids: Eerdmans, 1986), pp.365-368.
25. Clifford, p.27.
26. Gutmann, pp.12-13; (cf. John A. Wilson, *"Egypt,"* in *Before Philosophy,* Hammondsworth: Penguin Books, 1949, pp.59-61).
27. Gutmann, p.14.

3. Baal's Mount Zaphon

Similar to Osiris' grave-turned-enthronement scenario, Canaanite mythology presents Baal warring against Mot (the god of death and the underworld) on the heights of Mount Zaphon and he too is buried in his holy mount—only to be reborn to build his temple on Zaphon.[28] Baal, the masculine god-force (his alter-ego goddess-force seems to be a mix between Anath, Asherah, and Astarte), is also known by his proper name, Hadad, which relates to his storm-god aspect (we will further explain Canaanite mythology in chapter six). But Baal is simply a title that means "lord." Baal and Yamm compete for kingship of the gods, and after Yamm's defeat, Baal has his palace built on Mount Zaphon. The Baal epic then continues to describe his annual fight against Mot. Yet Baal maintains his residence on Mount Zaphon.

> [Baal] informs Anat, his ally, to put on the face of the goddess of fertility and to hasten to him. A temple which is to celebrate and bring about fertility and cosmic harmony is to be built...Baal will seek the temple for his holy place, on the mountain which he has acquired by his victory over the forces of evil...Zaphon is a place where messages are delivered to Baal, where Baal works that a temple may be built there. It was stormed by enemies, though they were beaten back by Baal and Anat...[therefore] Baal's mountain is a place of combat in which issues of life and death are decided; it is a place which commemorates victory.[29]

Zaphon as the location of Baal's burial and regeneration, his battles, and his attempt to create cosmic harmony clearly ties into Satan's cosmic mountain imagery of the ziggurats and pyramids.

Many mountains are designated to be the sacred sites of Baal-Zaphon, "lord of the north," but only two are mentioned

---

28. Clifford, pp.58-61.
29. Clifford, pp.74-75,79,97.

in the Bible: 1) in Egypt, northeast of the Nile delta near where the Israelites cross over in their miraculous exodus (Ex.14:2; Numb.33:7), and 2) in Syria (Ezek.14:2,9). The typical biblical understanding for Baal's dwelling place is "the mountain of the far north (*zaphon*)," (cf. Isa.14:13) but this geographical designation appears to be only one of *zaphon*'s meanings.[30] Firstly, *zaphon* identifies a national enemy located north of Israel (i.e. Isa.41:25; Jer.1:14; 4:6; 6:1, 22; 10:22; Jer.50:9; 51:48; Ezek.26:7; Joel 2; Zeph.2:13). These passages pertain to Assyria and Babylon, the literal foes "from the north (zaphon)," who fulfill the typology necessary to foreshadow the eschatological kingdom of darkness that threatens to encompass the true kingdom-city of God, the people of God in the latter days.

Secondly, *zaphon* suggests the place of "the heights"—or what Christians refer to as the heavenly or spiritual realm. The "northern heights" or heavenly battlefields are essentially the dimension that symbolizes the realm where Yahweh upholds victory and lordship (Job 37:22; Psa.48:2; Ezek.1:4ff.). From these references it appears that "heights" symbolize lordship.[31] Yet the spiritual heights of zaphon also indicate the place where Satan's obtrusive, tyrannical reign threatens to intrude into God's territory and spiritually dominate (Ezek.38:6-15; 39:2).

> The north, then, becomes a harbinger of evil. In various mythologies it is the seat of demons...In Canaanite mythology the north was considered to be the place for the meeting of the assembly of the gods. The gods assembled on Mount sapân; sapân may be taken as a proper name. Here Baal reigned supreme. The mountain is usually identified with Mount Casius, Jebel el Aqra`, to the north of Ras Shamra. Kapelrud suggests that the tower for sacrifices in Baal's temple may have been called Sapan, a mythical

---

30. Clifford states that Zaphon of the "north" is its secondary meaning (p.57).
31. Whitney, J.T. "'*Bamoth*' in the Old Testament," *Tyndale Bulletin*, 30, (Cambridge: Tyndale House, 1979), p.136.

connection between the mountain and the cultic shrine (p.58).³²

If heights symbolize lordship in the Bible, then this concept "may help us understand why shrines were first erected on heights, thereby claiming the symbol of lordship for the gods."³³ Remarkably, Baal's Mount Zaphon is brazenly declared to be Lucifer's headquarters. It is Lucifer himself who openly asserts:

> I will ascend to heaven; I will raise my throne above the stars of God; I will sit enthroned on the mount of assembly, on the utmost heights [*yerekah*, meaning, "flank, extreme parts, recesses, sides, coasts, borders"] of [zaphon]. I will ascend above the tops of the clouds; I will make myself like the Most High (Isa.14:12-14).

This avowal not only divulges that Lucifer is Baal, but also reveals his arrogant attempt to usurp God's lordship. His plan is to: 1) broaden his authority over "the stars of God" (former angels turned demonic), 2) gather his own "mount of assembly" (deceived congregation of followers), 3) extend his dominion from the peak (headquarters) of Zaphon to its outermost borders [yerekah]. Isaiah 14:12-14 affirms the spiritual reality of Satan's plan to build a cosmic mountain-structure, a spiritual *axis mundi* throughout the whole world.

4. Canaan's Corresponding High Places

The imagery and symbolism of Mount Zaphon is reflected in microcosmic proportions in the sexual-fertility rituals of the Canaanite "high place" (*bamah*).³⁴ According to Scripture, *bamah* seems to litter the ancient land of Canaan. These

---

32. Harris, R., Archer G., Waltke. B., editors. *Theological Wordbook of the Old Testament*, vol. 2, (Chicago: Moody Press, 1984), p.774, (cf. Kapelrud, A. S., Baal in the Ras Shamra Texis, Copenhagen: G. E. C. Gad, 1952).
33. Whitney, p.136.
34. See William Creighton Graham and Herbert Gordon May, *Culture and Conscience*, (Chicago: University of Chicago, 1936), p.133.

Canaanite establishments are built on mountains (1 Sam.9:13-25; 1 Kgs.11:7; 2 Kgs.16:4; 17:9,10; Ezek.20:28,29), but they also dwelt in towns (1 Kgs.13:32; 2 Kgs.17:29; 23:5), in the bustling city of Jerusalem (2 Kgs.23:8),[35] and in the valleys (Jer.7:31; 32:35; Ezek.6:3).

> Such a survey [of the biblical texts, especially 2 Kings 23] shows that in the closing years of the monarchy period many types of cult centre were thought of as bamoth—small gate shrines, royal centres to foreign gods, large public shrines, local rustic shrines and even Topheth [where child sacrifices were made to Molech]. Their situations are as varied as their cults—on hills, in cities and settlements, by the city gate and in a valley. The inescapable conclusion is that by this period bamoth was a general word for a small shrine...Their demise is lost in the obscurity of the post-exilic era. All that can be said is that they disappear from both the literary and archaeological evidence at the time when Judaism began to emerge.[36]

It is certain then, that the term "high place" means something much more that just a physically elevated sacred site. Because they are described as being constructed and destroyed, such a possibility indicates that "they were man-made structures requiring considerable effort to build or to demolish."[37]

---

35. Emerton, J.A. "'The High Places of the Gates' in 2 Kings XXIII 8," *Vetus Testamentum*, vol. 44, No. 4, (Leiden: E.J.Brill, Oct. 1994). Whitney suggests that these "gate-bamoth were doubtless very simple affairs and are to be associated with threshold superstitions" (p.141) and possibly guardian deities (J. Gray). H. Hirschberg thinks the gates of bamoth are columns that represent phallic symbols or are columns with engraved pictures of female genitals (*VT* 11, 1961, p.381). Yigael Yadin believes that the location of the "gates of the bamoth" in 2 Kings 23:8 were not in Jerusalem, but in Beersheba ("*Beer-Sheba: The High Place Destroyed by Josiah*," *BASOR*, Missoula: Scholars Press, April 1976, pp.5-17).
36. Whitney, pp.137-138, 146.
37. Whitney, p.142.

Although it is still difficult to ascertain the exact composition of bamoth (plural), most theories develop around the Old Testament text and little archaeological evidence.[38]

The evidence that is available seems to indicate that the open-air bamoth are probably artificial, truncated, cone-shaped structures that have stairs leading to a flat oblong platform on the top.[39]

The following are definite features characteristic of bamoth: 1) the messabah, a commemorative upright stone that signifies an unholy alliance, 2) the Asherah, the mother-fertility goddess of the Canaanite pantheon, 3) the altar for animal and child sacrifice, 4) pagan priests, 5) burning of incense, 6) a stairway that led to an oval platform, and 7) additional rooms.[40] The rituals performed in Canaanite worship involve excesses in alcohol and sexual deviation. Ezekiel 22:9 states: "In you are slanderous men bent on shedding blood; in you are those who eat at the mountain shrines and commit lewd acts" (cf. Ezek.18:6). The worship of Baal is essentially a drunken orgy in which the Canaanite priests and other participants indulged a frenzy of perversity and violent behavior. Such a precarious ritual is their attempt to arouse Baal to send his semen-rain on their crops (see Appendix A for a display of the peculiarities of the Canaanite ritual system and God's prohibition and commands for the destruction of its demonic order).

Through a careful etymological analysis of the word *bamah*, these Canaanite high places have similarities to the symbolism of the cosmic mountain imagery of the ziggurats and pyramids of ancient history. Vaughan concludes that the meaning of *bamah* is reflected in three senses: topological, cultic, and anatomical

---

38. See W.F. Albright, *"The High Place in Ancient Palestine," Supplement Vetus Testamentum,* IV, (Leiden: E.J. Brill, 1957), pp.242ff., and Albright's *Yahweh and the Gods of Canaan, A Historical Analysis of Two Contrasting Faiths,* (Garden City: Doubleday and Co., 1968), pp.203-205.
39. Vaughan, Patrick H. *The Meaning of 'Bama' in the Old Testament,* A Study of Etymological, Textual and Archaeological Evidence, (Cambridge: Cambridge University Press, 1974), p.45.
40. de Voux, Roland. *Ancient Israel, Vol.2, Religious Institutions,* (New York: McGraw-Hill, 1961), pp.284-285.

senses.[41] To this I would add a fourth sense: the spiritual level of bamah. It is true that bamah is simply a location (topological level), but it is also a platform for satanic rituals in operation (cultic level). It is imperative that one takes the concept of bamah a step further in order to analyze the human experience in taking part in the occult ritual (anatomical level). Ultimately, one must then form a conclusion about the participant's mystical encounter with the demonic realm (spiritual level).

Bamah

Bamah are "high places" because they are impregnated with spiritual forces. " 'Height', 'what is higher' becomes transcendent, super-human. Every ascent [spiritually] is a breakthrough…a passing to what is beyond, an escape from profane space and human status."[42] The Canaanites tap into demonic forces when participating in the occult rituals at the bamoth. Participants in these rituals align themselves with the demonic realm and seal their allegiance through sexual-fertility ceremonies and death-ritual covenants. "The transcending of the human condition by entering a sacred place [in the case of Canaan, bamah], by some ritual consecration, or by dying, is expressed concretely as a 'passage', a 'rising', an 'ascension.'"[43] So bamah's open-air platform is not only constructed for occult rituals, it also represents and actualizes the inner spiritual experience of those who adhere to Canaan's belief system.

If these ancient Near Eastern bamah-structures really did provide a means to transcend human existence in order to connect with the three-fold axis of the heavenly, earthly, and underworld, then this would explain the dangerously demonic trigger-mechanisms that infect the spiritual health of God's people. If they create a spiritual experience where human beings and demonic entities can move from one spiritual zone to enter another, then the human experience at the bamoth is at odds

---

41. Vaughan, p.51; cf. *TWOT*, vol.1, p.113.
42. Eliade, *Patterns in Comparative Religion*, p.101.
43. Ibid, p.102.

Spiritual Level: Canaanite Ritual in its Mystical Dimension	A cognate of bamah is found in Akkadian and Ugaritic and implies: "ridge, heights, lofty spot"
Anatomical Level: Canaanite Ritual in its Human Experience	In Ugaritic bamah means: "rib-cage, middle-of the body, flank" of a person or animal
Cultic Level: Canaanite Ritual in its Operation	Ugaritic and archaeology convincingly argues that bamah infers a "cultic platform and by extension, altar and sanctuary"
Topological Level: Canaanite Ritual in its Location	The biblical text and archaeological evidence locates bamah in the "hillside, town, city, valley"

with the law of God as revealed in the Scripture. Because Israel did not carry out the holy war mandate, the Canaanite bamoth offered to replace true worship and in due course desecrate the dwelling place/meeting place of Yahweh with his people. Ezekiel pronounces God's judgment on the mountain-shrines that covered the land of Israel:

> This is what the Sovereign Lord says to the mountains and hills, to the ravines and valleys: I am about to bring a sword against you, and I will destroy your high places. Your altars will be demolished and your incense altars will be smashed; and I will slay your people in front of your idols...They will loathe themselves for the evil they have done and for all their detestable practices (6:3,4, 9).

Baalism seeped into the very fabric of Yahwistic worship practices and therefore heaven responded with severe judgment.

Dabbling in the occult proves to be extremely harmful. It opens the way for demonic spirits to inflict bondage on those who tap into their powers (Psa.106:35-38; 1 Cor.10:20). The lure of the occult is simple: it promises power and control over people and events. The devil's tactic is the same as it was with Adam and Eve: "your eyes will be opened...and you will be like God" (Gen.3:5). Satan's religion, the occult, lures its victims into believing that the devil holds some mystical, hidden power. It purports that one can tap into its forces to manipulate one's circumstances and transcend God's sovereign rule. Resisting any subjection to God, people seek to manipulate spiritual forces. Control, however, is always just an illusion. Occultism is the futile attempt to determine one's destiny and to take the place of God. "These demonic forces allow themselves to be used. The price for such a service means the complete enslavement of the individual...Even though the person involved is able to manipulate these powers for a while, in the end he is completely enslaved."[44] Building the tower of Babel is not just the construction of another skyscraper. It is the strategy of Satan to seduce people into participating in the demonic *axis mundi*, to connect the people of the earth with his wicked cosmic mountain-structure.

God characterizes the people as being totally unified and as they begin to build this occult pyramid: "nothing they plan to do will be impossible for them" (Gen.11:6). Unity is usually a praiseworthy quality, so why is God's response so dramatic? Apparently, unity that is based on evil intent destabilizes society and is a serious menace to God's worldwide purposes. At the tower, humanity is uniting themselves with demonic forces bent on executing Satan's diabolical takeover. Satan is plotting to fill the earth with evil—obviously reminiscent of the days preceding the flood. The Lord averts another bid to accelerate the fruition of the antichrist kingdom. Satan desires to unveil his man of sin, the son of perdition, who will attempt to encroach on God's divine timetable. When referring to the days preceding Christ's Second Coming, Paul explains that there is a divine restraint on the devil's infringement into God's celestial schedule.

---

44. Thompson, Carroll. *Possess the Land*, (Dallas: CTM Publishing, 1977), p. 60.

> Don't let anyone deceive you in any way, for that day will not come until the rebellion occurs and the man of lawlessness is revealed, the man doomed for destruction...And now you know what is holding him back, so that he may be revealed at the proper time. For the secret power of lawlessness is already at work; but the one who now holds it back will continue to do so till he is taken out of the way. And then the lawless one will be revealed, whom the Lord will overthrow with the breath of his mouth and destroy by the splendor of his coming. 2 Thessalonians 2:3,6-8

Paul refers to the man of lawlessness in eschatological and apocalyptic terms. This terminology is exactly the same point that God makes in Genesis 11. God has determined an appointed time for the end of the age and nothing can thwart his schedule. The tower of Babel presents a type of the latter day falling away that John characterizes in apocalyptic form as Mystery, Babylon the Great, the Mother of Harlots (Rev.17:5). Revelation 17:13 reflects the end time fulfillment of Genesis 11 when the apostate, antichrist harlot Babylon system unites itself and hands her power to the beast. This graphically demonstrates the enslavement of those in contact with the occult. The delusion is that in Genesis 11, it appears as a ziggurat-mountain to the people of the world, but in Revelation, John exposes its true essence. Behind the tower lies a seductive whore who craves the honor, worship, and allegiance of mankind.

Paul comforts us by emphasizing the divine restraint on the man of sin, "that he may be revealed at the proper time"(2 Thess.2:6). The mystery of lawlessness has always been in operation; it is designed to prematurely preempt God's prophetic schedule. Satan is building his cosmic mountain structure. Seekers crave spiritual experiences and Satan will not disappoint them with his attractive, idolatrous construction sites. To enter into his spiritual zones is to encounter demonic entanglement and eventual enslavement. It is a spiritual reality that the Church must come to grips with in the latter days.

Tongues of Judgment, Tongues of Fire

How does God respond to the fabrication of Babel? One might guess that God would launch hail and brimstone down from heaven to level the tower. Or maybe an earthquake would sufficiently tumble this monument of defiance. As oftentimes happens, God chooses none of our options. Rather, in his infinite wisdom, God chooses to frustrate the devil's scheme by diversifying tongues and scattering the nations. The Lord says, "'Come, let us go down and confuse their language so they will not understand each other.' So the Lord scattered them from there over all the earth, and they stopped building the city" (Gen.11:7,8).

This certainly is adequate to take care of the problem, but why did God choose this particular form of judgment? The answer takes on a significantly profound, redemptive meaning in the New Covenant. On one hand, the judgment of tongues impedes the momentum of the antichrist movement by injecting confusion into the unified construction of the City of Man. It also sets the stage for a wondrously ironic twist of events for the righteous seed and the building of the City of God.

God's plan is initiated at Babel and then repeatedly set forth throughout the prophetical books. God scatters the nations to the ends of the earth and promises to search them out, like a shepherd looking for his sheep, to gather them unto himself (Ezek.34:11ff.). "I will bring your children from the east and gather you from the west. I will say to the north, 'Give them up!' and to the south, 'Do not hold them back.' Bring my sons from afar and my daughters from the ends of the earth—everyone who is called by my name" (Isa.43:5,6). The gathering is to Christ the banner who stands on top of Mount Zion (Isa.11:1,10-12).

This piece of the redemptive program begins with the dispersion at Babel and is fulfilled in the re-gathering of believers on the day of Pentecost. Here we find tongues again at the center of controversy. God will oftentimes work an ironic twist into the events of history. The judgment of tongues is just one of many ironies displayed in the Bible. Under judgment, human beings are scattered all over the earth. They constantly face chaos, solitude, bigotry, and the turbulence that is caused by the upheaval of the ethnocentricity of various languages. Babel represents humanity's alignment with evil forces and their attainment of false unity and false peace. Pentecost is God's reversal of his judgment at Babel.

The prophet Zephaniah remarkably discloses the divine plan to reverse the judgment on tongues in the New Covenant. God will "purify [*barar* meaning, "pure, clear, clean"] the lips (language) of the peoples, that all of them may call on the name of the Lord and serve him shoulder to shoulder" (3:9). The Lord gives the gift of the Holy Spirit to unify his people. By giving them "pure lips" or "clear language," God reverses the antagonism of Babel and releases the supernatural baptismal enablement for his new creational disciples to rise up as his witness to the ends of the earth (Acts 1:4,8). What God implements as equipment for the Church to call on the name of the Lord and to serve him with one accord, has instead gyrated into just one of the many heated theological battlefields on which the Body of Christ has been dismembered.

Whatever controversy tongues may bring to the Church, we cannot deny that the magnificent heaven-sent gift of the Holy Spirit is designed to redeem our fractured world. In Acts 2:1-6, Luke dramatically records Babel's reversal.

> When the day of Pentecost came, they were all together in one place. Suddenly a sound like the blowing of a violent wind came from heaven and filled the whole house where they were sitting. They saw what seemed to be tongues of fire that separated and come to rest on each of them. All of them were filled with the Holy Spirit and began to speak in other tongues as the Spirit enabled them. Now there were staying in Jerusalem God-fearing Jews from every nation under heaven. When they heard this sound, a crowd came together in bewilderment, because each one heard them speaking in his own language.

They are stunned to hear people from every nation under heaven speak in other languages the wonderful works of God (Acts 2:5-11). They ask the question most Christians have asked themselves, "What does this mean?" (v.12). This is the fulfillment of Joel's prophecy concerning the outpouring of the Holy Spirit on all nations (Acts 2:12-21). The descent of the Holy Spirit not only results in the salvation of three thousand souls, it also produces a fellowship of believers who enjoyed genuine unity (Acts 2:41-47).

There are "all sorts of languages in the world, yet none of them is without meaning... For this reason anyone who speaks in a tongue should pray that he may interpret what he says" (1 Cor.14:10, 13). Without interpretation, the gift of tongues is nothing more than unintelligible babbling. Without interpretation, tongues cannot edify the individual (v.4) or the corporate Church (vv.6-19). Paul exhorts us to be mature in our understanding of the matter by quoting Isaiah 28:11,12. Just as the Babylonians' foreign language was a sign of judgment on Judah, so again tongues is a sign of judgment, not for believers but for unbelievers (1 Cor.14:20-22). Tongues of fire are a sign to the unbeliever that Christians are now aliens to their world (Eph.2:12).

Believers in Christ are not of this world; they are citizens of the kingdom of God. As citizens of God's commonwealth, we are given a purified tongue of fire to use to witness to the world the wonderful works of God. Our lips can reflect the dialect of our heavenly country, meant to be expressed in a decent and orderly fashion (vv. 26-33,40). Tongues are not given to cause confusion and division. It is one of many supernatural gifts that enable the Body of Christ to be edified and empowered for world evangelism (1 Cor.14:4; Acts 1:5, 8).

The Greek word, "separated, divided" or "cloven" (*diamerizo*) means, "to part in two." On the day of Pentecost, the fire of tongues appear divided. Since the tower of Babel, humanity has been divided by language barriers and scattered throughout the earth. But now in the New Covenant age, the Holy Spirit is the purifying "fire" of God that rests on believers to unify and empower them.

Throughout the Bible, Scripture attests to manifold ways that God "speaks" to his people. The list of the gifts of the Spirit attest to the variety of ways that God still "speaks" to his people. He "speaks" through healing and he "speaks" through miracles. Of course, more obviously, he "speaks" through prophecy and words of wisdom and knowledge. In 1 Corinthians 14:21, Paul quotes Isaiah 28:11,12 to affirm that yet one other way that *God speaks* to his people is through the gift of tongues: "Through men of strange tongues and through the lips of foreigners *I will speak to this people*, but even then they will not listen to me." Paul also refers to the second way the gift of tongues opens up communication with God: "For anyone who speaks in a tongue does not speak to men but *to God*. Indeed, no one understands him; he utters mysteries with his spirit...He who speaks in a tongue edifies himself" (1 Cor.14:2,4). The "cloven" interchange of tongues of fire provides one of many avenues for God to speak to us and for us to speak to God (cf. Isa.32:3,4, 15; 50:4,5).

It is only on Mount Zion that one can encounter a genuine spiritual experience with the one true God through Jesus Christ. Ancient cultures throughout the history of the world may esteem physical and artificial mountains as sacred sites and the details may vary as to their form and mythology, but they all seem to provide a point of contact with evil entities that unfortunately seals unholy allegiances to Satan. Artificial cosmic mountain-structures such as the Sumerian ziggurats, Egyptian pyramids, and Canaanite high places are complex simulations meant to counterfeit the true representation of the biblical cosmic mountain of Yahweh. They may appear as a ziggurat-mountain to the people of the world (as we saw in Genesis 11), but in Revelation, John exposes the true essence: the spiritual reality behind the religious mountain-structures of the world is a seductive whore who settles for nothing less than complete servitude and allegiance.

The rebellious and shattered human race is now scattered across the globe. We are still created in God's image; we have never been abandoned. In fact, God sends us to our appointed place in the world so that we might find him. Our human lineage may stem from a specific culture and bloodline, but now that we are children of God through Jesus Christ, our spiritual lineage may be redeemed and purified. It is to be rebuilt on the foundation of the true Lord Jesus Christ of Nazareth.

Chapter Six

The Spiritual Reality of Contemporary Canaanite Culture

Jesus may be referring to the Israelite underdogs when he asks: "Suppose a king is about to go to war against another king. Will he not first sit down and consider whether he is able with ten thousand men to oppose the one coming against him with twenty thousand?" (Lk.14:31). The first king obviously wants to go to war against the second king, but why does he want to tackle an army twice the size of his forces? No king in his right mind would think of such aggression—unless he is provoked. Something must motivate him to action. The king is no fool, so before making any advancement toward enemy territory, he first sits down and considers whether his troops can overcome the odds. Is victory remotely possible for an arsenal that is half the size of the other king's stockpile? Or as Jesus points out, can underdogs sit still long enough to contemplate the weight of the reality against them? Dwelling in Yahweh's presence gives underdogs direction and empowerment, the defining edge in battle, even if the odds are stacked two to one against them.

Spiritual Reality

Just as God commands Israel to go and take possession (*yarash*) of the land of Canaan, so Christ commissions his disciples to go (*poreuomai* "carry over, transfer, pursue the journey on which one has entered") and join in the occupation of land. Jesus' Great Commission breaks beyond the walls of Israel's inheritance of the promised land to include all nations. Jesus, the new Joshua under the New Covenant, broadcasts an astounding reality: the precise location of the land of promise now expands to encompass all the nations of the world. Believers merge with the saints of old on an excursion that takes them beyond the borders of Israel to the ends of the earth. By encouraging his followers to "go and make disciples of all nations," Jesus transfers Moses' "go and take possession of the land" into a worldwide mission. Moses, Joshua, Jesus, and Paul link up the promise to dispossess evil forces, from Canaan to the uttermost parts of the earth, and restore God's kingdom of priests to their destined inheritance.

MOSES	JOSHUA	JESUS	PAUL
Deuteronomy 4:1	Joshua 1:3-9	Matthew 28:18-20	Romans 4:3,13-17
"Hear now, O Israel, the decrees and laws I am about to teach you. Follow them so that you may live"	"Be careful to obey all the law… Do not let the Book of the Law depart from you mouth; meditate on it"	"Make disciples… teaching them to obey everything I have commanded you"	"Abraham believed God, and it was credited to him as righteousness… Therefore, the promise comes by faith, so that it may be by grace"
"Go in and take possession of the land"	"I will give you every place where you set your foot, as I promised"	"Go and make disciples of all nations, baptizing them"	"As it is written, 'I have made you a father of many nations'"
"Take possession of the land that the Lord, the God of your fathers, is giving you"	"Be strong and courageous… the Lord your God will be with you wherever you go"	"All authority in heaven and on earth has been given to me"	"Abraham and his offspring received the promise that he would be heir of the world"

In his triumphal resurrection, Jesus is given all authority in heaven and earth. Since his ascension, Christ makes those whose righteousness is by faith, heirs of the world (Rom.4:13), heirs of God and coheirs with Christ (Rom.8:17). The Son of God shares his eternal birthright and inheritance with all the children of God.

Yahweh's War

As Christians, we may not refer to the Old Testament's concept of "treading," but we do discuss at length its New Testament counterpart: Jesus' Great Commission. Paul prefers to describe the Great Commission in terms of spiritual warfare, but Moses understands it to be Yahweh's war (1 Sam.18:17; 25:28). Christian scholars, beginning with Gerhard von Rad, use the phrase "holy war."[1] The concept of Yahweh the warrior (*gibbor*) is prominent throughout the Old Testament. Even the extensive occurrence of war (*mihamah* about 300 times) and the phrase "Lord of Hosts/Armies" (approximately 200 times) reveal that cosmic warfare is one of its major themes.

"Treading" on enemies fulfills Yahweh's war mandate of *herem*, which means, "to utterly destroy" (Deut.7:2-6). Herem is the comprehensive eradication of God's enemies through warfare. Yahweh's war projects onto an earthly battlefield the invisible spiritual war between God and evil forces (Isa.13:10; 24:21-23). The wars of Israel are the wars of Yahweh; our enemies are God's enemies.

God alerts Abraham about his war plan, way before Israel enters the land of promise (Gen.15:16).[2] The seed of the serpent, through the line of Canaan, have migrated directly to the promised land. Is this a coincidence? No, on the contrary, the spiritual seed of evil heads straight towards the land designed

---

1. Yahweh's war must not be confused with the Islamic concept of jihad. Jihad holds a wide spectrum of understanding among Muslims, from the personal internal struggle against evil to aggressive war. Extremists compel all Muslims to spread Islam by force. It summons war against all infidels and guarantees Muslim martyrs a ticket to paradise.
2. "Amorites" is used interchangeably with "Canaanites" within the Bible and in the ancient Near Eastern extra-biblical Amarna tablets and Mari documents.

by God to be Israel's inheritance. And just like in the days of Noah and Nimrod, the Canaanites are steeped in occult practices (Deut.18:9-12). This explains why the seed of the serpent is so threatening to the life of God's people and why such drastic measures as the *herem* is commanded by God to combat them. They are satanists (Deut.7:10). Realizing the extreme wickedness of the Canaanites, we can better understand the radical measures exacted in Yahweh's war regulations.

The divine warrior-God spearheads war (cf. Ex.15:3; Psa.24; Numb.21:14; 1 Sam.18:17; 25:28; Isa.42:13). It is Yahweh who fights for Israel, not Israel battling to defend her God. The Spirit of God clothes himself with soldiers (Jud.6:34; Zech.9:13), but if the Lord cannot find even one, he will at times act alone (Ex.14:13,14; 2 Kgs.19:32-35; Isa.37:33-36; 59:16-18; 63:1-6). The commander of the army of Yahweh must be consulted prior to every battle (Josh.5:14). The people of God must adhere to the rules and regulations of *herem* (Deut.20:1-10; 21:10-14; 23:9-14; 24:5; 25:17-19; 1 Sam.21:3-5). Unless otherwise directed, all Canaanite artifacts are banned (*herem*) from Israelite use or possession and must be completely destroyed (Deut.7:2-5,16,25,26; 9:1-5).

The struggle between Yahweh and Baal-Satan/gods of the Canaanite pantheon is played out on both a historic level (Israel's war mandate against Canaan) and a spiritual level (heaven's war against demonic hordes). The divine warrior-God is victorious in battle as his enemies flee before his presence (Psa.68). When Yahweh treads on the enemy territory of Zaphon, the result is deliverance for his people and a re-gathering to himself.

> God promises to bring his people back from the north (Isa.43:6; Isa.49:12; Jer.16:15). There is no location where an earthly power can banish them from his concern (Jer.31:8). Job says that God stretches out the north over the void (Job 26:7). This statement shows that God created even the sinister places or the mountain of the gods from nothing. No evil power or god or divine assembly, therefore, has any existence

co-eternal with God or any power or existence outside of God's creative power (cf. Psa.89:12).[3]

When Yahweh conducts a march, both Amos and Micah contend that Yahweh *treads* on the "high places" of Baal. "He who forms the mountains, creates the wind, and reveals his thoughts to man, he who turns dawn to darkness, and *treads the high places* of the earth—the Lord God Almighty is his name" (Amos 4:13, emphasis mine). As does Micah: "Look! The Lord is coming from his dwelling place; he comes down and *treads the high places* of the earth" (Mic.1:3, emphasis mine).

In light of both historic and spiritual levels and Isaiah 14:12-14, we must reconsider Psalm 48:2—the proof-text for many scholars today to equate Zaphon with Zion—and instead see that Mount Zaphon is not Yahweh's mountain at all. Psalm 48:2 deploys synthetic rather than synonymous parallelism as Yahweh is depicted as "treading" (*darak*, "to tread, bend, march") on Baal-Zaphon.

> Beautiful [when it is] in elevation [*nowph*, the heights],
> The joy of the whole earth [because it brings deliverance]
> *Is* Mount Zion [when it treads] *on* the sides [*yerekah*, recesses] of the north [*zaphon*], [because it establishes itself as] the city [domain] of the great King (Psa.48:2, personal translation).

The cosmic clash of these two mountains fit well with the warrior-theme and virtual tour of Zion in rest of Psalm 48. When enemy forces gather to assault Zion, they see Yahweh in the midst of her. They attempt to flee but are shattered and destroyed by his Spirit (vv.3-7; cf. Ezek.38:11,12).

Yahweh's historical enemies are personally in league with his cosmic enemies. The wars of Yahweh are divine judgments on human-demonic alignment. When God declares war on the

---

3. Whitney, p.775.

seven nations of Canaan (Deut.7:1), it is in fact God's justice-*herem*; it is capital punishment on a wicked culture. By demolishing the Canaanite altars, idols, and artifacts, Israel executes Yahweh's verdict on Canaan (Deut.7:2, 4,5) and restrains the acceleration of evil.

Yahweh's war also serves as a dedication-*herem* (Lev.27:28,29; Mic.4:13); it is a cleansing and repossession of the land that belongs to Yahweh and to the righteous as their inheritance (Gen.12:1-3; 17:1-8). So on one side, there is judgment on the wicked for embracing evil, and on the other, there is salvation for the righteous for remaining faithful to God. *Herem* is heaven's judgment on human-demonic alliance and the repossession of lost territory.

In the Old Testament, *herem* serves to deter the acceleration of evil through physical force—a necessary component exercised in the period between the deluge and the triumph of Jesus Christ in The Holy War on Calvary.

> His exorcisms are the inauguration of a holy war which reaches its climax in His death and resurrection wherein He decisively defeated the Devil and his hordes. In this capacity He is acting as the divine warrior. The demons cringe before Him, confessing him to be the Holy One of God...The NT presents Jesus not only as the divine warrior but also as the human martyr...who by vicarious suffering, the just for the unjust, makes expiation for sin and thereby breaks its binding power. At the same time He destroys the power of Satan as an accuser. At this point, Jesus as the human martyr-warrior joins the divine Warrior Who defeats demonic forces, as presaged by His exorcisms...We are called upon to enter His holy war; but "our weapons are not carnal."[4]

---

4. Brownlee, William H. "*From Holy War to Holy Martyrdom*," *The Quest for the Kingdom of God*, Studies in Honor of George E. Mendenhall, ed. H.B. Huffmon, F.A. Spina, A.R.W. Green, (Winona Lake: Eisenbrauns, 1983), pp.286,290-291.

In his resurrection, Christ restores humanity's position as king-priests in God's kingdom. He issues to his disciples the divine authority to corporately restrain and personally destroy the works of Satan—not through physical force, but through the more effectual means of spiritual warfare.

As believers under the New Covenant, we realize that the Old Testament's concept of holy war is meant to be a type and shadow of a spiritual reality. We do not fight with steel swords or guns in hand: "For though we live in the world, we do not wage war as the world does. The weapons we fight with are not the weapons of the world. On the contrary, they have divine power to demolish strongholds" (2 Cor.10:3,4; cf. Jn.18:36). We war with the sword of the Spirit, the word of God, against the demonic forces of evil in the spiritual realm. We do not fight against coworkers, neighbors, family, or government leaders: "For our struggle is not against flesh and blood, but against the rulers, against the authorities, against the powers of this dark world and against the spiritual forces of evil in the heavenly realms" (Eph.6:12). We battle against the unseen demonic hosts of hell (Deut.7:22).

There are risks in spiritual warfare. Battling against the forces of evil can be rough and intense, but the rewards of living in the promised land abound for those who engage in spiritual battle. While it is true that the promised land is occupied by swarms of enemies, it is also true that it is "a land flowing with milk and honey… [it] is not like the land of Egypt, from which you have come, where you planted your seed and irrigated it by foot as in a vegetable garden. But the land you are crossing the Jordan to take possession of is a land of mountains and valleys that drinks rain from heaven. It is a land the Lord your God cares for; the eyes of the Lord your God are continually on it from the beginning of the year to its end" (Deut.11:9-12). To the extent that we tread on enemy territory and dispossess the demonic penetration into our inheritance is to the extent that we enjoy the abundant blessings from heaven raining down on our promised land.

Let us not be afraid of spiritual warfare. The victory has already been won at the cross; weapons of mass spiritual destruction can now be disarmed. Jesus Christ has ascended to the right hand of God and has given the keys to the kingdom of our inheritance back to us (Dan.7:13-27). We need only to go to the nations and dispossess all evil intruders.

> The god of this world has established his strongholds and authorities in the land...A passive attitude will not conquer and possess. Consequently, the enemy remains in the land and God's people suffer. It is never God's will for His people to suffer from the oppression of the enemy. God wants His people to be a victorious people; a strong people that can rule in circumstances rather than be ruled by circumstances; a people that can determine the will of God and take direction rather than being directed by a turn of events.[5]

Yes, there are innumerable enemies scattered throughout the earth, but victory is assured on the basis of the redemptive work of Christ. The promised land is worth the spiritual fight. If we do not fight to enter the promised land, we will wander through life in the wilderness of carnality, grumbling about trivial matters of life, ruled by circumstances and paralyzed by passivity. Soldiers who are entangled in civilian affairs are not equipped to fight the complexities of Canaanite culture in the new millennium. We must "endure hardship...like a good soldier of Jesus Christ. No one serving as a soldier gets involved in civilian affairs—he wants to please his commanding officer" (2 Tim.2:3,4) in order to face the challenge of contemporary Canaanite culture.

We must determine the will of God in every battle and tread (*darak*) upon the darkness by spiritual force—yet victory will hang on our obedience to God's word.

> If you carefully observe all these commands I am giving you to follow—to love the Lord your God, to walk in all his ways and to hold fast to him—then the Lord will drive out all these nations before you, and

---

5. Thompson, C. *Possess the Land*, p. 4.

you will dispossess nations larger and stronger than you. Every place where you set [tread] your foot will be yours...No man will be able to stand against you. The Lord your God...will put the terror and fear of you on the whole land, wherever you go [tread]. Deuteronomy 11:22-25

The Spirit of God clothes the soldier of Christ and equips him or her with a spiritual sword—a directive word from the divine-warrior. Ultimately, Jesus' Holy War reflects the reality of the invisible cosmic war between good and evil that lies behind all earthly battlefields.

Canaanite Mythology

Baalism and the whole Canaanite culture are the Old Testament's ancient description of contemporary satanism. The religion of Baal has spread across the world. It may surface with various names and different disguises, but the roots of satanic culture remain unchanged. It comes in such forms as Islam, Buddhism, New Age religion, Egyptology, Freemasonry, Astrology, and innumerable false belief systems. Whatever label covers Baalism, we must recognize that its essential doctrines are alive and thriving throughout the earth.

Pulling together some of the similarities of various deities, we can see the integration, assimilation, and transformation of satanic mythology as it unfolds into a synthesis of demonic gods and goddesses throughout history. If we believe false gods are not simply sociological phenomena (human innovations), but they are actually conduits for demonic entities and ultimately represent Satan, the adversary of God, then we can trace the origin of these deities back to Canaan, Egypt, and Mesopotamia. The multiplicity of gods and goddesses present various mythologies and are known by different names in every culture, yet from a biblical perspective, we can deduce some common characteristics. Such commonalties lead us to believe that even though demonic spirits are autonomous, they are all subservient to the mastermind behind the world's complex system—Satan himself.

Spiritual Reality

Satan gives the impression that he is a dichotomous being; he appears to carry a bisexual presence throughout history, manifesting both masculine and feminine forms. In polytheistic modes of expression, Satan is worshipped as a god or goddess and in many cases, it seems as though he is worshipped as a combined, androgynous god(dess). Since the fall of humanity, Satan's perverse dichotomy has successfully seduced the world into following various forms of idolatrous practices. In the Old Testament, prince Baal appears alongside his alter ego, the queen of heaven. The metamorphosis of the concept of the queen of heaven is depicted in virtually every culture of the world.

Of the many scholars who focus on the Babylonian and Canaanite cultures, the majority believe that these ancient mythologies greatly influenced Israel's belief system as it is revealed in the Old Testament. This presumption, however, contradicts Yahweh's own denouncement of Israel's syncretistic association with Baalism and is contradictory to God's message through Moses and the prophets (Numb.25:1-9; Deut.23:18f.; 1 Kgs.14:24; 15:12; 22:46; 2 Kgs.23:7; Hos.4:12-14; Amos 2:7f.). Yahweh's intolerant jealousy over any adaptation of satanic Babylonian or Canaanite ritual is clearly illustrated in his historical acts of judgment.

There is a need to reexamine the Mesopotamian and Ugaritic texts, not as an influential force behind the formation of the Old Testament text, but as a key source that unlocks the mystery of satanic mythology as it unfolds in ancient Near Eastern religion. If there is any similarity between Canaanite mythology and Yahwehism it is because Satan, the adversary of God, has presented a twisted, perverse belief system to the Mesopotamian-Canaanite cultures to counterfeit the truth of salvation history as revealed in the Bible. The prophets merely use and rework satanic mythology to typologically illustrate the cosmic war between a dark, rebellious, perverse kingdom and God's righteous kingdom of light.

El, the head god over the epic Canaanite pantheon, is depicted as the inert creator. He is the impersonal latent force over the earth. Apparently, El and his goddess-wife Asherah create seventy offspring who receive territorial assignments. The most widely known offspring-god is Aliyan Baal ("the son of Dagan"), otherwise known as Hadad, the hero of the Canaanite assembly.[6] Baal has two sister-mistresses: Astarte, the glamorous, seductive-goddess, and Anath, the bloodthirsty-warrior, sex-goddess. Other key players are Yamm, known as Judge River (the lord of the sea), and Mot, the god of death. These are the main players who make up the divine assembly, the family or circle of El, who congregate around the distant mountains furthest to the north (cf. Isa.14:13). We will see that Canaanite mythology presents Baal as the primary stimuli for affecting earthly events, and remarkably, for influencing the disposition of the high god, El.[7]

The Ugaritic creation mythology begins with Yamm, the jealous lord of the chaotic sea. Yamm insists that Baal relinquish his position on the heavenly council, a council that also functioned as the judicial high court. El surrenders to Yamm's directive by ordering Baal to be Yamm's slave or prisoner. With the use of a scepter and lightning-shaped spear (fashioned by Kathir and Khasis, two celestial artisans), Baal rises from this humiliation to hurl decisive blows to Yamm's head and chest.[8] In a heroic effort, Baal claims eternal kingship over the cosmic

---

6. The Phoenician Baal is identified with Dagon and Hadad-Ramman, the weather-god of heaven. Hadad-Ramman's wife is named Ashratu. This leads one to believe that Baal, Dagon, and Hadad are the same spiritual entities.
7. The Sumerian pantheon is also similar to this Canaanite council. Out of the hundreds of deities of the Sumerians, the four prominent ones parallel El and his assembly: 1) An (Anu), the heavenly sky-god, 2) Enlil, the air or wind-god, 3) Enki, the water-god of wisdom, and 4) Ninhursag (Ninmah or Nintur), the mother-goddess. Just like Canaanite mythology, Enlil takes over as the dominant god over heaven and earth. There are also three other important astral deities: 1) Nanna (Sin), the moon-god, 2) Utu, the sun-god, and 3) Inanna, the goddess who became the most important goddess in western Asia, later known as the Akkadian Ishtar. The Sumerian belief is that humanity is created solely to carry out orders from these immortal gods. See S. N. Kramer, *The Sumerians*, (Chicago: University of Chicago Press, 1963), pp.118-119; 122-123.
8. The Ugaritic stele portrays a sketch of Baal, the warrior, standing on the chaotic waters, with a club in one hand and a lightning spear in the other.

Spiritual Reality

waters with which he will stimulate the earth's resources. Baal is Aliyon, which means "the victorious one," "the valiant warrior," or "the conquering hero."[9] El, the elderly creator god, now loses his place of power, while Baal, the young warrior, quickly gains the kingship.[10]

> Baal's kingship, unlike its human counterpart, is not hereditary; it is not designated by a vote of the pantheon. His royalty is not present because of some natural right from eternity, or by virtue of El's choice of a favorite son. It must be won by combat. And that combat...involves a rise from humiliation and servitude to glory...After the submission of chaos there follow the release of life and the creativity of the god of the cosmos.[11]

Baal is honored with a banquet to celebrate his reign as king, judge, and prince over all. However, this is no ordinary banquet. Instead, Anath, Baal's sister-mistress, revels in a cruel ritualistic massacre of the attendants of the banquet. The blood bath of Anath represents a rite of imitative magic meant to stimulate the flow of demonic activity (the demon's spiritual life essence). Anath's fetish-like association with bloody rituals is directed at humans, not divine beings.[12] She exclaims, "What enemy would dare [presumptuously] to rise up against [and challenge] Baal" as cosmic overlord of heaven and earth (Baal V iii 52-58)? Even though El created the universe, when Baal asks Anath to meet him on the land of warfare, she assumes the position of the goddess of love, peace, and fertility. In his inauguration address, Baal essentially introduces a new world order and settles down on Zaphon, his holy mountain-sanctuary.

---

9. Habel, Norman C. *Yahweh Versus Baal, A Conflict of Religious Cultures*, (New York: Bookman Associates, 1964), p.51.
10. Miller, Patrick. *The Divine Warrior in Early Israel*, (Cambridge: Harvard University Press, 1973), p.48.
11. Habel, p.54-55.
12. Miller, p.47.

> I will create lightning which the heavens do not know,
> Thunder (*rgm* "a roaring word" or "stone/hailstone") that mankind does not know,
> Nor the multitudes of the earth understand.
> Come now and I will show it to you
> I, God of Zaphon, in the midst of my mountain,
> In the sanctuary, in the mountain of my inheritance,
> In the pleasant abode, the hill of victory. (Baal iii 41-46)

Herein lies the foundation from which the storm-god motif develops in both the Ugaritic and biblical texts. Baal is now the rider of the chariot-clouds, the lord of wind, rain, and stormy weather. Yet, for all his power, "the rider of the storm clouds requires the confines of a particular heavenly structure within which to operate effectively as a king in the forces of the storm."[13] Baal must express his stormy nature through the edifice of a royal temple, a replica of some spiritual archetype.

Baal's authority is limited. El must grant him permission to build his own residential complex. So Anath secures a building permit from El by bribing Asherah with a piece of furniture built by Baal's artisans. The description of Baal's house suggests that this is not an earthly, physical temple, but an intricate construction of a temple of cosmic proportions. Baal's "magnificent palace...is burned until it turns into gold and silver, and a celebration is prepared."[14] In one of the towers in the temple, a staircase winds up to a skylight window. This window of the cosmic sanctuary provides the exit and entryway for Baal to manifest his terrifying storm capabilities.[15]

> Henceforth Baal sits [enthroned] over his mansion!
> Shall king or commoner make the earth a dominion for himself? (Baal II vii 30-41)

---

13. Habel, p.75.
14. Miller, p.33.
15. See C. Schaeffer, *The Cuneiform Texts of Ras Shamra-Ugarit*, (London: Oxford University Press, 1936), p.68.

Spiritual Reality

The erection of the temple incites another banquet, this time with the seventy territorial offspring of El and Asherah.

Apparently, "the Canaanite could not consider a Baal theophany a sovereign act free from cultic involvement."[16] In other words, sacrifices and cultic rituals relating to food and gifts honor the god or goddess, and thus, persuade them to act. The Canaanite belief is that when Baal has intercourse with his mistress-sisters or his mother-goddess Asherah, the result is rain falling upon Canaan's harvest. The only thing that terrified the courageous Baal-warrior is Mot, the underworld's god of death.

> Certain passages depict Mot with dragonlike characteristics. Thus the jaws of death can reach, if Mot wishes to extend himself, from the earth below to the heavens above. To die means to be swallowed by Mot himself and literally to enter the bowels of the earth that his appetite might be satisfied.

When Baal falls into Mot's clutches, he exclaims, "Hail, Mot, son of El, I am your slave, your perpetual slave" (Baal I ii 12). The death of Baal propels El to mutilate himself in some kind of hysterical lament (Baal I VI 11-16, 19-20) while Anath mourns by going on a massive, bloody rampage of sacrificing a large quantity of animals. The result is a curse upon Canaan. The people begin to experience a drought on their livelihood.

When harvest time finally arrives, Anath destroys Mot and Baal is resurrected from death (Baal III ii 30-36; iii 10-21). As Baal resumes his erotic behavior, he rapes Anath 88 times while she is in the form of a heifer and their offspring is a male bull. Baal's rape of Anath may have occurred just prior to or just after his stay in Mot's netherworld. Nevertheless, this violent combination sexual intercourse and animal sacrifice produces Baal's progeny (cf. Baal I v 18-22; Baal IV iii 35-37).

The yearly ritual harvesting of Mot (death) induces Baal to resurrect and excites him to perform. The followers of Baal who

---

16. Habel, p.79.

participate in cultic rituals focus primarily on sexual perversion that is closely associated with human and animal sacrifices. Chambers are set up on the high places for cultic prostitution for both male and female sacred harlots.

Babylonian and Ugaritic mythology provides Satan's perverted view of creation (Enuma Elish), his decisive battle to kingship over the earth, the flood (Epic of Gilgamesh), and his exaltation as cosmic overlord. Contrary to most scholarly work, any similarity between Babylon's or Canaan's mythology and Yahwehism is not because of assimilation or influence on Israelite belief, but is because of Satan's false belief system runs counterfeit to the truth of salvation history as revealed in God's word. We must acknowledge four fundamental aspects when sifting through satanic mythology: counterfeit parallelism, twisted truth, falsehood, and confusion. Therefore, we must always keep in mind that satanic mythology will never fit into a completely logical framework (see Appendix B for a display of the nine aspects of satanic mythology that reveal twisted parallels to the truth revealed in God's word).

The Dichotomy of Satan:
Prince Baal of Earth and Queen of Heaven

The dualistic character of Satan is portrayed in every culture, yet through a variety of disguises, using different names. The essence of the dichotomy of Satan is found in his masculine form, Baal, the prince of the earth, and in his feminine side, the queen of heaven. A good example of this dualistic element within demonic manifestations is Ishtar, the transgender Mesopotamian deity. Ishtar appears as both a god and a goddess. Another example is Anath, a Canaanite goddess, who looks like "a man-like woman, dressed as a man but girded as a woman...[Anath] has long been recognized as a man-like goddess, with slender shoulders uncurved body in female dress but fully armed."[17]

Because of the apparent association with many gods-goddesses who possess similar features, the queen of heaven

---

17. Albright, W.F. *Yahweh and the Gods of Canaan*, (New York: Doubleday, 1968), p.129.

probably suggests not one single entity, but a syncretistic conglomeration of masculine and feminine demonic beings. It seems that all the female goddesses represent different aspects of the fertility principle that underlie Canaanite mythology and yet they seem to merge into a single great entity. The LXX supports this theory by using "host" (noun fem. sing.) in place of "queen." Host can mean "an army of angels" or "a multitude of supernatural spirit beings" (cf. Acts 7:42). While it is certainly true that the term "host of heaven" can refer to Yahweh's heavenly court (1 Kgs.22:19; 2 Chron.18:10; Isa.40:1ff.), in some cases, the "host of heaven" infers in some way to the queen of heaven, the demonic goddess-network whose seductive operation proceeds from Satan's cosmic council (Deut.17:3; 2 Kgs.17:16; 21:3-5; Psa.82; 89; Jer.8:2; Dan.8:10).

1. Prince Baal

The Canaanite religion is a mixture of violence and perversity. Baal's ancient name is Satan and his persona reflects a perverse dichotomy of masculine and feminine manifestations. His cruel and erotic rituals compel his priests to employ cultic prostitutes to sacrifice children. Realizing the extreme wickedness of the Canaanites, we can better understand the radical measures exacted in the Old Testament's war regulations. It is heaven's judgment on luciferian disciples. Though "Baal" simply means "lord," his personal name is Hadad.

The worship of Baal is evident in Moab and Midian (Numb.22:41). These nations quickly influence Israel to participate with them in cultic prostitution at Baal-Peor (Shittim; Numb.25:3-18; 4:3). Baalism spread upward toward Phoenicia and even the ancient British isles may have been influenced by it. Baal appears in many forms, such as Babylon's Bel (Isa.46:1) and other compound names: Baal-berith ("Baal who covenants," Jud.8:33; 9:4), Baal-Zebub (Ekron's "Baal of the fly," 2 Kgs.1:2,3,16), Baal-Peor ("Baal of the opening," specially named to symbolize the opening for others to join in its heinous ceremony rites, Numb.25). He is believed to be of one essence, but in actual Canaanite practice there is a representation of Baal for each territory.

Not only is there an evolution of Baal's name, Baal also spreads his domain as displayed in the many prefixes to the names of several towns in Palestine: Baal/Baalath-Beer, "lord of the well" (1 Chron.4:33; Josh.19:8), Baalah or Kirjath-Baal, "mistress" (Josh.15:9,10; 19:44; 1 Chron.13:6), Baal-Gad, "lord of fortune" (Josh.11:17; 12:7; 13:5), Baal-Hamon, "lord of the multitude" (Song.8:11), Baal-Hazor, "Baal's village" (2 Sam.13:23), Baal-Hermon, "lord of Hermon" (Jud.3:3-9; 1 Chron.5:23), Baal-Meon, "lord of the house" (Numb.32:38; 1 Chron.5:8), Baal-Perizim, "lord of divisions" (2 Sam.5:20; 1 Chron.14:11; Isa.28:21), Baal-Shalisha, "lord of shalisha" (2 Kgs.4:42), and Baal-Tamar, "lord of the palm tree" (Jud.20:33). Psalm 106:28 also states that Israel "ate sacrifices to the dead" (cf. Baal-zephon in Numb.33:7, Baal-gad in Josh.11:17, and Baal-hazor in 2 Sam.13:23). Each emphasizes a particular aspect of Baal as he is revealed in Canaanite mythology.[18]

By the time of Christ, Baal-zebub meant Prince Baal, or the head Baal, and was widely used for the name for Satan. As we shall see, the worship of prince Baal and his alter ego, the queen of heaven, is simply the Old Testament's designation for the veneration of Satan.

2. *Queen of Heaven*

It appears that scholars have reached no consensus as to the identity of the queen of heaven; she has been remarkably elusive to any definitive archaeological data. By the time of Jeremiah in the sixth century B.C., all of Israel's neighbors are in some degree devotees of the queen of heaven (Deut.4:19). It is not just the women of Judah who pour out libations and burn incense to her (Jer.44:15,19,25). Her worship permeates "the cities of Judah and the streets of Jerusalem" (Jer.7:17; 44:17). The multitude of followers of the queen of heaven brazenly worship her on the rooftops of their homes (Jer.19:13;

---

18. Habel, p.35.

Spiritual Reality

Zeph.1:5), on every high place (2 Kgs.23:5), and in all the villages of Judah (Deut.17:2,3). She is everywhere.

Jeremiah's long list of her devotees suggest that just about everyone is somehow involved in the worship of the queen of the Hinnom Valley (1:18; 17:20, 25; 19:3; 24:8; 25:18; 26:19,20; 29:1; 34:19; 37:2). Even king Manasseh flagrantly dedicates cultic vessels and erects altars to the host of heaven in the temple court (2 Kgs.21:5; 23:4). They all bake cakes in her image (Jer.7:16-20; 44:17, 19, 21), but both Hosea and Isaiah condemn the rituals surrounding raisin-cakes (Hos.3:1; Isa.16:7).

A remarkable illustration of this odd ritual surrounding the queen of heaven may be depicted in a Hellenistic votive model.[19] This model shows six figures: four females are seated, one pregnant female is standing, and the sixth is a male. All are positioned around a domed or beehive-shaped oven. This Phoenician scene depicts a cake-baking ritual for a multiplicity of goddesses who most likely represent the queen of heaven. The queen of heaven, as revealed in the Akkadian goddess, Ishtar, may explain what image is represented in the cakes. Several clay molds found at Mari, a site in northern Mesopotamia, portray a nude female figure with large hips who cups her hands under her breasts. These molds must have been used to shape cakes in the image of Ishtar and offered to her as part of the sacrificial cult.[20] The Sumerian cult of Tammuz is closely tied to the Ishtar cult in that both baked cakes to their idols. Those who grieve over the death of Tammuz are at the same time worshippers who bake cakes for Ishtar, the queen of heaven. While Ezekiel is exiled in Babylon, he receives a vision of the Jerusalem temple being used for full-blown worship of this multi-faceted deity (Ezek.8). Apparently, the Israelites extend their worship of the queen of heaven beyond the borders of Israel to a temple in Egypt (Jer.44).

---

19. Culcan, W. "A Votive Model," *Palestine Exploration Quarterly* 108 (1976), p.122.
20. Ackerman, Susan. "'And the Women Knead Dough': The Worship of the Queen of Heaven in Sixth-Century Judah," *Gender and Difference in Ancient Israel*, Peggy L. Day, ed., (Minneapolis: Augsburg Fortress, 1989), pp.115-116.

3. Semiramis – Inanna – Ishtar – Astarte

According to satanic mythology, Cush, his wife Semiramis, and their son Nimrod, conspire to control the world through occult manipulation at the tower of Babel (Gen.10:8-10; 11:1-9). The plan unfolds when Nimrod marries his mother. Statues of a young Semiramis holding her infant son, Tammuz (the reincarnated Nimrod, her dead husband/son) reflects the image of the queen of heaven. God restrains the acceleration of evil by breaking apart and scattering this unified human-demonic rally.

When the demonic concentration eventually shifts to Egypt, Satan's twisted view of the cosmic order is simply reworked as it moves to Egyptian soil. The names of the gods and goddesses change, and there are some additional twists to the mythology. Semiramis becomes the Egyptian Isis and Nimrod transforms into Osirus. Osirus is later believed to be reincarnated in his son, Horus (Tammuz), the husband/son-god. Horus still holds a prominent place as the all-seeing eye of Horus at the top of the Egyptian pyramid. Many of the pagan deities can be traced back to Semiramis (i.e. Cybele of Rome, Ceres and Irene of Greece, Shing Moo the holy mother of China, Diana of Ephesus, and Isi of India).[21]

The Sumerian goddess, Inanna, possesses much power over civilization and human activity. She is the aggressive war-goddess of sex and fertility in the Mesopotamian pantheon (third millennium B.C., leading up to the time of Abraham). During this time in Sumer, Dumuzi rules over the prominent city-state of Erech, whose main deity is Inanna. The Sumerians believe that the king of Sumer must become the husband of the goddess Inanna to ensure the prosperity of all Sumerians. "After the initial idea had become accepted dogma, it was carried out in ritual practice by the consummation of a marriage ceremony, which was probably repeated every New Year, between the king and a specially selected hierodule from Inanna's temple in Erech."[22]

---

21. For further information see Alexander Hislop, *The Two Babylons*, (Neptune: Loizeaux Brothers, 1959), pp.19-21.
22. Kramer, p.141.

The mythology takes Inanna down into the netherworld's temple of lapis lazuli where she is tortured and dies. She is resurrected and released with a company of demons, but is compelled to find a substitute to send back down. Inanna finds Dimuzi celebrating her apparent death and hands him over to the demons. At this point, Dimuzi prays to the sun-god Utu and Dimuzi changes into a gazelle. Three times he is severely beaten by the demons and eventually he dies—a victim of Inanna's love and bitter hatred. Dimuzi later becomes Tammuz, the shepherd-god.[23]

Inanna evolves into the Akkadian Ishtar, and then into the Canaanite Astarte. In other words, the Akkadian goddess Ishtar is the east Semitic counterpart to the west Semitic Astarte. Astarte is associated with the worship of the heavens or astrology. A star symbolizes her iconography and so she is commonly identified with the Greek sexual goddess, Aphrodite or Venus, the morning and evening star. Philo of Byblos relays a tradition about Astarte's discovery of a fallen star during her worldwide tour (cf. Isa.14:12). She consecrates it on Tyre, the "holy land" (cf. Ezek.28:12ff.).

Astarte bears the Egyptian title: "the Lady of Heaven," "the holy Queen."[24] Not surprisingly, the Mesopotamian Ishtar is also known as the "Queen of Heaven" or "Lady of Heaven" and "the lady of the battle and of the fight." Astarte is also known to the Egyptians as the "Lady of Combat," and "Astarte, Mistress of Horses, Lady of the Chariot."[25] This makes sense of 1 Samuel 31:10, when the Philistines take Saul's armor as a trophy into the temple of Astarte because she is the lady-warrior goddess (cf. Jud.2:13; 10:6; 1 Sam.7:4; 12:10; 1 Kgs.11:5, 33; 2 Kgs.23:13). The origin of the Canaanite veneration of the syncretistic deity of the queen of heaven begins with Semiramis.

---

23. See Kramer, pp.153-164.
24. Ackerman refers to the Kition Tariff inscription that mentions "the two bakers who baked the basket of cakes for the Queen" (line 10) and believes that "the Queen...must be Astarte" (p.113). The baked cakes that are prepared for Ishtar are also mentioned in Akkadian texts and in the Epic of Gilgamesh (cf. Gilg.6:58-60 and Ackerman, p.115).
25. Ackerman, pp.110-115.

4. Asherah

Asherah, El's consort and Baal's mother-wife, is mentioned forty times in the Old Testament. Asherah seems to be the proper name of the goddess and a cult object (Jud.3:7). Her carved image is displayed in tree trunks that stand beside the Baal altars on the high places (2 Kgs.17:10, 16) and in the Jerusalem temple (2 Kgs.21:7). These poles are usually translated "sacred tree," "wooden pillar," and "grove" (cf. Deut.16:21; 2 Kgs.18:4; 23:6,14; 2 Chron.33:19). However, the best rendering is probably to simply transliterate the word, "Asherah" (1 Kgs.14:15,23). Our focus would then be on the human construction of a phallic maypole or wooden column-like cylinder that represents the veneration of the goddess Asherah (Jud.2:13; 3:7; 2 Chron.24:18).[26]

Further enforcing the multiplicity and bisexual image of Satan, the word *Asherah* appears in singular and plural feminine endings (cf. Deut.16:21; Jud.6:25; 1 Kgs.15:13 and Jud.3:7; 2 Chron.19:3; 33:3) and in plural masculine endings (cf. 1 Kgs.14:22; 2 Kgs.17:10; 23:14; 2 Chron.14:3; Isa.17:8; 27:9). Asherah "is represented as being the female side of Baal, exceedingly sensual in character, whose worship involved sacred prostitution."[27] Asherah's sacred prostitution is based on the fertility rituals of Canaanite mythology, but in real practice, Satan's diabolical kingdom is built on these perverse sexual rituals that seal a person's allegiance to the devil.

Asherah seems never alone. She is always standing beside Baal's altar in many or all of the Canaanite high places. "Since the Asherah was associated with the altar of this deity [Baal], it would appear to have been an object which was in some way useful in his worship, if not directly to him, then to his consort."[28] The fact that high places are found on hills, in valleys, and in cities, reveal

---

26. See William H. Ward, "*The Asherah*," *American Journal of Semitic Languages*, XIX (1902), pp.33-34 and A. Kuenen, *The Religion of Israel to the Fall of the Jewish State*, translated by Alfred H. May, (London: Williams and Norgate, 1882), p.88.
27. Reed, William L. *The Asherah in the Old Testament*, (Fort Worth: Texas Christian University Press, 1949), pp.23-24.
28. Reed, p.46.

that these cultic sanctuaries or meeting places provide access to demonic spirits in the heavenly realm, the "high places."

Surely, Asherah commemorates humanity's inaugural access to the demonic realm with the Edenic tree of the knowledge of good and evil. She is known as "the Lady Who Traverses the Sea" (Yamm, the chaotic spiritual world). She is "the Mistress of the Lions," "the Princess of Zaphon." While standing on her sacred lion, she holds lotus blossoms in her right hand and serpents in her left that clearly disclose her status as the naked advocate of diviners.[29]

5. Anath

Anath (or Anat), Baal's sister-mistress, is the high powered warrior-goddess. Her royal position may have stationed her in the city of Anathoth, the hometown of Jeremiah (Jer.1:1). Anath is known as the "Mistress of the Lofty Heavens" and the "Radiance of the Face (Presence) of Baal," thus projecting the ominous image of protector and avenger.[30] She apparently delights in ritualistic slaughter, plunging her knees into human blood. Anath's cruel acts of violence toward humans seem to arouse and intensify the essence of demonic spiritual life. As Baal's consort, she aids in his resurrection by destroying Mot. Yet ironically, Baal turns around and rapes her 88 times while she is in the form of a heifer. The violent combination of sexual intercourse and human sacrifice disseminates the Anath-Baal progeny.

Whenever Anath is associated with Baal-hammon, she is known as "Tinnit, the face of Baal."

> On a number of occasions Baal-hammon is simply called Baal, with no accompanying epithet. That this is the case is clear from the fact that we find dedications not only of the type "to the lord to Baal-hammon and to the lady, to Tinnit" (e.g. KAI 105.1), but also "to the lord to Baal and to Tinnit face of Baal" (e.g. KAI 137.1). Moreover, there are

---

29. Albright, p.122.
30. Albright, pp.131,135.

many dedications to Baal-hammon and Tinnit in which Tinnit is referred to as 'face of Baal,'... and whilst there is dispute over her precise identification—Anat or Astarte are often thought to be intended.[31]

This ties Anath specifically to the cult of Molech (Baal-hammon), which is renowned for its human sacrifices in the valley of Hinnom. Much debate surrounds the word "molech" (*mlk*) as to whether it refers to the name of a deity or merely a sacrificial term.[32] All the Old Testament evidence suggests that Molech is a god of Canaanite origin and that his name reflects the cult ritual of human sacrifice (Lev.18:21; 20:2-5; 2 Kgs.23:10; 16:3; 21:2, 6; Psa.106:37,38; Jer.32:35). "The human sacrifices of the Carthaginians mentioned in their inscriptions are regularly represented as having been offered to the god Baal-hammon or to Baal-hammon and his consort Tinnit."[33] Anath-Tinnit and her involvement in the Molech cult probably dramatizes Anath's defeat of Mot and, more importantly, represents the depraved substructure of the satanic religion of Baal.

Human sacrifice is obviously the most hideous aspect of satanic ritual, but what does it mean to "cause your son or daughter to pass through the fire"? In view of Leviticus 18:21, the cult of Molech is denounced for combining human sacrifice and sexual deviancy. It is probable that children from cultic prostitutes and children from other Molech devotees are offered as sacrifices. The person who commits this horrific act is making a covenant with death and Sheol (Isa.28:15, 18). This is no less than a pact with the devil himself. In these verses Isaiah tells us of the apparent payoff for committing such a drastic hideous act of murder: to avert personal calamity. Day

---

31. Day, John. *Molech, A god of human sacrifice in the Old Testament*, (Cambridge: Cambridge University Press, 1989), p.38.
32. See O. Eissfeldt, *Molk als Opferbegriff im Punischen und Hebraischen und das Ende des Gottes Molech*, translated 'Molk as sacrificial term in Punic and Hebrew and the end of the god Molech,' (Halle, 1935).
33. Day, p.37.

Spiritual Reality

makes this summation: "Desperate circumstances required desperate measures (cf. Mesha's sacrifice in 2 Kgs.3:27 and Carthaginian human sacrifice in time of need) and the offering of human sacrifice was thought to possess especially strong apotropaic power" (pp.62-63).

It is the classic double bind. The truth is that Satan's rituals are all based on manipulation and falsehood. Jeremiah addresses Israel's participation in the Molech-Tinnit/Anath cult (32:35; 19:5). He says to Judah: "How can you say, 'I am not polluted, I have not gone after the Baals'? See your way in the valley; know what you have done… For shame [*boset*, euphemism for Baal][34] has devoured the labor of our fathers from our youth—their flock and their herds, their sons and their daughters" (Jer.2:23l 3:24). The "covenant with Death is spoken of as involving taking refuge in 'lies' (*kazab*)."[35]

One of the main features of the Hebrew language is the communication of truth through parallelisms that compare and contrast. Often, parallelisms will infer some kind of compensation within the given text. In other words, a verse or thought may be assumed in the successive lines that follow. We see this happen in a remarkable display of chiastic parallelism when Jeremiah connects the Molech cult to the queen of heaven (7:17-32). Notice the balance of thought in Jeremiah's parallelism and how the queen of heaven is assumed to be the recipient of Judah's attention throughout these verses.

    a) Synopsis of the Situation in Judah (vv.17,18)
       "Do you not see what they do in cities of Judah and in the streets of Jerusalem?"

       b) <u>Multi-generational Participation</u>
          Children gather wood, fathers kindle fire, women knead their dough, to make cakes **for the queen of heaven**

---

34. Cf. Jer.11:13; Hos.9:10; 2 Sam.2:8,12,15.
35. Day, p.63.

c) <u>Yahweh's Response:</u> Anger (vv.19-29)

b) <u>Multi-generational Participation</u>
Since the day their fathers came out of Egypt until this day...they did not obey God or incline their ear, but stiffened their neck...They did worse than their fathers

a) Activity inside Jerusalem (v.30)

b) <u>Participation Inside:</u> Abominations in Temple (**for the queen of heaven**)

a) Activity throughout Judah (v.31)

b) <u>Participation Outside:</u> High Places of Tophet-Hinnom (**for the queen of heaven**)

c) <u>Yahweh's Response:</u> Judgment (vv.32-34)

Here we see multiple generations participating in occult activities. The worship of the queen of heaven is deliberate and unashamedly brazen. It has infiltrated the Jerusalem temple complex and all the cities of Judah. Worst of all, the people of God are openly participating in the cult of Molech as part of their homage to this diabolical queen. Israel's god is now a syncretistic deity that represents part of the dichotomy of Satan. And what was Judah's response to all of this?

> We will not listen to you! But we will certainly do whatever has gone out of our mouth, to burn incense to the queen of heaven and pour out drink offerings to her, as we have done, we and our fathers, our kings and our princes, in the cities of Judah and in the streets of Jerusalem. For then we had plenty of food, were well-off, and saw no trouble. But since we stopped burning incense to the queen of heaven...

we lacked everything and have been consumed by the sword and by famine (Jer.44:16-18).

Jeremiah clarifies the truth for them. Their troubles have come, not because of their lack of reverence for the queen of heaven, but as the result of God's judgment on their participation in her cult rituals (44:20-23). She can only provide a false peace and a prosperity that is merely a façade for eventual implosion.

There is certainly a need for more scholarly work on the mythology of ancient Near Eastern religions. I am convinced, however, that our focus must shift to treating ancient mythologies as a major source that will help the Church understand Satan's bizarre world of the occult. We must begin to see that if there is any similarity between Canaanite mythology and Yahwehism, it is only because the Canaanite belief system is a counterfeit presentation of twisted parallelism that runs contrary to salvation history as revealed in the Bible.

Chapter Seven

The Spiritual Reality of the Anti-Kingdom

When an unexpected event occurs, when unexpected information surfaces, when people astonish us with their actions—doing things we never anticipated—what is our response? My response to all these situations is, "Well it depends." Unexpectedness can be good or bad—obviously! When God suddenly breaks into our schedule with something good, something we do not expect, the unexpected news can be exhilarating. We marvel at his loving kindness and his sheer goodness for he "is able to do immeasurably more than all we ask or imagine, according to his power that is at work within us" (Eph.3:20,21). Responding to the unexpected, awesome blessings of God is sheer delight because it causes unspeakable joy. It is easy to adjust to blessings that we do not anticipate happening.

The disciples were always responding to the unexpected. Just about everything Jesus did caught them off guard. He always talked to someone they didn't anticipate, like the

Samaritan woman. He always did something miraculous, like walking on water. Such a feat hadn't even entered the minds of the disciples. He always taught them eternal, timeless truths in ways, like the parables, in which they did not expect. Even John the Baptist was perplexed because the fulfillment of prophecy did not take place along his expectations. Responding to the unexpected was an everyday experience for Jesus' disciples. It was not that they got used to the unexpected, but living with Jesus would probably cause a disciple of Christ to anticipate good things.

But what happens when God breaks into our schedule and does something unexpected, yet it is something disconcerting, something unsettling? The disciples did not expect a friend to betray Jesus. They did not anticipate such an illegal process in his arrest and trial. They did not imagine such cruelty and severe beatings that led up to Christ's torturous death on a cross. Who in the world expected Jesus Christ (who was from Nazareth of all places) to die on a cross for the sins of the whole world? Nobody, not even one of the disciples expected Jesus to be resurrected on the third day. When some of the graves opened and the saints of old appeared with him for forty days between his resurrection and ascension—well, who expected that?

Living, moving, and having our being centered in God, walking in the Spirit and beholding him daily, causes true disciples of Christ to expect the unexpected. Whether there are exciting or bewildering events that break in to our lives, we can be confident there is always a redemptive purpose in whatever God does. "We know that in all things God works for the good of those who love him, who have been called according to his purpose" (Rom.8:28). When we nurture a love relationship with God and are faithful to his call and his purpose, then God works all things for our good. In everything we experience being re-molded and refashioned to conform to the image of Christ (Rom.8:29). Will our response to the unexpected result in our conformity to the likeness of Christ?

There is, however, another element to the unexpected that we must address and face. It is critical to fulfilling our call in ministry. While we are busy in our ministry, laboring in our fields of harvest, sometimes the war in the heavenly realm suddenly, without warning, crashes into our labor field.

This is extremely disruptive and annoying. It is diversionary and oftentimes confusing. We are busy fulfilling our ministry and something gets hurled at us. Sometimes the unexpected comes from a different source than God. When the spiritual realities of war unexpectedly break into our lives, we need to get a clue: they are a direct hit upon our call and ministry in God's kingdom.

When there is an unexpected direct hit from the demonic realm we cry out to the Lord:

> Oh, that you would rend the heavens and come down, that the mountains would tremble before you! As when fire sets twigs ablaze and causes water to boil, come down to make your name known to your enemies and cause the nations to quake before you! For when you did awesome things that we did not expect, you came down, and the mountains trembled before you. Isaiah 64:1

When the enemies of God do something we do not expect, God's response is likened to fire. He desires to rend the heavens to make his great name known to the enemy and to cause everything to shake!

God encourages us to expect miracles from him, but he also warns us to anticipate unexpected evil to surface and accelerate. Jesus alerts us to some unexpected, disheartening, discouraging conditions that will permeate the latter days (Matt.24). When the disciples ask Jesus what is the sign of his coming and the end of the age, it's impossible to get into their thoughts to know for certainty what they expected Jesus to say. Yet we might guess that they did not anticipate Jesus' answer. He is clearly concerned about the horrendous onslaught of demonic activity that believers will have to face before the end of time. Why point this out? Because most of us do not anticipate the onslaught of demonic activity that we are facing in the *present* time—but we need to learn to. We're not expecting someone to deceive us everyday and yet Jesus tells us, "Watch out that no one deceives you" (v.4). This is not paranoia; it is a warning from Jesus himself concerning those who live in the latter days. Jesus is clearly concerned with deception.

"For many will come in my name, claiming, 'I am the Christ,' and will deceive many" (Matt.24:5). They will come in the name of *Jesus*, but their presentation is a false Jesus. They will take upon themselves a messianic element to their ministry, claiming "I am *Christos*" (*one who has been anointed*), but they are self-appointed saviors who possess a pseudo-counterfeit anointing. They will deceive (*planao*: "to cause to stray, to lead astray from the truth, to lead into error in order to wander, roam about, ultimately, to sever and fall away") many. "Many" may refer to a quantity (the majority or widespread extent of deception), or it may mean a quality (the magnitude of deception, a deep, profound, or severe deception).

There will be turmoil and conflict not only with the nations in the natural realm, but with kingdoms in the spiritual realm (Matt.24:6,7). Jesus tells us not to be alarmed, upset or even shocked—we are to expect these things! And this is just the beginning of birth pangs (v.8)—which may be understood from the Greek as "intolerable anguish" (*odin*). We are to expect conflict in both the natural and spiritual realms and this conflict will lead to great persecution (vv.9,10). Believers will suffer betrayal and hatred because of their relationship with Christ. Others will be offended and will alienate themselves from the wider Body of Christ. Without accountability, isolation sets people up for deception, namely by false ministries (Matt.24:11). Staying with the context, we can understand that the increase of wickedness refers not to the immoral decay of society. He strikes directly at the rampant presentations of false Christs, the pseudo-counterfeit anointing, the turmoil and spiritual conflict of kingdoms, the persecution, betrayal, and hatred of true believers, and the increase of false ministries. This is the "increase of wickedness" that Jesus warns us about. So when falsehood infiltrates the

Church, will our love grow cold toward God, toward others, and the Church? Will our love grow cold in such an unexpected situation?

The Babylon Harlot

> The angel...said to me, "Look up and see what this is that is appearing." I asked, "What is it?" He replied, "It is a measuring basket." And he added, "This is the iniquity of the people throughout the land." Then the cover of lead was raised, and there in the basket sat a woman! He said, "This is wickedness," and he pushed her back into the basket and pushed the lead cover down over its mouth. Then I looked up—and there before me were two women, with the wind in their wings! They had wings like those of a stork, and they lifted up the basket between heaven and earth. "Where are they taking the basket?" I asked the angel who was speaking to me. He replied, "To the country of Babylonia to build a house for it. When it is ready, the basket will be set there in its place." Zechariah 5:5-11

Truth will always expose falsehood. True spirituality will cause counterfeit spirituality to surface. The kingdom of God will force the anti-kingdom of false spirituality to materialize. The story line of history is how Satan, the adversary of God, attempts not only to set up his apostate antichrist world kingdom, but also to set up his harlot anti-kingdom in the dwelling place of God (2 Thess.2; Rev.17). Zechariah describes the Babylonian harlot as sitting in a basket with a lead top over it. She lies hidden in a basket until an appointed time when the top is lifted. When the Babylonian harlot is released she will build her house and lure her victims to the chambers of death (Prov.7:7-27).

Who is the Babylonian whore? John sees her riding on the back of the beast (Rev.17:7). The spiritual reality of the Babylonian whore is that she is "a home for demons and a haunt for every evil spirit" (Rev.18:2). Throughout history, people have joined in with her prostitution (Ex.34:15,16; Lev.17:7; 20:6; Deut.31:16; 2 Chron.21:11, 13; Jer.2:20,23,24; Ezek.23:22-30; Hos.4:12; Rev.17:15). She is the anti-bride, the anti-church, the anti-kingdom, that is deliberately contrasted to the Bride of Christ, the Church triumphant of the kingdom of God (Rev.17:1-6; 19:6-9; 21:1-27). "Anti" signifies "in the place of" and "opposed to" the genuine Bride. The anti-kingdom counterfeits the true kingdom of God.

If we understand that Satan holds two main objectives to his plan: to deceive the world and to desecrate the sanctuary of God, then we can grasp his goal. What does Satan have in mind? His aim is to merge the worldwide deception with the desecration of the temple of God to set up his antichrist kingdom. His pseudo-religion is founded on deception and since the fall he has converted many followers, but Satan's target is the temple of God. His aim is to desecrate God's dwelling place so that it will suffer "the abomination of desolation" (Dan.8:13; 9:27; 11:31; 12:11; Jer.32:34). Baal-Satan desperately wants to get in the sanctuary to set up his evil throne. The abomination of desolation is the great deception of the latter days (Matt.24:15).

We see the abomination of desolation occurring in the days of Samuel and his mother, Hannah. The abomination of desolation offers the kind of spirituality that makes eyes so dim they cannot see and ears so deaf they cannot hear (1 Sam.3:2-18). In response to this, God reveals himself as the great Yahweh-Zebaoth, "the Lord of hosts" (1 Sam.1:3, 11)—the divine general of the heavenly army. Yahweh-Zebaoth confirms that the divine-warrior God has at his disposal the enlistment of a vast angelic army. "He will guard the feet of his saints, but the wicked will be silenced in darkness. It is not by strength that one prevails; those who oppose the Lord will be shattered…He will give strength to his king, and exalt the horn of his anointed" (1 Sam.2:8-10). Yahweh-Zebaoth wants to guard and give strength to his Church so they may courageously grasp the reality of spiritual conflict in the midst of the sanctuary.

Infiltration of the Anti-Kingdom

Samuel's linen ephod reflects his authentic relationship with God: he grew up in the presence of the Lord and ministered before him (1 Sam.2:11,18,21,26; 3:1,19-21). In those days, genuine spirituality was hard to find outside of Samuel (1 Sam.3:1), but God promises to establish a future Zadokite priesthood who will enjoy the same intimate fellowship with God as Samuel did (1 Sam.2:35; cf. 1 Kgs.2:35; 1 Chron.29:22).

Joshua establishes Shiloh as the community center for the Levitical priesthood (Josh.18:1; Jud.18:31), but by the time of Samuel, the priesthood of Eli and his sons Hophni and Phinehas veer off into a syncretistic Baalism-Yahwehism perversion (1 Sam.2:12-22). This explains the rise of prophetism (cf. Acts 3:24; 13:20). Such an abomination in the sanctuary opens the way for the Philistines to defeat Israel and capture the ark of the covenant. It signifies the evacuation of Yahweh's presence from Shiloh (4:1-22). It is "Ichabod"—the "glory has departed" (1 Sam.4:21)—the anti-kingdom has desecrated God's dwelling place and made it desolate.

It is at Shiloh that God exposes the spiritual reality of the anti-kingdom. Eli and his sons outwardly perform their religious service, but they are "wicked men; they had no regard for the Lord...[and] they were treating the Lord's offering with contempt" (1 Sam.2:12-17). They are not lovers of God; they are "lovers of themselves, lovers of money, boastful, proud, abusive...lovers of pleasure rather than lovers of God—having a form of godliness but denying its power" (2 Tim.3:2-5). These priests were involved in occult rituals right in the midst of the sanctuary for they "slept with the women [religious prostitutes] who served at the entrance to the Tent of Meeting" (1 Sam.2:12:22; cf. Deut.23:17,18; 1 Kgs.14:24; 15:12; 22:46). The enemy permeates into the very fabric of God's habitation: the sanctuary (1 Sam.2:32). This perverse element makes the supernatural gifts and revelatory word of the Lord rare (1 Sam.3:1).

The ark makes its way around Philistia but ends up in Kiriath Jearim (or Baalah), a Gibeonite city (4:1-7:2). They take it to Abinadab's house "on the hill" (*ba gib`eah*) and consecrate Abinadab's son Eleazar to guard the ark of the Lord where it stays for twenty years (7:1,2; cf. 2 Sam.6:3). The strange thing about this time in Israel's history is that the ark, the bronze altar, and even Moses' tabernacle are taken to the *high place* (*bamah*) of Gibeon (1 Chron.21:29; 2 Chron.1:2-6). Why a high place of all places? These references certainly infer something suspicious about the spirituality of the Gibeonite cult.

It is important to clarify the three scriptural references that appear to legitimize the use of high places by the Israelites (1 Sam.9,10; 1 Chron.16:39; 1 Kgs.3:4). Let us address all three in light of the anti-kingdom's agenda.

When the Israelites make their initial entry into Canaan, the Gibeonites of Canaanite-Hivite origin use pretense to deceive Joshua into making a pact with them (Josh.9:3-21; 11:19; cf. 1 Chron.1:13).[1] Because of their clever sting operation, Joshua consigns them to servitude (Josh.9:21), yet the Gibeonite men maintain their status as mighty warriors (*gibborim* Josh.10:2). The city of Gibeon is allotted to Benjamin and becomes a Levitical city (Josh.18:25; 21:17). During the Judges era, Benjamin advances their association with Gibeon (now referred to as Gibeah)[2] to a hideous level of fidelity

---

1. "The list of four Gibeonite cities with which Israel entered into treaty-relationship (Joshua ix.17) warns us that such a study cannot be confined to the city of Gibeon... In Joshua ix.7 and xi.19 the Gibeonites are described as Hivites (*hiwwi*) and in 2 Sam.xxi.2 as non-Israelite, 'part of the residue of the Amorites,'" Joseph Blenkinsopp, *Gibeon and Israel, the Role of Gibeon and the Gibeonites in the Political and Religious History of Early Israel*, (Cambridge: Cambridge University Press, 1972), pp.1, 14, cf. pp.15-22.
2. Blenkinsopp clarifies this issue by stating that after the account of the Gibeon-Israel treaty, Gibeon is not mentioned until David transfers the ark to the Gibeonite city of Kiriath Jearim (1 Sam.6:21-7:2). "During the long period of the Judges and the reign of Saul...there is not a single occurrence of the name in M.T., despite the fact that it is precisely at this time that we would expect this 'great city' and the 'great high place' to have played a significant role...the silence of the tradition about Gibeon during this crucial period...has tempted many scholars to suppose that, in some instances at least, *haggib`ah* [Gibeah] has either replaced *gib`on* [Gibeon] or refers indirectly to it" (p.3; cf. Jud.19:14; 20:4; 1 Sam.13:2,15; 14:16; 1 Sam.11:4; 15:34; 2 Sam.21:6).

The Spiritual Reality of the Anti-Kingdom

(Jud.19-20)—and enters into covenant-marriage with them (Jud.19-21; 1 Chron.8:29-33).[3]

If the Gibeonites are rooted in satanic Canaanite Baalism and are at the same time aligned with the tribe of Benjamin, they may be suspect in introducing a counterfeit priesthood, a false "anti-kingdom" if you will, that threatens to infiltrate and destroy the true theocracy of God. If this is true, then it makes sense that from this unholy alliance would come its most famous descendent: Saul of Gibeah (1 Sam.11:1).

In 1 Samuel 9-10, Samuel, along with the prophets of God, anoint Saul as the leader over Israel at the high place of Gibeah. Why pick Saul? Who is he? Why would Samuel and the prophets do this at a bamah when the Scripture so clearly condemns their use? Why, of all places, is he anointed at the bamah of Gibeah to be leader over Israel? The answer lies in the convoluted character of Saul. Even Saul's vicious actions toward Gibeon (2 Sam.21), may be explained by an attempt to make Gibeon his capital city, "the centre of his kingdom and to authenticate his rule from the religious point of view by means of the ark-sanctuary established there."[4] We will see that Samuel and the prophets "use" the bamah of Gibeon to "anoint" the wicked appeal of the people, thereby demonstrating Israel's rejection of Yahweh and insistence in inaugurating the anti-kingdom. A life in alignment with bamoth is evidenced in the tormented life of Saul.

Israel succumbs to an anti-theocratic spirit, an attitude that blatantly rejects the reign of God through the Spirit (1 Sam.8:1-7). It is critical to note that it is at the bamah of Gibeah that Saul is anointed as *nagid*, the leader or commander (1 Sam.9:16;

---

3. "In the tribal coalition against Benjamin (Judges xx-xxi) the men of Jabesh-gilead were the only ones who did not contribute to the war of extermination (xxi.8f.), and the ensuing narrative seems to presuppose ethnic affinities between Gilead and Benjamin (verses 12-14)" (Blenkinsopp, p.61). Saul defends the people of Jabesh Gilead against Nahash the Ammonite to secure his leadership position (1 Sam.11), and in the end, the people of Jabesh Gilead regain Saul's dead body to give it proper burial (1 Sam.31:11-13; 2 Sam.2:4,5; 21:12).

4. Blenkinsopp, p.68.

Spiritual Reality

10:1) of the "anti-kingdom" (1 Sam.8-10). Yahweh chooses Saul to be *nagid* ('he who restrains' in the sense of a tyrannical suppression) over Israel, but it was the people of Israel who deemed him *melek* ('king').

Samuel's dramatic, albeit symbolic, gesture of anointing Saul as the anti-kingdom's pseudo-prince is distinctly dramatized at the bamah of Gibeah. The irony is revealed in Samuel's simultaneous denouncement (1 Sam.8:1-22; 10:17-19; 12:13-17) and as one would suspect, in the condemning content of the prophecies coming from the group of prophets as they expose the bamah for its representation of the anti-kingdom (1 Sam.10:9-16; 19:23,24). The details of these prophecies are not given, but we might assume that because these men are true prophets of God, the content of their prophecies must relate to the plan of Yahweh—his very heartbeat in this situation.

What would God say to Saul at this critical point in history? If Israel has rejected Yahweh as their king, Saul has only two options: 1) he can try to replace Yahweh as king of Israel, or 2) he can join with Samuel and the prophets and reinstate Yahweh as king over Israel's theocracy. It is probable that Saul affirms the theocratic reign of God through his prophecies and such spiritual behavior is so out of character that a sarcastic proverb spreads quickly throughout Israel (1 Sam.10:11). Yahweh genuinely touches his heart, but nevertheless, he will soon choose a path away from God.[5]

Saul is soon feeling a bit embarrassed about moving in the prophetic gift of the Spirit (1 Sam.10:9-22). He might think: "Those crazy charismatics influenced me to be carried away by all those prophecies. It's probably just ecstatic emotionalism! I'm going to lie low for a while and maybe the whole thing will blow over." Saul is wrong about that spiritually-charged experience. His encounter with the Spirit of God is designed to save him from participation in the anti-kingdom that is about to penetrate the people of God.

---

5. Blenkinsopp confirms this: "and we might note in this connection that while his first son, Jonathan, bears a good Yahwist name, later sons have names formed with Baal" (p.54).

Destructive Fruit

The book of 1 Samuel reveals to us what the anti-kingdom looks like "above ground" (1 Sam.8:10-18; 10:25ff.). To build the anti-kingdom, a spiritually abusive environment must be created—one that is based on usefulness rather than on personal value (1 Sam.8:10-18). Unfortunately, when a person's usefulness is no longer needed, neither is the person. One is only valuable if one is beneficial to the anti-kingdom's agenda. The anti-kingdom forces people to run in front of its chariots (v.11), it positions people like pegs in holes (vv.12,13), it exploits them (vv.14-16) and enslaves them (v.17). Amazingly, when the leaders of the anti-kingdom "rule by their own authority...people love it this way" (Jer.5:31). The Lord will eventually give them what they want (1 Sam.8:19-22). The anti-kingdom uses the flock as a means to serve themselves (Ezek.34:2-5). Without having a living relationship with God, the anti-kingdom is stuck in the precarious seat of false authority. There is the appearance of religious duty, but the anti-kingdom merely interferes and obstructs those who desire the experience of true spirituality in God's kingdom (Matt.23:1-13; 2 Tim.3:5).

The anti-kingdom concentrates on projecting an image. The first prince of the anti-kingdom is Saul, a tall handsome fellow from a wealthy family (1 Sam.9:1,2). There's obviously nothing wrong with these qualities, but they represent an emphasis on outward appearance that the anti-kingdom demands. Impressive persona is of utmost importance and Saul fits the bill. In contrast, the kingdom of God seeks a heart after God's own heart and deliberately rejects outward appearances: "The Lord does not look at the things man looks at. Man looks at the outward appearance, but the Lord looks at the heart" (1 Sam.16:7; cf. 13:14). The anti-kingdom exhausts all its efforts to project the right image "above ground" to cover for the lack of spiritual substance and integrity underneath.

Although the anti-kingdom gives God the credit, its verbal testimony is misleading (1 Sam.11:13). Saul learns to use Samuel's vocabulary and refers to God as Yahweh, even

Spiritual Reality

though he shows no evidence of any genuine relationship with God. Its mesmerizing capabilities "above ground" causes the anti-kingdom to fool the spiritually naïve. It sounds spiritual, looks righteous, and acts noble. Just as cubic zirconium looks like a diamond, so also the anti-kingdom looks authentic, but it's not real. The outward appearance of spirituality is a façade. The anti-kingdom's god is not Yahweh; its god is merely a force to rein in to advance the "underground" agenda. The word of God is not transformational and life giving; it is simply a tool used to manipulate. This is the spirituality of the anti-kingdom. There are no personal, face-to-face conversations with God, no life-changing encounters with the Holy Spirit; there is only god-talk: "These people honor me with their lips, but their hearts are far from me. They worship me in vain; their teachings are but rules taught by men" (Matt.15:8,9; cf. Isa.29:13).

Samuel appears worried. He discerns the spirit of the anti-kingdom and so at Gilgal he attempts to get back on course and renew the vision of the true kingdom of God (1 Sam.11:14). "What may be meant by the 'renewal of the kingdom' may be not the renewal of Saul's mandate to reign so much as the renewal of the kingdom structure within Israel."[6] But the people can only envision becoming like all the other nations, so they make Saul their king and Israel celebrates in their newly formed anti-kingdom (v.15). Samuel is beside himself and he unloads a denunciation of the entire scene (1 Sam.12:1-17). The whole incident demonstrates the permeating force of the anti-kingdom and the influx of the antichrist spirit within the dwelling place of God (1 Jn.2:18; 4:3). It looks good "above ground" but "underground" it looks like an abomination of desolation.

The anti-kingdom's true colors do come to the surface when the kingdom of true spirituality moves forward against the enemy. While the anti-kingdom is engrossed in rearranging

---

6. Dumbrell, W.J. *Covenant and Creation*, (Nashville: Thomas Nelson, 1984), p.135; cf. J.R. Vannoy, *Covenant Renewal at Gilgal*, (Cherry Hill: Mack Pub., 1978), pp.61-91.

The Spiritual Reality of the Anti-Kingdom

its regime, the true kingdom is fighting real battles. But of course, the anti-kingdom must assume full credit for victory (1 Sam.13:2-4). The tyranny of the anti-kingdom not only feeds off the genuine exploits of the righteous, it demands performance from them.

> If you perform as they say you must: (1) it will make them look good; (2) their self-righteousness will escape the scrutiny of the cross of Christ as the only means to God's favor; (3) it will allow them to examine you instead of themselves; (4) they will be able to "boast in" or gain a sense of validation from your religious performance.[7]

The anti-kingdom siphons from genuine spirituality to improve its image "above ground."

When the Philistine army encamps around Saul's army at Michmash, the people of God hide in caves and pits (1 Sam.13:6). The anti-kingdom cannot protect the sheep against the onslaught of the enemy; it divides, scatters, and jeopardizes the safety of God's flock (cf. Ezek.34:1-10; Prov.14:12). The anti-kingdom alienates sheep and drives them into isolation (Jn.10:12,13). To maintain damage control, it must do something religious, something that will appear spiritual so that others will take notice and submit once again to its authority. The wheels of Saul's mind begin to turn, "Gilgal! That's it! I'll go to Gilgal and wait to hear from Samuel and the prophets" (1 Sam.13:7,8). Neither Samuel nor the school of prophets is there. The anti-kingdom presumptuously assumes all ministerial positions (1 Sam.13:9). Even when the true kingdom confronts the anti-kingdom with truth, Saul gives Samuel a poor performance review—apparently, Samuel is the unspiritual one (vv.10-12). Religious rituals soothe and temporarily relieve the anti-kingdom's conscience from experiencing any true conviction. Samuel rebukes him for not following the

---

7. Johnson and VanVonderen, p.37.

Lord wholeheartedly and announces the withdrawal of the Spirit from the anti-kingdom (1 Sam.12:20; 13:13,14).

The anti-kingdom maneuvers its "underground" agenda through power posturing "above ground." The soldiers of Israel are faint and in distress because Saul had bound the people under an oath: "Cursed be any man who eats food before evening comes, before I have avenged myself on my enemies!" (1 Sam.14:24,28). Insecurity propels the anti-kingdom to constantly reassert its position and, unfortunately, its power posturing techniques only curse those who dwell under its oppression. Saul's religious oath sounds virtuous enough, but its consequences are disastrous. Saul's fast is bent on manipulating God and rallying the troops, but it is just another indication of his false spirituality. His spiritual authority is not real because it does not come from personal integrity that stems from real fellowship with God. The anti-kingdom appears to be something it's not.

The army is afraid to confront their leader for fear of being branded disloyal or not submissive to authority. "For many reasons, followers sometimes obey...to avoid being shamed, to gain someone's approval, or to keep their spiritual status or church position intact. This is not true obedience or submission; it is compliant self-seeking."[8] The conscience is overruled by the pressure to blindly obey the anti-kingdom's false spirituality (1 Sam.14:25,26). The anti-kingdom's demand for subordination to abusive shepherding strangely appeals to sheep who refuse to confront the obvious bad fruit "above ground" and who are afraid to discern the bad fruit's diabolical roots "underground." Undoubtedly, the anti-kingdom is built on spiritual and emotional manipulation between false shepherds and their flock.

In contrast, Jonathan is free to partake of some honey and is refreshed. When he finds out about Saul's threatened curse, he breaks the "can't talk" rule. "My father has troubled the land. Look now, how my countenance has brightened because I

---

8. Johnson and VanVonderen, p.66.

tasted a little of this honey" (1 Sam.13:27-30). The false spirituality of the anti-kingdom is counterproductive and causes the starving army to sin (vv.31,32). The legalistic foundation of the anti-kingdom first demoralizes the troops, then fosters rebellion. The anti-kingdom focuses much of their effort on meaningless obligation. It is meaningless—yet not without its consequences. False spirituality mutates people's perception of God's word and his character and this faulty image can enslave them to twisted imaginary revelations from God.

Saul builds the anti-kingdom's first altar (1 Sam.14:35). Ahijah suggests that he draw near to God and so Saul asks God, "'Shall I go down after the Philistines? Will you give them into Israel's hand?' But God did not answer him that day" (v.37). No answer? Who is causing the doors of heaven to slam shut? The anti-kingdom accuses the one who truly nurtures an intimate relationship with God of being in its way (vv.38-44). Even the people see through this madness and rescue Jonathan: "Shall Jonathan die—he who has brought about this great deliverance in Israel? Never! As surely as the Lord lives, not a hair of his head will fall to the ground, for he did this today with God's help" (v.45). The sad irony is that when God intrudes into the anti-kingdom to bring salvation to its adherents, Saul doesn't recognize him. In fact, the authentic move of God in the midst of the anti-kingdom propels Saul to clutch even tighter to control the reins of his anti-kingdom (v.47). The anti-kingdom always battens down its hatches when the Holy Spirit is loosed among the people (vv.48-52).

Spiritual pride is a distinctive earmark of the anti-kingdom's "above ground" activities. When commanded to carry out Yahweh's war against the Amalekites, Saul brings home Agag, the king of Amalek, as his trophy (1 Sam.15:1-9). Jonathan Edwards believed that the main cause of aborted revivalism is spiritual pride: "[Pride] is the main door by which the devil comes into the hearts of those who are zealous for the advancement of religion…[pride is] the main handle by which the devil has hold of religious persons, and the chief source of all the mischief that he introduces, to clog and hinder the work of God."⁹ The anti-kingdom is threatened by the genuine move of God because it will expose its true nature. It is totally immersed in self-congratulation and spiritual self-interest. It seeks to construct monuments to itself (1 Sam.15:12). Yet when the true kingdom of God once again confronts the anti-kingdom about its hypocrisy, Saul is quick to blame the people (vv.13-21). This is the last straw that breaks Samuel's back.

Samuel discloses the key difference between the true spirituality of God's kingdom and the counterfeit spirituality of the anti-kingdom:

> Does the Lord delight in burnt offerings and sacrifices as much as in obeying the voice of the Lord? To obey is better than sacrifice, and to heed is better than the fat of rams. For rebellion is like the sin of divination, and arrogance like the evil of idolatry. Because you have rejected the word of the Lord, he has rejected you as king. 1 Samuel 15:22,23

True spirituality hears the voice of the Lord and obeys it. False spirituality hears nothing from God. It only carries out the anti-kingdom's intricate system of self-righteous deeds. The arrogance of the anti-kingdom drives its citizens to unwittingly sin against God because it idolizes the appearance of spirituality, glorifies works, and covets the immediate recognition and admiration of everyone "above ground."

Samuel lashes out a strong indictment against the anti-kingdom. He accuses the anti-kingdom of empty spirituality and calls such rebellion "divination." Offering pious, yet meaningless, sacrifices deeply offends Yahweh.

> "The multitude of your sacrifices—what are they to me?" says the Lord. "I have more than enough of burnt offerings...I have no pleasure in the blood of bulls and lambs and goats. When you come to

---

9. Edwards, Jonathan. *Thoughts on Revival*, (New Haven: Yale Univ. Press), p.414.

appear before me, who has asked this of you, this trampling of my courts? Stop bringing meaningless offerings! Your incense is detestable to me. New moons, Sabbaths and convocations—I cannot bear your evil assemblies...your appointed feasts my soul hates. They have become a burden to me; I am weary of bearing them." Isaiah 1:11-14

People who are caught in the "above ground" zone of the anti-kingdom have the tendency to turn their beliefs into a formalized religious system rather than a life of Spirit-led service. Entanglement in counterfeit spirituality accentuates outward observance and leaves the soul entrenched in a prison house of performance.

The anti-kingdom is proficient in spiritual manipulation. Samuel defines the rebellion of the anti-kingdom as divination. This is not simple disobedience—its defiance has regressed to a diabolical level. Therefore, it should not surprise us when Saul consults with the witch at Endor in the near future (1 Sam.28). What kind of "rebellion is like the sin of divination"? The rebelliousness of the anti-kingdom will eventually seek knowledge and power through unholy connections. Searching for enlightenment outside of the Spirit of God, the anti-kingdom will find assistance "underground" to fulfill its destiny. Though it may sound extreme, if the anti-kingdom dabbles in rebellion while trying to keep up its religious appearance, then it is operating in spiritual manipulation—otherwise known as divination.

Spiritual manipulation lays the foundation of the anti-kingdom. It preaches a false Jesus, it imparts a different spirit, and it promotes a different gospel. Paul describes the anti-kingdom to be like a masquerade parade:

> For if someone comes to you and preaches a Jesus other than the Jesus we preached, or if you receive a different spirit from the one you received, or a different gospel from the one you accepted...such men are false apostles, deceitful workmen, masquerading

Spiritual Reality

> ["above ground"] as apostles of Christ. And no wonder, for Satan himself masquerades ["above ground"] as an angel of light. It is not surprising, then, if his servants masquerade ["above ground"] as servants of righteousness. Their end will be what their ["underground"] actions deserve. 2 Corinthians 11:4,13-15

They "masquerade as servants of righteousness" yet with a different spirit, a manipulative spirit—the spirit of divination.

When Samuel uncovers the anti-kingdom's unholy disguise, Saul cries out: "I have sinned. I violated the Lord's command and your instructions. I was afraid of the people and so I gave in to them. Now I beg you, forgive my sin...But *honor me* before the elders of my people and before Israel; come back with me, so that I may worship the Lord *your* God" (1 Sam.15:24,30, emphasis mine). Is this true repentance or false humility? It's clear that confession of sin does not necessarily mean that repentance has occurred. Support groups are full of confessions, but without repentance within those confessions, there is no transformation (2 Cor.7:10). In the anti-kingdom, it's easier to psychoanalyze and explain sin than to truly repent.

Saul's request to receive honor reveals his pretentious humility. "Another infallible sign of spiritual pride is when persons think highly of their humility...It is the very nature of false humility to be highly conceited about itself...the deluded hypocrite...is so blind that he never sees his pride and yet is quick sighted about any show of humility."[10] Even in the anti-kingdom's show of humility there is spiritual pride. But Saul's reference to "the Lord your God" discloses the true condition of his counterfeit spirituality (1 Sam.15:30). The anti-kingdom's referral to Samuel's Lord is obviously not Saul's god.

So the Spirit of the Lord departs from Saul, and an evil spirit from the Lord torments him (1 Sam.16:14). Although this might upset our theology, God is the one who sends the evil spirit to trouble Saul. This impediment is not due to

---

10. Edwards, Jonathan. *Religious Affections*, ed. James M. Houston, (Minneapolis: Bethany Pub. House, 1996), p.136.

God's viciousness, but rather due to the breakdown of the structure of the anti-kingdom. It is the inevitable consequence to participating in its system. God, in his infinite wisdom, will allow a problem to intensify and permit the escalation of demonic activity. We might call it hitting the bottom, but from heaven's perspective, it is God's appointed time to look up and reach for redemption. Satanic influence is designed to destroy, but God uses the enemy for redemptive purposes. This evil spirit gains entrance into Saul's life because the door of his heart is closed to God—but it is wide open to demonic forces. As a last resort, God uses this evil spirit to provoke Saul to repentance.

So we see that because of its rebellious nature, the anti-kingdom is vulnerable to demonic assailants. Rebellion creates an environment in which the devil can subtly gain entrance. In phase one, oppression enters gradually through many invitations to admittance. These invitations are so subtle the victim may be completely ignorant of the cost. The devil begins phase one by accepting invitations to set up strongholds of falsehood in the mind. Over the years, Satan gradually captivates Saul's mind with pseudo-spiritualism. Demonic strongholds convince the mind that good is evil and evil is good, that truth is false and lies are true. This is demonic oppression of the mind.

Once Satan has a foothold in a person's mind, he moves to phase two: demonic obsession. In the case of Saul, the Holy Spirit becomes so grieved by his resistance that the Spirit departs completely from him. Saul becomes demonically obsessed. Psychologists call it obsessive-compulsive or neurotic behavior. Neurotics act very normal most of the time, but certain things set off irrational, abnormal reactions. Though antidepressants may stabilize the nerves, they cannot deliver from demonic oppression. Demonic oppression makes reasonably sane people susceptible to paranoia and warped suggestions of reality. Saul is a classic case. Saul receives ample opportunities for deliverance under David's anointed ministry (1 Sam.16:23; 18:10; 24:17-22; 26:21-25), yet he habitually regresses into paranoia and invites the obsession to advance.

Later, the evil spirit comes on Saul again and this time Saul prophesies and throws a spear at David (1 Sam.18:10,11). Saul's obsession with David manifests itself through jealousy and hatred. His religious spirit links up with demonic obsession and produces a counterfeit manifestation of prophecy (cf. 2 Thess.2:9-12). Although Saul's prophecy is not stated, one could guess that its content is a message from the anti-kingdom's "underground" well. Its perverted utterance probably sounded something like this: "Thus says the Lord, 'Saul is My anointed king—not David! Though Israel may ascribe to David slaying ten thousands, and to Saul but thousands...David is an enemy of this kingdom!" The anti-kingdom always misrepresents and persecutes the true kingdom of God—but to no avail (1 Sam.18:17-30; 19:9,10).

God provides many opportunities for Saul to repent and receive deliverance through the ministries of Samuel, David, and the prophets (1 Sam.19:20-24). Even in his last encounter with the Spirit of God and the prophets, Saul experiences a moment of freedom—freedom from delusion and freedom to grasp truth. He realizes he is way off course; his throne is slipping through his fingers (1 Sam.20:30-31; 24:17-22; 26:21-25). Tragically, this truth does not set him free. Knowledge alone cannot deliver the captive soul. Only through the power of the Holy Spirit can a contrite heart be delivered from demonic influence.

"Now Samuel was dead, and all Israel had mourned for him and buried him in his own town of Ramah. Saul had expelled the mediums and spiritists from the land...When Saul saw the Philistines army, he was afraid; terror filled his heart. He inquired of the Lord, but the Lord did not answer him by dreams or Urim or prophets" (1 Sam.28:3,5,6). He then seeks another means strictly forbidden by God (Lev.20:6; Deut.18:11). Saul is panic-stricken and completely deranged. He throws out all the occult practitioners in his kingdom and then consults a witch!

All legitimate means of communicating with God are closed. So now Saul's demonic obsession aims to maneuver Saul into the presence of a spiritualist medium. Demonic operations have moved to phase three: the anti-kingdom will eventually align with the antichrist kingdom. It is best to understand this level of demonic operations in terms of full demonization rather than "possession." The New Testament uses two words "*diamonizomai*" (under the power of) and "*echo*" (to have hold of, adhering, clinging to) to describe the idea of demonization rather than its having possession or ownership over a person. Full demonization takes control of thoughts, emotions, and actions of its victim.

There are four ways in which occult power and oppression may enter: 1) through heredity (generational succession), 2) willful subscription of one's self to Satan, 3) occult involvement, and 4) occult transference. Christians can continue to suffer from occult oppression because of pre-conversion or generational participation. "The door opened to the powers of darkness will remain open until he closes it by an act of his will."[11] One must renounce the hidden works of darkness to enjoy the freedom of deliverance from occult penetration.

In principle, however, obsession turns into legal possession when a person bonds in an unholy alliance with a demon. This is exactly what Saul does in a séance with a medium (*ba`alah* "enchantress, sorceress, necromancer"). In 1 Samuel 28:7 Saul's request literally reads, "Seek me a woman who has a voice from the pit." The witch at Endor actually "brings up" (`*alah* "cause to ascend") a familiar spirit from the pit and channels into communication with the demon—not Samuel. A familiar spirit is a demon who, by assignment, observes a family or individual to assess how they respond to various circumstances in order to determine their strengths and weaknesses. Though demons cannot read people's minds, they can anticipate certain patterns of behavior. This explains the impersonation of Samuel in the séance at Endor. It is the sad account of spiritism, the quest to enter contact with the dead.

If all the biblically legitimate ways of contacting God were severed, certainly God would not speak through a witch and

---

11. Thompson, C. *Possess the Land*, p.72.

thereby break his own law! The witch sees a vision of an old man and spirits ascending out of the earth (v.13). This should have been a dead give-away! Those spirits are ascending out of the pit of hell. Saul is duped into believing that Samuel has come to his rescue.

He confesses to the familiar spirit impersonating Samuel that God has stopped speaking to him via the prophets (1 Sam.28:15). Was not Samuel a prophet? If this were really Samuel, a genuine prophet would have kept silent like his God. The familiar spirit impersonating Samuel tortures Saul with the threat of death (vv.19,20). The chronicler settles the whole matter: "Saul died because he was unfaithful to the Lord; he did not keep the word of the Lord and even consulted a medium for guidance, and *did not inquire of the Lord*. So the Lord put him to death and turned the kingdom over to David son of Jesse" (1 Chron.10:13,14, emphasis mine).

By contacting a *ba`alah*, Saul opens the door for deception by a familiar spirit that impersonates Samuel and falls prey to the transference of the ba`alah's occult power. Both Saul and the ba`alah connect with the demon and thereby participate in divination (*nahash* "enchantments, sorcery"). To participate in divination is to fall under a spell (*haber* "to join, unite, bind together, be coupled, be in league, to make an alliance," namely "to tie up a person by magic") and such an unholy alliance opens communication lines to hear (*lahash* "whispers, charms") from the demonic realm.[12] Just looking at Saul's consequences, one can easily understand why the Lord vehemently opposes any occult involvement by his people (Deut.18:10-12).

Saul's sad story dramatically illustrates a life caught in the web of the anti-kingdom. The anti-kingdom will eventually align itself with the apostate antichrist kingdom. Such a merger makes a shipwreck of the faith and destroys the lives of those involved in its diabolical system. The anti-kingdom may look good "above ground," but "underground" it's in league with the antichrist kingdom.

---

12. It is not a coincidence that divination (*nahash*) and the casting of charms (*lahash*) are similar to the word serpent (*nāhāsh*).

This is how the Babylonian harlot system worked in the time of Saul and how it works in the latter days: "By your magic spell (*pharmakeia* "sorcery, magical arts, poisoning, administering of drugs") all the nations were led astray" (Rev.18:23). The technique used to deceive the nations is divination. The system is designed to seduce the nations into making legal, binding associations with demonic powers. The Babylonian system "ties up" its participants to demonic strategies by triggering them with temptations, torment, and the condemnation of devious whisperings. And this system creates the abomination of desolation.

After the death of Saul, David takes the ark of the covenant from Kiriath-Jearim, from Abinadab's house "on the hill" (*ba gib`eah*) to the house of Obed-Edom, and then finally to his tent in the city of David (2 Sam.5:25-6:12). Oddly, David installs Abiathar as priest in his tent but leaves Zadok as priest at the anti-kingdom's bamah of Gibeon (1 Chron.16:39). Yahweh does not judge this situation until David takes a census of his mighty army (2 Sam.24; 1 Chron.21). When God sends a plague that spreads throughout Israel, an angel of the Lord commands David to buy the threshing floor of Araunah the Jebusite to erect an altar (1 Chron.21:18-28). In the following verses it is clear that David's fear of the angel of the Lord is connected to his uneasiness about Gibeon's bamah and he soon comes to this remarkable revelation:

> The tabernacle of the Lord, which Moses had made in the desert, and the altar of burnt offering were at that time on the high place at Gibeon. But *David could not go before it* to inquire of God, *because he was afraid of the sword of the angel of the Lord*. Then David said, "*The house of the Lord God is to be here, and also the altar of burnt offering for Israel*" (1 Chron.21:29-22:1, emphasis mine).

The angel of the Lord ultimately judges David's syncretistic use of this bamah. David is to prepare his son Solomon to extract all aspects of worship away from Gibeon's anti-kingdom to Jerusalem's true kingdom (1 Chron.22:2-29:20). Alignment with the anti-kingdom's bamoth only proves to be a stumbling block to the worship of the one true God.

The last passage that appears to legitimize the use of bamoth is the story of Solomon in 1 Kings 3:4. However, the context of 1 Kings 2-3 reveals the legacy of Israel's battle with the anti-kingdom's syncretism and the reality of its affects on Solomon and Israel. What we see in this period is spiritual fragmentation: Solomon nurtures affectionate devotion to Yahweh, but still "offered sacrifices and burnt incense on the high places"—most notably at the Gibeonite bamah of the anti-kingdom (1 Kgs.3:2-4).[13]

The excuse given that the temple had not yet been built may explain Solomon's actions, but it does not justify him (1 Kgs.3:2; 2 Chron.1:3). The bamoth, especially the one at Gibeon, represents the anti-kingdom, the kingdom of false spirituality that infiltrates the sanctuary—the designated meeting place of Yahweh with his people (1 Sam.9:12-25). It is imperative that Solomon builds the true temple of Yahweh and destroys the syncretism of the bamoth for it is at the bamah of Gibeon in particular, that Satan's Canaanite pseudo-kingdom accesses the seed of the righteous. Does Solomon do this? He constructs the magnificent temple in Jerusalem (1 Kgs.5:1-9:9), but in his senior years he builds bamoth for numerous idols (1 Kgs.11:1-8). Alignment with the anti-kingdom's bamoth proves once again that it will only obstruct and destroy true spirituality. It causes division and sets the stage for the abomination of desolation within the temple of God.

---

13. Blenkinsopp may be correct in connecting Saul's bamah of Gibeon and the sacrificial offerings by Solomon: "'The great stone which is in Gibeon' (2 Sam.xx.8) has sometimes been identified with the altar upon which Solomon offered sacrifices as recorded in 1 Kings iii.4. While this is hypothetical, it may find support in the reference to 'the great stone' set up by Saul after his victory over the Philistines. This constituted the first altar erected by him to Yahweh and was certainly in the Gibeonite region (1 Sam.xiv.33-5; cf.v.31)", p.7.

The Abomination of Desolation

As we have observed the influence of the Canaanite culture throughout the era of the kings, we can see how the Israelites incorporate Baalism-satanism into their belief system. During the time of Jeremiah, the Israelites participate in occult rituals right in the temple of Jerusalem (Jer.7:6). They stand in the sanctuary of God and say, "We are safe"—safe to take part in the disgusting ceremonies to Baal, the queen of heaven, and Molech (vv.9,10,17,18,30,31; cf. 1 Kgs.11:5). The Canaanite practices performed inside the temple complex are offerings of occult sacrifice. The house of God became "a den (*me`arah* "cave, hideout") of robbers" (v.11)—a safe place for occult rituals. These abominable practices within the house of the Lord bring God's judgment of desolation, a withdrawal of God's presence and blessing.

There are numerous theories about the fulfillment of the phrase "abomination of desolation." Surely it refers to Antiochus Epiphanes IV's slaughter of pigs to Zeus, the Hellenized version of Canaan's Baal, inside the Jerusalem temple in 169 B.C. (2 Macc.6:2). It may also refer to the Roman seizure of the temple and its destruction (A.D. 40-70). Others believe that the abomination of desolation will occur in the future when the antichrist appears in a rebuilt Jewish temple in Jerusalem.

If we define the abomination of desolation as a "period of unholy alliance, the disruption of temple worship, [and] its replacement by an apostate alternative,"[14] then we will understand that it pertains to a time when "the sanctuary and the truth are overthrown, and sanctuary and army are given over to be trampled down. Army, sanctuary, and truth are all portrayed as victims of the goat's charging and butting"[15] (cf. Dan.8:11). But it is vital to notice that "the rebellion that causes desolation, and the surrender of the sanctuary and of the host" refers not to a rebellion by the true worshippers of Yahweh, but to a rebellion

---

14. Goldingay, John. *Word Biblical Commentary, Daniel,* 30, (Dallas: Word, 1989), p.267.
15. Ibid, p.210.

by "the Prince of the host (demonic army)"—the little horn of antichrist and his evil minions (Dan.8:12,13). This demonic rebellion infiltrates and desecrates the temple so that the glory of God's presence departs and the temple is left desolate.

A key, but admittedly difficult, verse is found in Daniel 9:27: "And on a wing of the temple he will set up an abomination that causes desolation, until the end that is decreed is poured out on him." The wing (*kanap*) "is often used figuratively of the extremity or skirt of the upper garment or cloak (1 Sam.xv.27; xxiv.5; Hag.ii.12)… [this] shows that not the pinnacle, i.e. the summit of the temple itself, is meant, but a wing or adjoining building of the sanctuary."[16] This implies more than a setup of an idol and idolatrous worship (although it is idolatrous in its essence); it implies the construction of a counterpart, a corresponding image built onto the true sanctuary. The abomination of desolation is a sacrilegious addition (*shiqquwts* noun masc. plural) that desecrates (LXX renders "to make foul" or "to cause to stink") the sacred place. The true temple of God, the true Bride of Christ remains faithful and stands pure (Eph.2:21,22; Heb.9:11,24; 1 Pet.2:5).

Paul exhorts us not to be deceived when "the rebellion [*apostasia* "the defection led by the Prince of the demonic army"] occurs and the man of lawlessness [antichrist] is revealed, the man doomed to destruction" (2 Thess.2:3). The apostasy is best understood as a demonic infiltration into the temple of God to cause defection (1 Tim.4:1ff.) and create the abomination of desolation. Antichrist "will oppose and will exalt himself over everything that is called God or is worshipped" and he will set himself up "in God's temple, proclaiming himself to be God" (v.4) in "a wing"—a sacrilegious counterpart, a perverse counterfeit addition (Rev.11:1,2) that is designed to mock the true temple of the Holy Spirit (1 Cor.3:16,17; 6:19; 2 Cor.6:16).

False peace and prosperity will be given to those "who forsake the holy covenant" to pacify their consciences and convince them of the benefits to aligning with darkness

---

16. Keil, C.F., Delitzsch, F. *Commentary on the Old Testament, Ezekiel, Daniel*, 9, (Grand Rapids: Eerdmans, 1985), p.369.

(Dan.11:30). Evil "armed forces will rise up to desecrate the temple fortress...Then they will set up the abomination that causes desolation. With flattery (*chalaqqah* "smoothness, fine promises") [antichrist] will corrupt those who have violated the covenant, but the people who know their God will firmly resist him" (Dan.11:31,32). Despite apostasy, the gospel of the true kingdom of God must continue to be preached to all nations (Matt.24:9-14). The true temple of God will resist the seduction and desecration, but not without price:

> Those who are wise will instruct many, though for a time they will fall by the sword or be burned or captured or plundered. When they fall, they will receive a little help, and many who are not sincere will join them. Some of the wise will stumble, so that they may be refined, purified and made spotless until the time of the end, for it will still come at the appointed time. Daniel 11:33-35 (cf. Dan.8:14; 12:10,11)

Jesus tells us ahead of time to look for "the abomination that causes desolation" for it is his signal to the disciples: 1) to discern the demonic infiltration in the temple of God, and 2) to courageously separate from its web of sorcery (Matt.24:14,25). Surely, this will cause "great distress, unequaled from the beginning of the world until now—and never to be equaled again. If those days had not been cut short, no one would survive, but for the sake of the elect those days will be shortened" (*koloboo* "mutilated, amputated" vv.21-22). The war on the saints oppresses them; it is literally bent on wearing them out (Dan.7:25).

When Daniel sees visions of the latter day abomination of desolation he is very troubled; he is appalled by the visions and lies ill for several days because it is beyond his comprehension (Dan.8:27). He fears for those who will live through the latter day abomination of desolation for the merging of the anti-kingdom and the antichrist kingdom will cause intolerable anguish. But Daniel is our hero. Although he is exhausted by visions of all the anti-Christian forces, he then "got up and went about the king's business" (v.27). Daniel 11:32 assures us that in spite of the reality of the anti-kingdom:

> "the people who know their God will display strength and take action" (NAS)
> "the people who know their God shall be strong, and carry out great exploits" (NKJV)
> "the people who know their God will firmly resist him" (NIV).

Can the Church come to terms with the spiritual reality of the abomination of desolation in her midst? Will we display strength and take action, advancing the gospel of the kingdom in the face of the anti-kingdom? Will we carry out great exploits and firmly resist the spirit of antichrist as it manifests in the abomination of desolation? Let us pray that "we will always be on the watch...that we may be able to escape all that is about to happen, all that is about to come upon the world; that we may be able to stand before the Son of Man when he appears" (Lk.21:34).

Chapter Eight

Our Hope and Final Destination: The Realization of Mount Zion

Throughout the Old Testament records we have found a spiritual heritage that is both rich and profound. It not only reveals our heritage in the family of God but it also brings out the spiritual reality behind our journey here on earth. We have come to understand that from the beginning all things possess a spiritual origin and mission. God's creation is not just a tangible presentation of his splendor; it contains a spiritual reality behind it. But since the first day of creation, a jealous archangel has tricked God's masterpiece, human king-priests, into making an unholy alliance with him. So we must come to terms with the dark side of spiritual reality.

The day Adam and Eve lost their place as joint rulers over the world is the day they traded their kingly position for slavery. The world has since become a hostile place for human beings because Satan's perverse mission has been inaugurated. Although many will follow his pernicious religion, a faithful remnant will refuse to join in the deception. So Satan and his demons will persecute the righteous and attempt to set up the abomination of desolation in their midst. Our ancient heritage includes a courageous multitude who have continuously withstood malicious assaults from the apostate antichrist kingdom.

We have all faced the spiritual reality of participating in the greater family of faith. We are part of an ancient sovereign plan that began in Eden and will consummate in the New Jerusalem. Mount Zion is our hope and final destination. In the fall, Eden disconnects with God's heavenly dwelling place; in Christ we reconnect with his holy mountain—Mount Zion, the city of the living God.

Ancient cultures throughout the history of the world esteem physical and artificial mountains as sacred sites for human-divine encounters. The details of the form and mythology may vary, but mountain-structures seem to provide a point of contact with evil entities that unfortunately seal unholy allegiances to Satan. Artificial cosmic mountain-structures, such as the Sumerian ziggurats, Egyptian pyramids, and Canaanite high places are complex simulations meant to counterfeit the true representation of the biblical cosmic mountain of Yahweh.

Christians must attempt to formulate their beliefs about Yahweh's holy mountain by using only biblical motifs associated with mountain imagery rather than borrowing from extrabiblical sources—especially Canaan's mythology. To stay within the boundaries of Scripture is to readily grasp the characteristics and significance of Yahweh's true cosmic mountain. One will clearly be able to contrast the Bible's portrayal of the true cosmic Mount Zion with the mythological traditions of cosmic mountain imagery that so many contemporary scholars now presume to assimilate into the biblical text.

The True Cosmic Mountain of Yahweh

Mountains can simply be a physical reality, but they can also be a symbolic literary motif or represent a mystical sacred space.[1] Although the ziggurat, pyramid, and bamah all presume

---

1. Cohn, p.25.

to be simulated, albeit diabolical, representations of the true mountain of Yahweh as presented in the Bible, in reality they are multifaceted pinnacles for humans to be accessed by the forces of evil. In contrast, what does Yahweh's true cosmic mountain *look* like? What is its significance? And how does *the Bible* describe its characteristics? Does the Bible describe Mount Zion as "the meeting place of the gods"? Does it portray Zion as "the battleground of conflicting natural forces"? Does the biblical text describe Mount Zion as "the meeting place of heaven and earth, the place were decrees are issued"?[2] Is Mount Zion, as so many contemporary scholars now assume, really Baal's Mount Zaphon? Before we attempt to answer these questions, let us first lay a foundation using only biblical motifs associated with mountain imagery rather than relying on Canaanite mythology.

Let us begin our study of biblical mountain imagery with the paradigm found in the Edenic linkage to the holy mount of God (Ezek.28:13-15). Lucifer's attempt to usurp the divine order sends him reeling from his post in the heavenly abode (vv.16,17) and in effect disconnects humanity from their connection with the sacred mount. Since the luciferic incident in Eden, a pattern develops where faithful believers experience spiritual encounters on various physical mountains (i.e. Mount Ararat in Gen.8:4-12 and Mount Moriah in Gen.22:1-5). However, mountain imagery achieves its clearest expression in the sacred mountain of Yahweh as it is displayed in two separate mountains that reflect one unified image. The first is Mount Sinai (or Horeb) and the second is Mount Zion. If we link Sinai with Zion we will gain an appreciation for redemptive history on a higher, cosmological plane and grasp its significance on a progressive, eschatological level.

The Goal of Mount Sinai: Mount Zion

As the Israelites make their way out of Egypt, Yahweh instructs them to encamp by the sea directly opposite a mountain called Baal Zaphon (Ex.14:2). It seems humorous that

---

2. Clifford, p.3ff.

Yahweh deliberately parades a demonstration of his omnipotence right in front of Baal's residence. Baal appears as the impotent onlooker, the helpless witness to God's sovereign deliverance of his people through the Red Sea. Mount Sinai then becomes "a beacon to the slaves of Egypt, a symbol of a new kind of master and a radically different relationship [with God]…Sinai is not the final goal of the Exodus, but lying between Egypt and Canaan, it does represent YHWH's unchallengeable mastery over both."[3] This miraculous deliverance brought Israel to a mountain called Sinai, but Yahweh states his real intention: "You yourselves have seen what I did to Egypt, and how I carried you on eagles' wings and *brought you to myself*" (Ex.19:4, emphasis mine). Mount Sinai, the mountain of God (Ex.3:1; Numb.10:33), and its analogous covenant of law establish a suzerain-vassal love-relationship between Yahweh and Israel (Deut.6:1-5; 7:7-9; 10:12,13; 11:1,13,22,23; 13:3; 30:6,20).

> To believe that he alone is lord is to do his will; to do his will is to enthrone him in lordship. The belief in the one true God, the love of God, and the observance of his commandments are inextricable; they are all ways of stating one fact, his suzerainty…at the core of the covenant relationship lies a twofold love, the mysterious love of YHWH for Israel and the less baffling love of Israel for YHWH, her benefactor…[The commandments] are the words of the language of love, the fit medium in which to respond to the passionate advances of the divine suzerain…The love of God moves Israel to embrace the norms of Sinai.[4]

The relationship is much more than dutiful, it is personal and highly intimate. The vassal's obedience to the suzerain's commands spring from a deep sincere love for God.

---

3. Levenson, Jon. *Sinai and Zion*, (Minneapolis: Winston Press, 1985), p.23.
4. Ibid, pp.70,77.

If the goal of Exodus is Mount Sinai, the establishment of suzerain-vassal kingdom relations, then by extension the aim of Mount Sinai is Mount Zion. Moses affirms this in his song: "You will bring them in and plant them on the mountain of your inheritance—the place, O Lord, you made for your dwelling, the sanctuary, O Lord, your hands established" (Ex.15:17). Mount Zion will symbolize the impact that the suzerain-vassal love-relationship has on all earthly affairs. Intimacy with Yahweh commences the suzerain-kingdom's transforming power throughout all the earth.

When Yahweh reappoints Israel as his king-priests at Sinai, he sets up a transportable tabernacle to be their meeting place. But it is not until after David's conquest of the Jebusite fortress that Mount Zion's imagery and theology begin to develop. Mount Sinai is the foundation and commencement of Israel's journey to Mount Zion. Israel's march from Sinai is directed toward the establishment of Yahweh's throne at Zion (Psa.68:1-17). To put it more succinctly, "Sinai has not so much been forgotten as absorbed...The transfer of the motif from Sinai to Zion was complete and irreversible, so that YHWH came to be designated no longer as 'the One of Sinai,' but as 'he who dwells on Mount Zion' (Isa.8:18)."[5] So Yahweh leaves Sinai (Deut. 33:2; Jud.5:4; Hab.3:3) to take up residence in enemy territory, the land of Canaan (Ex.15:17; Psa.78:54). With David's transfer of the ark of the covenant to Jerusalem, Mount Zion then becomes the great King's chosen abode (Psa.78:68,69; 132:13). Zion becomes Yahweh's divine capital city (Psa.46:5; 48:2,3,8,9; 87:2).

Salvation history reveals that "through time and the movement of Israel into the Promised Land, Zion displaces Sinai as God's dwelling place on earth. The movement of the mountain of God from Sinai to Zion tracks with the progress of redemption."[6] Scripture focuses on the historicity of Sinai and its symbolic emphasis on deliverance from evil, while it depicts Zion

---

5. Levenson, p.91.
6. Ryken, Wilhoit, Longman, p.573.

as being cosmic in character and its symbolic emphasis on transformation through Yahweh's conquest over evil. Israel's historical experience with Yahweh as its liberator is memorialized at Mount Sinai, yet a "whosoever-will" encounter with Yahweh is advanced to a grander cosmic scaffold in the symbol of Mount Zion.[7]

What brings the national experience of Yahweh to an international level? The Davidic Covenant. The next step to formulating our conception of Zion theology must integrate the preexisting motif of Sinai with the Davidic tradition as revealed in the Davidic Covenant.[8]

> This Davidic covenant, then, is distinct in kind from the Sinaitic. The focus of the Mosaic covenant sealed at Sinai is twofold: history and morality…In the case of the Davidic covenant…[it] fixes attention to that which is constant beneath—or perhaps I should say, above—the flux of history…Jerusalem and, as we shall see, especially Mount Zion, are a sign that beneath and beyond the pain and chaos of the realm we call history, there is another realm, upheld by the indefectible promise of God.[9]

The symbolism of Mount Zion points to a reality that is above linear earthly history (or what Eliade calls "profane time") into the realm of eternal life. Because of this, Zion takes on primal paradisiacal characteristics that demonstrate a concrete yet immeasurable bearing on the universe.

---

7. Cf. Ben C. Ollenburger, *Zion, the City of the Great King, A Theological Symbol of the Jerusalem Cult,* JSOT Sup.41, (Sheffield: JSOT Press, 1987), p.156.
8. Renz, Thomas. "The Use of the Zion Tradition in the Book of Ezekiel," *Zion, City of our God,* ed. Richard S. Hess and Gordon J. Wenhem, (Grand Rapids: Eerdmans, 1999), p.83,85. Although the word covenant (*berith*) is not used in 2 Samuel 7, other scriptures clarify this encounter as a covenant between God and David (cf. 2 Sam.23:5; Psa.89:3; 132:11,12).
9. Levenson, pp. 100-101.

Integrating Sinai with the Davidic Tradition

Building on the foundation of the Mosaic Covenant and staying within the framework of the Davidic Covenant, the prophets begin to develop Zion theology, a theology that paints a vivid portrait of Yahweh's cosmic mountain. Zion exhibits eternal characteristics and radiates eschatological significance. Even if the Israelite understanding of the Davidic tradition of 2 Samuel 7 focused on human government, the prophets clearly expound on this eternal kingship-covenant in terms of Yahweh's cosmic governance from Zion.[10]

> This "kingdom" must be placed in the category of an "anticipative" realization in proper keeping with the entire scope of Old Testament experience. The shadow-kingdom of Israel was real. God was reigning in their midst. But it was nonetheless only a shadow of the reality to come…David's line anticipated in shadow-form the eternal character of the reign of Jesus Christ. While God actually was manifesting his lordship through David's line, this human monarchy was serving at the same time as a typological representation of the throne of God itself. David's reign was intended to anticipate in shadow-form the reality of the messianic Redeemer who was to unite with finality the throne of David with the throne of God.[11]

The historical conquest of the Jebusite fortress "signified Yahweh's right of possession of the land of Canaan"[12] and connects

---

10. Cf. Renz, pp.84-85. I concur with Renz's position that both traditions affirm Zion as the center of government, but I would break from his assertion that "the Zion tradition can be imagined without the Davidic tradition" (p.85) for it appears that Zion tradition is founded on the Davidic tradition and therefore inseparable. "This election of Mount Zion was indissolubly connected with the divine election of David and his dynasty" (Clements, p.49).
11. Robertson, O.P., pp.241,249.
12. Clements, p.50.

David's throne with Yahweh's throne. Ultimately, "Yahweh's holy mountain must refer to the whole land of Palestine, if not the whole world, which is signified by Mount Zion as a world-mountain"[13] and the King-Priest, Son of David-Son of God reigning over all.

The Davidic Covenant (2 Sam.7:13-16) identifies three basic motifs of the cosmic Mount Zion:

Davidic Covenant	Zion as Yahweh's Cosmic Mountain
Yahweh's Mediator-Priest will build a "house" (*bayith*) for God's Name.	Zion is a theological institution that utilizes Yahweh's priestly order of Melchizedek-Zadok. Zion secures the spiritual transformation of the faithful vassal-remnant into a city-temple.
Yahweh's King reigns over a "kingdom" (*mamlakah*) that will endure forever.	Zion is an eschatological kingdom that symbolizes Yahweh's kingship. Zion projects the redemptive reign of God in the earthly realm.
Yahweh's Son will establish his lordship or the "throne" (*kicce'*) of his eternal kingdom.	Zion is a cosmological symbol that represents Yahweh's lordship. Zion reflects the divine governance of his cosmic holy mount in the heavenly realm.

Let's look more closely at the characteristics of Mount Zion, the majestic cosmic mountain of Yahweh.

Characteristics of Yahweh's Cosmic Mount Zion

1. Yahweh's Cosmic Mountain: A City-Temple under the Priesthood of Melchizedek-Zadok

The cosmic mountain of Zion is founded on the divine Father-Son dynasty: "I will be his father, and he will be my son... Your house (*bayith*)...will endure forever before me" (2 Sam.

---

13. Ibid, p.82.

7:14a, 16a). The Davidic Covenant directs its fulfillment to a messianic king's intimate Father-Son relationship with God. When David offers to build a permanent house (*bayith*) for Yahweh, God's response infers a clever play on words. It will be through the dynasty (*bayith*) of David's Son/God's Son that an everlasting dwelling place (*bayith*) will be constructed (2 Sam.7:11-14). "House" is a metonymy, a figure of speech that implies "dynasty." The builder of this bayith-complex is Jesus Christ who is both Son of David and Son of God (Amos 9:11; Matt.1:1; Lk.1:32,33; Acts 2:29-36; 15:13-17; Rom.1:3,4; Heb.1:5; 3:4-6). Interpreting the Davidic Covenant in this way makes it easier to see that God's chastening of Solomon in rending the kingdom does not extinguish the overarching perpetual covenant that is inaugurated and realized in Christ (2 Sam.7:14; 1 Kgs.11:13, 32-36; 15:4; 2 Kgs.8:19; 19:34; 20:6).

As the Davidic-throne succession falters and eventually ceases, the prophets' message is placed within an eschatological framework. They foretell of a worldwide movement, a second exodus from every nation that will stream to Mount Zion.[14] Israel's historical exodus to Mount Sinai parallels this "whosoever-will" cosmological exodus to Mount Zion—where "geography is simply a visible form of theology."[15]

The "God the Father-Son of God" dynasty is portrayed in horticultural imagery. The great Davidic dynasty will sprout up from a "tender sprig" planted on Mount Zion.

> This is what the Sovereign Lord says: I myself will take a shoot from the very top of a cedar and plant it; I will break off a tender sprig from its topmost shoots and plant it on a high and lofty mountain. On the mountain heights of Israel I will plant it; it will produce branches and bear fruit and become a splendid cedar.

---

14. Cf. Bernhard W. Anderson, '*Exodus Typology in Second Isaiah*,' *Israel's Prophetic Heritage, Essays in Honor of James Muilenburg*, Bernhard Anderson and Walter Harrelson editors, (New York: Harper and Brothers, 1962), pp.177-195.
15. Levenson, p.116.

> Birds of every kind will nest in it; they will find shelter in the shade of its branches (Ezek.17:22,23).

The fruitful messianic Branch on Yahweh's cosmic mountain provides "whosoever-will" a shelter—a place to call home (2 Sam.7:10; Isa.11:1; Jer.23:5; 33:15; Zech.3:8; 6:12; cf. Matt.13:32). The Branch-event signals the gathering of all nations to Zion. A scattered remnant responds to the new worldwide exodus and enters the highway of holiness that leads them on an exuberant journey to Mount Zion (Isa.11:1-16; cf. Isa.19:23-25; 27:12-13; 35:8-10). Ezekiel portrays this "whosoever-will" exodus as an essential part of the true cosmic mountain experience:

> For on my holy mountain, the high mountain of Israel, declares the Sovereign Lord, there in the land the entire house of Israel will serve me, and there I will accept them...I will accept you as fragrant incense when I bring you out from the nations and gather you from the countries where you have been scattered, and I will show myself holy among you in the sight of the nations (Ezek.20:40,41; cf. 11:17; 28:25; 34:13; 39:28).

The four-fold purpose for this gathering to Yahweh's cosmic mountain is to be cleansed from defilement, to experience spiritual transformation, to be taught God's laws, and receive the Spirit's empowerment to obey (Isa.2:1-3; Mic.4:1-3).

> For I will take you out of the nations; I will gather you from all the countries and bring you back into your own land. I will sprinkle clean water on you, and you will be clean; I will cleanse you from all your impurities and from all your idols. I will give you a new heart and put a new spirit in you; I will remove from you your heart of stone and give you a heart of flesh. And I will put my Spirit in you and move you to follow my decrees and be careful to keep my laws (Ezek.36:24-27).

Our Hope and Final Destination: The Realization of Mount Zion

Yahweh's high and lofty cosmic mountain is not only a secure home, it is also a life-changing meeting place where decrees are issued and spiritual empowerment is provided.

Even though the term "Zion" never appears in the book of Ezekiel, his message relays the significance of Zion's expansion and completion of the temple imagery begun in the Mosaic era. The departure of the *shekinah* glory from Jerusalem's temple is similar to the departure of the glory from the tabernacle when Philistia captured the ark (Ezek.8-10; 1 Sam.4:21). There is an "abomination of desolation" because the enemy has entered the sanctuary of the Lord. This happens a third time when the Jews refuse Christ as Messiah and Jesus announces: "Look, your house is left to you desolate" (Matt.23:38) and the temple is razed in A.D. 70 (cf. Dan.9:26,27). Amazingly, Jesus foretells of yet one more departure—one more abomination of desolation in the temple of God in the latter days (Matt.24:15; 2 Thess.2:3,4).

When the glory of the Lord went up from Jerusalem it "stopped above the mountain east of it," thus placing Yahweh's concentrated presence in—of all God-forsaken locations—Babylon (Ezek.11:23). Ezekiel's vision testifies to the profound truth that the glory of God will forsake the sacred-turned-apostate temple, but he will not forsake the faithful remnant, the devout that dwell on Yahweh's holy cosmic mountain in the midst of unholy territory. The Lord says: "Although I sent them far away among the nations and scattered them among the countries, yet for a little while I have been a sanctuary for them in the countries where they have gone" (Ezek.11:16). The biblical concept of Yahweh's cosmic mountain is clearly a sanctuary-dwelling place where the faithful enjoy intimate covenant relations with him anywhere, anytime, in the midst of any circumstance.

Although "Ezekiel never uses Zion in any sense, and never uses the name Jerusalem in a positive context...he uses other terminology to speak of future blessings—city, mountain, hill, and sanctuary."[16] Ezekiel receives a vision of the inauguration of

---

16. Gowen, Donald. *Eschatology in the Old Testament,* (Philadelphia: Fortress, 1986), p.9.

the new temple on the cosmic mountain of Yahweh. "In visions of God he took me to the land of Israel and set me on a very high mountain, on whose south side were some buildings that looked like a city" (Ezek.40:2). He goes to great lengths to describe the sanctuary as a city set on a high mountain (cf.Psa.48:1; Matt.5:14; Rev.21:10). Not only will Yahweh return to Zion, his return to the new Jerusalem results in its transformation into "the City of Truth... and the mountain of the Lord Almighty will be called the Holy Mountain" (Zech.8:3). Ezekiel 40-48 closes with renaming this mountain-city-temple as: Yahweh Shammah, the Lord is there (Ezek.48:35). Therefore the old city of Jerusalem symbolizes those who adhere to the Judiastic letter of the law; the new heavenly city-temple symbolizes those who enjoy the grace and liberty found in Christ (Gal.4:21-31). Believers "have come to Mount Zion, to the heavenly Jerusalem, the city of the living God...You have come to God, the judge of all men...to Jesus the mediator of a new covenant" (Heb.12:22-24; cf. Heb.11:10,16).

When Christians come to Jesus Christ, the living Stone, they become like living stones that are being built into a spiritual house; they become a holy priesthood that offers spiritual sacrifices acceptable to God (1 Pet.2:4,5). So the imagery of the new city-temple includes a new holy priesthood in the New Covenant. Did the Old Testament prophets foresee a new priesthood in the future Zion? They did characterize the eschatological remnant as a dedicated few that worship Yahweh with a new heart under a new covenant (Joel 2:32; Zeph.3:12,13; Jer.31:31-34; Ezek.11:18-21). Israel's restoration is not to her homeland, but to Yahweh as a spiritually cleansed, faithful community (Ezek.20:32-36; 36:24-33; 37:22-26). The restoration is inclusive of all nations, both Jew and Gentile (Zech.9:7; 14:16; Isa.66:19; Dan.7:27; 12:1-3).

Ezekiel saw the new priesthood of believers. In the middle of Ezekiel's vision of the city-temple-mount, Yahweh lays down three basic regulations regarding the temple (Ezek.44:5). First, the uncircumcised in heart may not even enter the sanctuary (v.9). Second, the Levitical priests of the same strain as the house of Eli may serve the people in the temple complex to fulfill their ministerial duties, but are not allowed to come near to God himself (vv.10-14; cf. 8:5-18; 22:26-29; 33:31,32; 43:8-10; 1 Sam.2:12-22; 3:11; 1 Kgs.2:27). Third, only those of the Zadok priesthood may minister before Yahweh and carry out in ministry only that which he has instructed (vv.15,16; cf. 1 Sam.2:31-3:4). In this city-temple-mount God makes a distinction between the defiled, compromised priesthood of Eli of Shiloh and the faithful, holy priesthood of Zadok (*Tsadowq* "righteous").[17]

Is Ezekiel advocating a reestablishment of the same legalistic rituals only under a new hierarchy?

> On the contrary...in the centre of Ezekiel's temple is his vision of a new reality, a mystical glimpse into the divine world...In the new community, risen from the dry bones of the old with a new spirit and new heart, the outward forms of worship will be penetrated and their inner meaning revealed.[18]

The true meaning of the worship of Yahweh will finally penetrate into a new community that has received a new heart and a new spirit. They will experience a new reality: insight into the divine world where Christ is High Priest after the order of Melchizedek (*Malkiy-Tsedeq*/Zadok).[19] In Genesis 14, Melchizedek is both the king of Salem (the future Jerusalem) and the priest of God Most High. In Hebrews 7, the "order of Melchizedek" is the order of the

---

17. Zadok anointed Solomon as king (1 Kgs.1:39,40) and is the high priest of the line from Eleazar, the successor-high priest, son of Aaron (1 Chron.24:3; comparing this to 1 Sam.22:20 which should read: "Zadok, and Abiathar the son of Ahimelech the son of Ahitub" thus emphasizing just Abiathar's lineage back to Eli and Ithamar). Some would accentuate the textual corruption in these two genealogies to propose that Zadok is a Jebusite refugee who joined David after he captured the city (Christian E. Hauer, 'Who was Zadok?' *JBL*, 82, 1963, pp.89-94; H.H. Rowley, '*Zadok and Nehushtan*,' *JBL*, 58, 1939, pp.113-141; and its critique by J.J.M. Roberts, '*The Davidic Origin of the Zion Tradition*,' *JBL*, 92, 1973, pp.329-344).
18. Sawyer, John. *From Moses to Patmos, New Perspectives on Old Testament Studies*, (London: SPCK, 1977), p.68.
19. All uses of *tsadowq* are variations of a state of being "righteous" or "just" (cf. *tsaddiyq*, *tsadaq*, and *tsedeq*, as in Melchi-zedek "king of righteousness").

priesthood to which Christ belongs. It is not by blood lineage but through spiritual lineage (Heb.5:6; Psa.110:1ff.). Ezekiel includes the priesthood of Zadok as active participants in the new temple complex—their inclusion also is not based on bloodlines but through spiritual adoption into the family of God.

> [Christ] has made us to be a kingdom and *priests* to serve his God and Father—to him be glory and power forever and ever! Amen (Rev.1:6).

> You have made them to be a kingdom and *priests* to serve our God, and they will reign on the earth (Rev.5:10).

> Blessed and holy are those who have part in the first resurrection. The second death has no power over them, but they will be *priests* of God and of Christ and will reign with him for a thousand years (Rev.20:6, emphasis mine).

The order of Melchizedek-Zadok is one that is chosen by God, one that exalts righteous and holy living. It includes people called to be "a royal priesthood, a holy nation, a people belonging to God" (1 Pet.2:9) to serve God in his holy city-temple cosmic mountain. Zion is therefore a theological institution that utilizes Yahweh's priestly order of Melchizedek-Zadok. The cosmic mountain of Yahweh secures the spiritual transformation of the faithful vassal-remnant into a city-temple.

2. Yahweh's Cosmic Mountain: An Eschatological Kingdom that Inaugurates the Redemptive Transformation of the Heart

The holy city-temple-mount has a King. In him all nations can receive redemption and experience sanctification through Zion's installment of the Davidic Shepherd-King.

> I will tend them in a good pasture, and the mountain heights of Israel will be their grazing land. There they

will lie down in good grazing land, and there they will feed in a rich pasture on the mountains of Israel (Ezek.34:14)

The messianic Davidic-Shepherd is sent to gather the lost sheep of the house of Israel to himself (Matt.15:24; cf. 12:30; Ezek.34:15,16, 23,24; Jer.23:3-5). The Gentiles are brought into his sheepfold as well (Isa.56:8; Jn.10:16; 12:32). Ezekiel portrays the gathering of Jews and Gentiles as the joining together of two sticks "on the mountains of Israel":

> Hold before their eyes the sticks you have written on and say to them…"I will *gather* them from all around and bring them back into their own land. I will make them one nation in the land, *on the mountains of Israel*. There will be one king over all of them and they will never again be two nations or be divided into two kingdoms…They will be my people, and I will be their God. *My servant David will be king* over them, and they will all have *one shepherd*. They will follow my laws and be careful to keep my decrees" (Ezek.37:20-24, emphasis mine).

F.F. Bruce confirms that "Jesus' calling of disciples around Himself to form the 'little flock' who were to receive the kingdom (Luke 12:32; cf. Daniel 7:22,27) marks Him out as the founder of the New Israel."[20] He is God's servant, the Davidic Shepherd-King who installs his twelve apostles to represent a new organism with its own structure and authority, and commissions them to begin their universal mission as the new Israel of God (Mk.3:14,15; Lk.22:29,30; Gal 6:16). Only when Yahweh is acknowledged as the Messiah, the new David, the Great Shepherd, will the "whosoever-will"—including both Jew and Gentile believers—come into the kingdom of the new theocratic order of the New Covenant. Zion is therefore an eschatological

---

20. Bruce, F.F. *The New Bible Dictionary,* ed. J.D. Douglas, (Grand Rapids: Eerdmans, 1979), p.558.

kingdom that symbolizes Yahweh's kingship. The cosmic mountain of God projects the redemptive reign of Yahweh on the earth.

The concept of the kingdom of God remains one of the most controversial topics within Christian doctrine. Swirling around this concept is a broad range of definitions, from social activism to apocalyptic thinking, from seeking political worldwide utopia to Christianizing culture, and from an inner mystical communion to simply supporting the Church as an institution. Some adhere to a "dominion now" kingdom, others view the kingdom to be ushered in a future millennial reign of God, while still others support the reality of a present kingdom that is not yet fully consummated.

The phrase "the kingdom of God" does not occur specifically anywhere in the Old Testament. However, the key to tying in an Old Testament understanding of kingdom theology with the cosmic mountain imagery is to focus on the ruling activity of God rather than on an abstract notion of a kingdom.

> It was Yahweh's sovereign action on which the attention of Old Testament writers focused, and it was the manifestations of his sovereign power that called forth their worship. Even when later writers did come to speak of the kingdom of God or of heaven, they did so chiefly in order to describe the rule of God.[21]

If we define the kingdom of God to simply mean the reign of God, then the anticipatory progression of the concept of the kingdom of God in the Old Testament will be clearly seen in Zion's cosmic mountain. Yahweh's holy mountain will be positioned within the omnipresent, omniscient, omnipotent realm of the Shepherd-King who reigns through the vassal-administration of his kingdom's image-bearing citizens.

Israel begins as an individual person (Jacob), then is transformed into a corporate nation (beginning with Moses and through the era of the kings) that eventually becomes ensnared

---

21. Beasley-Murray, G.R. *Jesus and the Kingdom of God*, (Grand Rapids: Eerdmans, 1986), p.17.

by idolatry and fails in their mission to the nations (by their exile to Assyria and Babylonia). The end of the monarchy signals the dismal failure of Israel to usher in the kingdom of God on the earth. Even when the exilic Jews return to Israel they do not generate any sign of a kingdom economy. The kingdom did not arrive until John the Baptist, the last of the great Old Testament prophets, paves a highway for Messiah to usher in the reign of heaven on earth.[22] The kingdom is now at hand.

A messianic individual fulfills the role of Servant-Israel to reconcile the world to God (cf. Isa.42:1-9; 49:1-13; 50:4-11; 52:13-53:12). Isaiah's Servant-Israel is Ezekiel's Davidic Shepherd-King who inaugurates his kingdom on earth and consummates it in his eternal reign. As the divine Servant-Israel and Shepherd-gatherer, Christ brings all nations to his Mount Zion-kingdom to create a new citizenship with its own heavenly capital, the New Jerusalem, the City of God in the heavenly sphere. The new Israel includes all nations, Jew and Gentile, slave and free, male and female, rich and poor, dark and fair skinned. If there is any exclusion, it is because one chooses to reject the free offer of citizenship in the new Israel of God. Sadly, the majority of the first ones whom Jesus invites reject his offer (Matt.23:37-38; cf. 8:11,12; 21:43). This sober indictment proclaims that the true Israel embraces only those who receive Jesus as their messianic Shepherd-King.

If Israel is the Old Testament paradigm for the Church then the theocratic rule of historical Israel is also a paradigm for the theocratic reign of the kingdom of God in Christ. The Davidic-Solomonic kingdom and its Zion theology typify the glorious kingdom that comes only through a supernatural event that breaks into history and inaugurates a higher, spiritual order. Jesus fulfills the prophetic hope of the cosmic mountain-kingdom by

---

22. Dispensationalism misconstrues the "kingdom of God" and the "kingdom of heaven" to be two separate kingdoms. Yet a close examination of Scripture will conclude that "kingdom of God," "kingdom of heaven," "kingdom of our Lord," and "kingdom of Christ," are all used interchangeably to describe the same kingdom (Matt.11:12 and Lk.16:16; Matt.4:17 and Mk.1:14,15; Matt.5:3 and Lk.6:20; Matt.10:7 and Lk.9:2; Matt.19:14 and Mk.10:14; Matt.19:23 and Lk.18:24).

Spiritual Reality

proclaiming: "the gospel of the kingdom of God...saying, 'The time is fulfilled, and the kingdom of God is at hand. Repent, and believe in the gospel'" (Mk.1:14-15, NKJV) and "I must preach the kingdom of God to the other cities also, because for this purpose I have been sent" (Lk.4:43, NKJV). Explaining and manifesting the kingdom is preeminent in Jesus' heart and mind for it reflects the prophetic establishment of Zion's mountain.

We must not make the same mistake as the Jews of Jesus' day. The kingdom of God is not a political kingdom (Jn.18:36; Rom.14:17) just as Mount Zion is not merely a physical mountain. Rather, the kingdom of God is an invisible spiritual realm: "The kingdom of God does not come with your careful observation, nor will people say, 'Here it is,' or 'There it is,' because the kingdom of God is within you" (Lk.17:20,21). Whatever expression is the preferred rendering of the Greek, "within you" or "in the midst of you," the force of the language concludes that the kingdom simply cannot be located or localized because the character of the kingdom must reflect the glory from which it exists—an eternal cosmic mountain-realm. Just as Ezekiel prophesied, Jesus transfers the kingdom from a piece of significant real estate to the soft, fleshly heart of born-again believers. A person must be born again—they must possess the kingdom's Spirit in order to see and enter the kingdom of God's presence (Jn.3:3-5).

To enter the kingdom of God is to come to Mount Zion, to be delivered from the power of darkness, translated into the kingdom of the Son, and be transformed by his love (Col.1:13). Gowen calls this experience "eschatological forgiveness."[23] Ezekiel likens eschatological sanctification to the delicate spiritual operation of removing a heart of stone in order to replace it with a heart of flesh (36:26).

> The problem is that in history the responsive, truly human heart has turned to stone; something of humanity has been lost so that love, obedience, and

---

23. Gowen, p.63.

knowledge of God are no longer possible. This is more appropriately called re-creation than new creation. To become truly human again, able to make the choice to follow God, must also be accompanied by the gift of the spirit to empower one to act on those choices.[24]

Zion's promise of human transformation is one of internal change through the circumcision of the heart. Transformed citizens of the kingdom of God rule and reign with Christ from the true cosmic mountain. They enjoy the blessings of God's presence, share in building God's city, and rejoice in the abundant life of Zion (Isa.33:13-16; Psa.24:3,4).

3. Yahweh's Sacred Mountain: Cosmological Governance through the Lordship of the Prince of Peace

Zion is also a cosmological symbol that represents Yahweh's lordship. Zion reflects the divine governance of his cosmic holy mount in the heavenly realm. God tells Ezekiel that his city-temple-mount "is the place of my throne and the place for the soles of my feet. This is where I will live among the Israelites forever" (43:7).[25] Zion is positioned as the cosmic center of the nations with countries all around her (Ezek.5:5; 38:12). The Davidic Shepherd-King is Zion's "prince forever" (Ezek.37:25). "The Lord has established his throne in heaven, and his kingdom rules over all" (Psa.103:19).

Ruling over divine governmental administration is none other than the Son of David-Son of God, the Davidic "Prince of Peace" (Isa.9:6; Ezek.34:24) who reigns forever in the presence of the Lord (Ezek.44:3;.45:7; 45:16,17,22; 46:2-12). The reign of the Prince of Peace is established through his death (Dan.11:22; Hos.3:4) and resurrection when God exalts him to his own right hand as Prince and Savior (Acts 5:31). "I will place on his

---

24. Ibid, p.74.
25. Levenson suggests that "What is certain is that the expression of the idea of Jerusalem as a cosmic center, the navel of the world, is fuller and more developed in rabbinic literature than in the Hebrew Bible" (p.120).

shoulder the key to the house of David; what he opens no one can shut, and what he shuts no one can open...All the glory of his family will hang on him" (Isa.22:22,24). "They will tell of the glory of your kingdom and speak of your might, so that all men may know of your mighty acts and the glorious splendor of your kingdom. Your kingdom is an everlasting kingdom, and your dominion endures through all generations" (Psa.145:11-13).

When the Prince of Peace begins to demonstrate Zion's kingdom power over evil, the Pharisees accuse him of operating under the power of another prince: Beelzebub (Baal-zebub), the prince of demons (Matt.12:24). Yet his government inauguration proved that this false prince over the world system had no hold on him (Jn.14:30). "Now is the time for judgment on this world; now the prince of this world will be driven out" (Jn.12:31). Before the Prince of the holy cosmic mountain of God "the prince of this world now stands condemned" (Jn.16:11).

Even though the cosmic Mount Zion reigns supreme and assures victory over the enemies of God, biblical imagery still portrays Zion to be the battleground of conflicting forces (Dan.8:25). A worldwide alliance of anti-Christian nations form to make a dramatic assault against the peaceful, holy mount of God (Ezek.38:1-23). The Lord tells Ezekiel to "set your face against Gog," an apocalyptic, albeit somewhat cryptic title to describe the hordes aligned with the antichrist prince of demons (32:2; 39:1; cf. Dan.8:11).

As believers take up residence in Zion, the spirit of the world resists this awesome reality all day, every day. "The kingdom of heaven has been forcefully advancing, and forceful men lay hold of it," but it is a bitter fight to throw off the pressures of the world that violently strip us of God's presence (Matt.11:12). Believers are to learn to vigorously lay hold of the presence of God's kingdom through decisions and actions that are based on biblical convictions. Paul and Barnabas encourage us to forcefully press into God's presence: "We must go through many hardships to enter the kingdom of God" (Acts 14:22). Spiritual vitality is available to those with the humility and tenacity to press into the Lord. To lay hold of the kingdom of God is to experience righteousness, peace, and joy in the Holy Spirit—in spite of the battle with conflicting forces of evil (Rom.14:17). Believers reign on God's cosmic mountain because of his presence.

Jesus' preaching of the gospel of the kingdom is accompanied by authoritative teaching, healing all kinds of sickness and disease, along with a powerful deliverance ministry (Matt.4:23,24). He explicitly says, "If I cast out demons by the Spirit of God, surely the kingdom of God has come upon you" (Matt.12:28).

> The presence of the Kingdom of God was seen as God's dynamic reign invading the present age without transforming it into the age to come...The meaning of Jesus' exorcism of demons in its relationship to the Kingdom of God is precisely this: that before the eschatological conquest of God's Kingdom over evil and the destruction of Satan, the Kingdom of God has invaded the realm of Satan to deal him a preliminary but decisive defeat.[26]

Yahweh's cosmic mountain-kingdom does not manifest merely in word, but in power (1 Cor.4:20). Therefore, knowledge about Mount Zion and all its theological implications is not evidence of authentic kingdom living. Simply researching, discussing, and teaching about it does not produce victorious kingdom living. When we lay hold of the timeless truths of Yahweh's cosmic mountain-kingdom, we encounter the supernatural power of God. "The Law and the Prophets were proclaimed until John. Since that time, the good news of the kingdom of God is being preached, and everyone is forcing his way into it" (Lk.16:16). To press into the kingdom is like pushing aside evil obstruction and—under duress—pressing into the presence of God. God's

---

26. Ladd, George Eldon. *The Presence of the Future*, (Grand Rapids: Eerdmans, 1974), pp.149, 151.

cosmic holy mountain is omnipresent. He is always everywhere actively present. We then must learn to refuse to succumb to the spirit of the world and press into his presence everywhere and at all times (Psa.139:7-10).

Pressing into the presence of God will bring bittersweet results. There will be immense pleasure in abiding in him as well as intense resistance from the kingdom of darkness. Walking in the Spirit means invading enemy territory—even to the recesses of Mount Zaphon. The fact that it is on Mount Zion that Yahweh will defeat the nations reveals the guarantee of its inviolability (Isa.31:4,5; Mic.4:11-13; Zeph.3:8-13; Ezek.38:17-23). Though assaulted by evil forces, God's cosmic mountain remains secure because of the serenity and immutability of the presence of the Lord in its midst (Psa.46:3,6; Ezek.48:30-35).

Toward the end of Ezekiel's vision of the city-temple-mountain of God, he sees the healing river of Zion flowing to the nations (Ezek.47:1-12). So the blessing of God "is not limited to victory of hostile armies, but extends also to the bestowal of all blessing and fertility from the temple where Yahweh is to be found. With this we must connect the belief in the fertilizing river which flowed through Zion to bless the land."[27] Jesus' disciples appear to join with Ezekiel in the river of Zion as they are sent to all nations to preach this message: "'The kingdom of heaven is near.' Heal the sick, raise the dead, cleanse those who have leprosy, drive out demons" (Matt.10:7,8; cf. 28:18-20). The Holy Spirit visibly manifests the cosmic kingdom of God on the earth. The observable demonstrations issued from Mount Zion aren't weird or paranormal. It is evidence that Yahweh's cosmic mountain reigns supreme. The gospel of the kingdom is to be preached and actively verified by supernatural, Spirit-led ministry (Mk.16:17,18). Citizens of the New Jerusalem go about the kingdom's business. Their ministry breathes refreshment, inexpressible joy, and incomprehensible peace to the weary and heavy laden.

---

27. Clements, p.71; cf. Psa.46:4; 65:9,10; Isa.33:21; Joel 3:18; Zech.14:8,9.

Mount Zion's joy is merely another divinely appointed avenue for deliverance. "When the Lord brought back the captives to Zion, we were like men who dreamed. Our mouths were filled with laughter, our tongues with songs of joy. Then it was said among the nations, 'The Lord has done great things for them'...and we are filled with joy" (Psa.126:1-3). When God reveals himself in life's pathways, he makes us full of joy in his presence (Acts 2:28; Psa.16:11). Joy in God's presence is like medicine (Prov.17:22a). It is supernaturally therapeutic and therefore life changing. Joy is just another sign of Zion's manifestation on the earth's premises.

Taking Up the Cultural Mandate

We have seen that as a result of the fall of humanity, generational sin has attempted to ravage our spiritual lineage. Yet in Christ we receive back an ancient spiritual heritage reserved for us in heaven since Eden. From the beginning, God gives a mandate to humanity to be fruitful, multiply, to fill the earth, and subdue it (Gen.1:28). Though sin will plague humanity, this mandate is still intact. It is best understood as a cultural mandate because of the two responsibilities that are associated with it. God has given us: 1) the innovative task to be fruitful and fill the earth, and 2) the assertive task to subdue and have dominion over the earth. To carry out the cultural mandate is to give a preview to the grand appearance of Yahweh's cosmic Mount Zion in the Second Coming of Christ.

The innovative task to be fruitful means that as priests of the order of Melchizedek, we are to be creative instruments of blessing. God intends that humanity tend and cultivate the earth (Gen.2:15). We are to explore this bountiful world and develop it that it might reflect our celebrated fellowship with the omnipresent God. Industry, music, science, art, commerce, technology, education, recreation, government—society as a whole—is meant to glorify our Creator. Human beings have the innate creative ability to progress in all areas of life. God ordains our work to be our ministry and commits six days of every week to it.

The other side of the cultural mandate is the assertive task. The assertive task to subdue and have dominion means that as kings of the order of Melchizedek, we are to be courageous instruments of restraint. To subdue the earth implies that the world needs to be made subservient. We are to creatively shape all aspects of culture and sanctify it for the distinct purpose of reclaiming creation for God's presence and service. Humanity's potential and earth's possibilities seem limitless, but in the holy Script there is a clear restraining order. God intends for Adam to guard Eden (Gen.2:15). Our royal task as ambassadors of Yahweh's holy mount is to take hold of the assertive task of the cultural mandate and reign over the affairs of culture and in effect restrain evil.

> Besides availing himself of the earth's hospitality man would have to protect himself from earth's inhospitable elements and moments. This is perhaps reflected in the language of the cultural mandate for its terms are vigorous...Man was to overcome whatever resistance or recalcitrance he encountered in nature and win from it its supportive service. However...it was not intended that man's dominion over the earth and his appropriation of its resources should be twisted into a process of destructive exploitation. Indeed, for man to lay waste, to spoil and poison his world, would be to turn it into an unmanageable monster...And that would of course be contrary to the objective of the cultural mandate.[28]

Human beings are born to shape history, to uphold God's standard, and to restrain insurrection. As depicted in the royal garden, both the innovative and assertive tasks of the cultural mandate embrace the divine ordination of both culture and government.

Sadly, the magnificent Edenic garden is now an untamed wilderness. Sin has poisoned every aspect of culture. It permeates

---

28. Kline, M. *Kingdom Prologue, Vol.1*, p.106-107.

and desecrates work and play. It separates life into social, political, and religious realms. Does sin cancel the cultural mandate?

> Despite [the] catastrophic effects, the fall did not end the cultural mandate. Eve still brings forth the generations, Adam still works the ground. In fact they cannot stop fulfilling this task, for that is how God made them and us. Even though we are fallen, we do not cease to work, or play, or pray, or bring up children, or make political decisions. We *have* to do these things, this is how God made us.[29]

The cultural mandate continues to *redemptively* counteract the pervasive corruption in the world. Although Eden is now the land of Nod, a world of aimless wandering in the wilderness of sin, Christ repositions us to our original place as king-priests unto God. The King of king-priests calls for the fulfillment of the cultural mandate—otherwise known as the gospel mandate. We must once again connect Eden's cultural mandate with the New Covenant gospel mandate and thereby connect Eden with the holy mountain of God.

The Great Commission is truly about the conversion of the soul. It is an internal transformation. When we transform inside, we transform outside. Redemption is meant to begin in the heart and extend far and wide into the realm of culture.

> A new heart must lead to a new life. A new life expresses itself throughout every part of God's world. God is not concerned with rescuing people from out of human existence, or only concerned with the internal life of believers, or only concerned with the internal relations of the Christian community itself. We must realize that God is concerned about politics, about architecture, about food and furniture, about poverty, suffering, about play, art

---

29. Marshall, Paul. *Thine is the Kingdom, A Biblical Perspective on the Nature of Government and Politics Today*, (Grand Rapids: Eerdmans, 1984), p.27.

and music, about neighborhoods and economics, about animals and trees, about sex and intimacy, about the *reconciliation*, the healing from sin, *of all things* within the creation.[30]

Because of the sin element in the world, the consummation of the cultural mandate cannot be fully realized until the end of time when Christ ushers in the eternal state. This stark revelation can burst our bubble and diffuse all our political and social efforts. It can, however, spark a worldview renaissance. Convinced of the perpetuation of the cultural mandate, we will push to see how far we can penetrate.

When the cultural mandate is carried out, it begins to expose the serpent's same old hideous plot to separate humanity from God and to divide the sacred from the secular. Satan not only wants to rip God's kingdom apart, he wants to tear up the music kingdom, the economic kingdom, the political kingdom, the educational kingdom, and all of society's kingdoms—to create chaos and ultimately destroy *every* kingdom. We, however, are called to *infiltrate and transform every kingdom.*

As an example of a Mount Zion representative, Elijah confronts the people of Israel and accuses them of leaping between God and Baal-Satan (1 Kgs. 18:19, 20). If the Lord is truly God, then Israel needs to be wholly devoted to him. But if Baal is their lord, then they must not attempt to syncretise their belief system. The people, nevertheless, are strangely silent in their response (1 Kgs.18:21). They are caught in the compromised position of leaping between alliance with demons and Yahweh. The assertive task of the cultural mandate must surface in our ministries, especially when compromised convictions blur into the abyss of syncretism. One cannot at the same time fellowship at the table of demons and the table of the Lord (1 Cor.10:21). We cannot serve Yahweh and Baal, for we will either hate one and love the other, or else we will be loyal to one and despise the

---

30. Marshall, p.35.

other (Matt.6:24). To leap between true Christianity and demonic fellowship obviously leads to a breakdown in our covenant relationship with God. At Mount Carmel Elijah exposes the danger of spiritual trysts with demons and is himself an instrument of restraint on the acceleration of evil.

With every great move of the Holy Spirit, there is a reaction of counterfeit demonic manifestations. The false prophets practice their occult rituals and pronounce demonically-inspired prophecies (1 Kgs.18:28,29). Satan desires to deceive anyone who is open to false spiritual revelation. He entices them unwittingly from full devotion to Yahweh. Some indiscriminately believe that the source of all supernatural manifestations is divine, yet throughout Scripture, false prophets appear as messengers of new light, hoping that their false signs and wonders will validate their deceptive words.

Satan injects counterfeit gifts of the Spirit into Christian revival movements. Elijah's encounter at Mount Carmel previews the end of the age (cf. 2 Thess.2:9,10). He is just as intolerant of evil deception as Peter is after Pentecost. The gift of the Spirit pulls back the curtain on the spiritual reality behind the scenes. Having received of the Spirit's downpour, Peter quickly recognizes evil penetrating the ranks of the Church (Acts 5:3). He speaks up and boldly announces the cultural mandate's assertive task to resist any abomination of desolation. We, too, must match belligerent demonic infiltration with bold aggression.

Elijah's faith soars to such great heights that he expects Ahab, king of Samaria, and his wife Jezebel, to repent of their wicked ways and turn to Yahweh (1 Kgs.18:44-46). Instead, Jezebel totally disregards her husband by devising an assassination plot to kill the revivalist (19:1-3). Suddenly, Elijah's great mountain-moving faith appears shipwrecked. Hiding in a cave at Beersheba, he is overwhelmingly depressed and wallows in self-pity (vv.4-9). The angel of the Lord who is a pre-incarnate appearance of Christ comes to him in his moment of need (vv.9,10).

When Yahweh speaks, we may not be able to hear him. To hear God's voice requires a hearing heart. So when Yahweh comes to Elijah in "a still small voice" the Hebrew words actually read "voice still small." "Voice" means "thunderous," while "still" means "reducing" or "grinding down." "Small" denotes "silence." Therefore, when Yahweh speaks, it is a thunderous voice that reduces us down to silence before him. In other words, it is undeniably clear! God speaks because he desires to confide in us (cf. Gen.18:16-19; Amos 3:7).

Why is Mount Zion's ambassador so fearful of Jezebel? Jezebel possesses a certain spirit that aggressively persecutes and assaults the righteous. Such belligerence scares Elijah. Historically, Solomon opens the door to religious syncretism, but it is Jezebel who institutes Baalism as Israel's official religion. Occultism disguised as Baalism hastens the spiritual decline and fall of Israel and Jezebel leads the charge. She instigates the collapse of the nation by craftily replacing Yahwehism with Baalism.

The spirit of Jezebel lives well into the future. In the last days, the spirit of Jezebel will again rear its ghastly head and threaten God's people (Rev.2:18-24). Jesus commends the church of Thyatira for its service, but he denounces their toleration of Jezebel's spirit. Believers need to nurture the spirit of Jehu and furiously drive their chariots of war, having no peace, so long as the harlotry of Jezebel and her witchcraft are so many (2 Kgs.9:16-22).

Jezebel's false teaching tricks God's servants to blatant rebellion and sin. Jezebel's prophecies put a spin on the definition of sin. Her charisma may be charming, but her cryptic prophecies of new things are in reality the depths of Satan (Rev.2:20,24). Jezebel's followers claim to be enlightened, but in reality the Jezebel spirit preaches hidden secrets that only the spiritually elite can understand. This abnormal pseudo-spirituality is witchcraft. She replaces simple, humble communion with Yahweh with communion with Baal-Satan. She is an integral part of the seductive mystery Babylon religion and represents doctrine based on spiritual manipulation and spiritual fornication. She encourages adulterous allegiance to falsehood. Jezebel's manipulative influence stirs up rebellion in all who come in contact with her (1 Kgs.21:25). Her spirit aggressively routs truth and righteousness out of town. The spirit of Jezebel wears out the saints—just like she wore out Elijah. But the Lord assures Elijah that he has reserved a remnant of faithful believers in Israel who have not dedicated themselves to Satan (1 Kgs.19:18).

God renews Elijah's vision of the cultural mandate and inspires him to become a political activist (1 Kgs.19:15,16). Before Ahab is removed from office, Jezebel, the corrupt power behind the throne, instigates a string of illegal activity: subordination of perjury, conspiracy to murder, and illegal seizure of property (1 Kgs.21:8-16). When the Israelite government turns perverse, Elijah must fulfill the mandate's assertive task in the political arena.

The cultural mandate demands involvement when the institution of government is exploited. Government is an ordained institution. Rulers may be good or evil, effective or incompetent, but government itself is an institution that is ordained to assist humanity to fulfill the cultural mandate (Rom.13:1-7; 1 Pet.2:13,14; 3:22). Paul Marshall clarifies the biblical role of government:

> Governments have *a particular task* and authority. They do not have authority to do anything they might please. Jesus said 'Render to Caesar the things that are Caesar's, and to God the things that are God's' (Mark 12:17; see also Acts 5:29). Clearly then Caesar cannot claim *all* things…Nor shall we think that in Romans 13 Paul gives government *carte blanche* in all its activities. He does not blandly accept the *status quo* of Roman Imperialism and advocate only a quiescent submission to it… Give [governing authorities] what is *due* to them, what is owing them, what is *right for them* to have. The order of justice determines the relation of ruler and subject, government and citizen, and delineates their

place in relation to one another. We do not surrender all to government, rather we give what is *due* it.[31]

Government serves the people and is therefore deserving of what is due. However, when government does not serve, but capitalizes on injustice, then believers must intervene as instruments of restraint. Mount Zion's assertive task extends grace and defers the acceleration of evil when authorities use and abuse the powerful institution of government for exploitation. Elijah does just that. He denounces the atrocities of the Ahab-Jezebel government and pronounces God's judgment (1 Kgs.21:17-29).

To grasp a biblical understanding of government, it is helpful to understand the Hebrew worldview. There are many biblical references that poetically illustrate a world submerged under hostile waters (cf. Psa.18:16-19; 69:1-3,14,15; 144:7). The diagram on the next page illustrates.

Leviathan, the twisted, seven-headed sea monster, and numerous other sea serpents ambitiously encroach upon the world in order to destroy it (Isa.27:1; Job 41; Psa.74:13,14). This image reflects Genesis 1:2, when God creates a world which becomes surrounded by a dark, chaotic watery void. When sin and rebellion reach their zenith, God dispenses the judgmental deluge to cover the earth (Gen.6-9). The Hebrew worldview retains the image of the flood and projects it into everyday life. Every aspect of the world's system is thoroughly soaked in dark, hostile, muddy water. The development of culture and the institution of government are ordained by the cultural mandate, but we must accept that they are submerged in the filthy waters of chaos, too.

Counteracting the true cultural mandate given by God is a demonically-inspired mandate. The satanic kingdom seeks to infect culture by instigating a perverted cultural mandate. Instead of developing culture to glorify the Creator, the demonic principalities and powers represented by predatory sea serpent-powers convince humanity to use and abuse it. Instead

---

31. Marshall, pp.48-49.

Our Hope and Final Destination: The Realization of Mount Zion

God
Sits Enthroned over the Flood
(Psa.29:10)

The Ark of God: In Christ
Joint-Heirs/King-Priests
(Rom.4:13-16; 8:17; 1 Pet.2:9; Rev.1:5)

Called to Fulfill the Cultural Mandate:
1) Innovative Task: Cultivate & Develop
2) Assertive Task: Subdue & Protect

The World: Submerged Under Chaotic, Hostile Waters
All Aspects of Culture & Government threatened by
Demonic Principalities & Powers: Twisted Sea Serpents
(1 Jn.5:19; Psa.74:13,14; Eph.6:12)

Instigates a Perverted Cultural Mandate:
1) Predatory Task: Use & Abuse
2) Annihilative Task: Exploit & Destroy

Satan
Leviathan Sea Dragon:
The World's god
(Isa.27; Job 41; Rev.12-13;
Eph.2:2)

of ruling under the righteous reign of God, fallen humanity exploits culture, lured by the perverted mandate of the Leviathan serpent.

Gregory Boyd emphasizes the importance of resisting the evil forces that encompass the world's system:

> For the ancient Israelites, there was no bifurcation between what occurs "in heaven" and what occurs "on earth," and neither should there be with us, if

our perspective is to be truly biblical. We might (and must) express and apply this ancient biblical conviction in our own times by identifying and then resisting "the cosmic serpent" in the structural evil that besieges our own culture and the church of God. For example, when we resist the spiritual complacency and empty religiosity that has deeply infected much of Western Christianity at a structural level, we participate in God's cosmic battle with Leviathan. When we fight the ongoing tendency to compromise the radicality of the gospel by identifying it with this or that political ideology, or by allowing it to be taken hostage by this or that cultural ideal or movement, we are resisting "the twisting serpent."[32]

Elijah takes on the assertive task of the cultural mandate by identifying and resisting the cosmic serpent that besieges his culture.

2. Mount Zion's Innovative Task: Becoming Instruments of Blessing

Elijah and Elisha typologically represent the powerful ministry of the Church in the latter days as symbolically depicted in the two witnesses of Revelation 11:6. The witness of the Church will move in miraculous demonstrations of the Spirit's might. The Antichrist, however, will persecute the Church to the point of martyrdom, while the world rejoices because the Church's testimony torments them (vv.7-10). Death will lose its sting as the victorious saints will rise from the dead and Christ will appear to usher in the eternal state (vv.11-19).

When Yahweh transfers Elijah's supernatural ministry to Elisha, Elisha asks for a double portion of Elijah's spirit on his ministry (2 Kgs.2:1-9). Elisha's double portion reflects Zion's assertive and innovative tasks of the cultural mandate. His first miracle demonstrates the mandate's innovative task to cultivate

---

32. Boyd, Gregory. *God at War, The Bible and Spiritual Conflict*, (Downers Grove: InterVarsity Press, 1997), pp.89-90.

and develop culture. By all outward appearances, the world system offers a pleasant, multifaceted, cultural smorgasbord. But the *source* of its life—the water supply—is bad, and the ground is barren (2 Kgs.2:19). So Elisha went directly to the source, threw salt in the water to bring life to a dying river (v.20). We, like Elisha, are the salt of the earth, the preservative of a putrefied world, the proactive seasoning that penetrates and resurrects a sterile society (Matt.5:13). We season the contaminated stew of the political arena (2 Kgs.4:38-41). We throw the tree of life into the murky waters of the entertainment world so that the Spirit of God can transform exploitive artistry into creative, effectual ministry (2 Kgs.6:1-7). Evil cannot exterminate Zion's innovative task to glorify God in cultural achievements.

Elisha's ministry transforms anything, anywhere, anytime. He does not restrict his ministry to religious settings only. The cultural mandate knows no ministerial boundaries. Kline alludes to the cultural mandate when he explains the sanctification of culture.

> All that [God's people] do is done as a service rendered unto God. All their cultural activity in the sphere of the city of man they are to dedicate to the glory of God. This sanctification of culture is subjective; it transpires within the spirit of the saints. Negatively, it must be insisted that this subjective sanctification of culture does not result in a change from common to holy status in culture objectively considered…the cultural activity of God's people is common grace activity. Their city of man activity is not "kingdom (of God)" activity. Though it is an expression of the reign of God in their lives, it is not a building of the kingdom of God as institution or realm. For the common city of man is not the holy kingdom, nor does it ever become the holy city of God, whether gradually or suddenly.[33]

---

33. Kline, M. *Kingdom Prologue, Vol. 2*, p.57.

We express the reign of God by being instruments of blessing. The task is treacherous—we must affect the world without being absorbed by it. Without assimilating into the doomed City of Man-harlot system (Rev.18:2-4) we remain faithful to Mount Zion's transformational task (Jn.17:14-18).

Elisha's social activism paves the way for the future ministries of Amos and Micah and their prophetic makeshift courtrooms. God's prophets are involved in all areas of life because the world is their arena for ministry. For example, a poor widow fears that her creditors will force her sons into slavery if she cannot pay her bills (2 Kgs.4:1). Elisha does nothing for her; he simply tells her to borrow empty vessels from everyone and pour oil into each vessel (vv.2-4). Empty vessels of potential blessing are everywhere in society. They are in our neighborhood, workplace, parks, concerts, restaurants, and ball games. Life is full of empty vessels of opportunity waiting to be filled by our little jars of blessing. If we fill some of the containers of culture with anointed oil, blessings will multiply (vv.5-7). When we cultivate all aspects of culture, fruitfulness will find innumerable creative ways to impact people and places beyond its initial destination.

The innovative task does not merely affect some abstract part of culture, it ministers to the human soul. The Shunamite woman miraculously conceives and bears a son according to the word of Elisha (2 Kgs.4:8-17). Unfortunately, tragedy soon strikes the boy and he dies (vv.18-20). Her journey to find Elisha tells us everything about her. She is expeditious, astonishingly calm, and forcefully confident. Staring straight into the face of dire circumstances, the Shunamite sings the familiar tune: "It is well with my soul!" (vv.21-26). Elisha prays and then stretches himself over the boy, putting his mouth on his mouth, his eyes on his eyes, and his hands on his hands, and the boy comes back to life (vv.33-35). This dramatic act portrays a life fully devoted to Mount Zion's innovative task to become instruments of blessing to the lost and dying.

A contemporary example of this may not be as dramatic, but might include a kind Christian dentist who spends most of his adult life drilling, sealing, and straightening teeth. His patients appreciate him and his family adores him. He ministers to hundreds of people with his expertise and kindness. Another example is a receptionist in an automotive company who generously shares the love and joy of the Lord throughout her faithful twenty-five years of service. Her employer is grateful and her family thrives on her robust personality. Are these two believers prophets? Are they evangelists or pastors or elders? Neither one is called to an official church ministry, but they are, however, called to fulfill Mount Zion's cultural mandate—whatever they do, they do it heartily for the glory of God (Eph.6:6,7; Col.3:22-24).

> Making music does not seem to be "social action," nor is it "evangelism," but God tells us to do it, and do it well. Making clothes and shoes and chairs that are good for people to use does not seem necessarily to be "social action," but it is an essential part of the "cultural mandate." Similarly for composing, choreography, dance, plays, poems, growing crops and eating good food, teaching mathematics well, enjoying games…In all these activities we are called to be new creatures taking our place as stewards of God's world, being servants of our neighbour and proclaimers of the good news of Jesus Christ.[34]

Elisha's ministry to the Shunamite's son demonstrates the incredible cost and outstanding results of fulfilling Zion's cultural mandate. The innovative task does not merely affect an abstract culture; it ingeniously soothes, heals, and resurrects wounded human souls.

To catch the vision of Mount Zion's cultural mandate and its two-fold task, we must receive a revelation of the spiritual reality that lies behind the scenes of the temporal world we face every day. When the world's system swirls around us, we need to see what Elisha and his servant Gehazi saw in Dothan. We

---

34. Marshall, p.37.

must not fear the antichrist world system or the anti-kingdom. We need only to pray that God may open our eyes to see that those who are fighting with us are more numerous than those fighting against us—for behold, the whole mountain is full of God's chariots of fire (2 Kgs.6:16,17). The world's system cannot see this angelic army behind us. But the enemies of God can hear the noise of these chariots of fire—and they flee (2 Kgs.7:1-7). The sea serpents that exploit all aspects of society flee at the sound of God's army. They must leave the culture intact so that the cultural mandate may continue until the Lord's personal return to earth.

After studying the two responsibilities associated with the cultural mandate—the innovative task to be fruitful and fill the earth, and the assertive task to subdue and have dominion—we can see that our mission is intensely arduous. Yet we must not lose heart over the fact that cultural achievements will never fully transform the world. We know that in the end, at the time of Christ's second appearance to the earth, he will fulfill the Noahic Covenant stipulations to unite heaven and earth. So the kingdoms of this world will some day become the kingdoms of our Lord and of his Christ and his reign will be eternal (Rev.11:15).

Daniel saw the cosmic mountain of the Great Shepherd-King. He saw the cosmic Mount Zion becoming a great mountain that filled the whole earth (Dan.2:35). Daniel declares: "the God of heaven will set up a kingdom that will never be destroyed, nor will it be left to another people. It will crush all those kingdom and bring them to an end, but it will itself endure forever" (2:44). When Jesus comes to announce the arrival of the kingdom, in reality he inaugurates the plan of God that originates in the Edenic connection to the cosmic mountain at the beginning of creation. He affirms that the divinely appointed goal of all the prophecies about Yahweh's cosmic mountain is now in full operation. The Church of Jesus Christ may actually press into the presence of Yahweh's cosmic mountain—this side of eternity.

John also saw Yahweh's cosmic mountain in all its glory. It looked like a city, a Holy City called the new Jerusalem, with foundations, walls, streets, and gates (Rev.21:2,12-21). It looked like a great and high *mountain* that shone with the glory of God (v.10). It looked more like a bride beautifully dressed for her husband, the Lamb of God, than it looked like a temple (vv.2,9). In fact, there is no temple in this brilliant city "because the Lord God Almighty and the Lamb are its temple" (v.22). It looked like a throne that issued forth the river of the water of life for the healing of the nations (22:1-2). "The throne of God and of the Lamb will be in the city, and his servants will serve him. They will see his face, and his name will be on their foreheads" (vv.3b,4). It sounds as though John experienced the same tour of Yahweh's cosmic mountain that Ezekiel received while exiled in Babylon.

Let us not grow weary living in the days of harlot Babylon. We must be faithful to the Lord when facing the spiritual reality of a very complex antichrist kingdom. Some day soon we, too, will experience a personal tour of Mount Zion for it is our spiritual heritage in Christ Jesus our Lord.

Appendix A

Canaanite Ritual System and Its Scriptural Prohibition Chart

Canaanite Ritual System	Scriptural Prohibition	Destruction of the System
Open-air Structure 1 Kgs.11:7; 13:2 2 Kgs.17:9-17	Lev.17:1-5	Numb.33:52; Deut.12:2 1 Kgs.13:2; 2 Kgs.17:11 Jer.19:5; 32:35; Ezek.6:3-6
Messabah (stone pillars) 1 Kgs.14:23; 2 Kgs.3:2;17:10	Ex.23:24;34:13 Deut.12:3; 16:21,22	Deut.7:1-5; 12:2-7 2 Kgs.18:4; 23:14 Hos.3:4; Mic.5:13
Asherah 1 Kgs.14:23; 16:33; 2 Kgs.13:6; 17:10-16; 21:3-7	Ex.20:1-6; 23:24; 34:13 Deut.16:21,22	Deut.7:1-5; 12:2-7 Jud.6:25-30; 1 Kgs.15:13 2 Kgs.18:4; 23:4-5, 14 Isa.17:8; 27:9; Jer.17:2; Mic.5:14
Animal & Child Altar for Sacrifice 2 Kgs.12:3; 14:4; 15:4; 16:3,4; 21:3-6; 2 Chron.14:3	Lev.17:7; 18:21	Deut.7:1-5; 12:2-7 2 Kgs.23:15
Pagan Priests 1 Kgs.12:31,32	Lev.19:31 Deut.18:9-12	2 Kgs.23:5
Burning of Incense 1 Kgs.22:43 2 Kgs.12:3; 14:4; 15:4; 16:4 Jer.44:17,25	2 Kgs.22:17	Lev.26:27-35 2 Kgs.23:5; Isa.17:8; 27:9 Jer.7:9; 11:12-13; 18:15; 32:29; 48:35
Stairs leading to oval platform	Ex.20:25-26	
Additional rooms for cultic prostitution, sacrificial meals 1 Sam.9:22; 1 Kgs.14:24	Lev.17:10	2 Kgs.23:7

Appendix B
Twisted Parallels of Satanic-Canaanite Mythology Chart

Satanic Counterfeit Mythology	Parallel to Biblical Truth
Baal defeats Yamm and is exalted as cosmic overlord of the earth.	Lucifer treacherously swindles Adam and Eve from their co-vassal positions as king-priests. His self-exaltation as the god of this world, the prince of the power of the air, is over the spiritual atmosphere of "Yamm"—a volatile demonic network-system that encompasses the whole earth.
El, the elderly creator god, now loses his place of power, while Baal, the young warrior, quickly gains rulership over the earth.	Humanity loses its place as co-regents over the affairs of the earth and hands the world kingdom over to Lucifer, now Satan, the adversary of God. In spite of this transaction, God remains sovereign over all.
Baal's banquet is celebrated by a bloody massacre due to Anath, the goddess of love, peace, and fertility.	Anath is simply the feminine *alter ego* of Satan. The reveling in cruel satanic rituals represents the rite of imitative magic meant to stimulate the flow of demonic activity (the demon's spiritual life essence) in and through human beings in order to usher in *malkhut* (the satanic kingdom of the new world order).
Baal introduces his new world order and settles down on Zaphon, his sacred mountain-sanctuary. Baal must express himself through a royal temple of cosmic proportions, a replica of some spiritual archetype.	Satan aggressively inaugurates his plan to pervert, desecrate, and counterfeit the kingdom of God in all its aspects. Satan must express his diabolical nature by dwelling in his own temple, namely devoted satanists, who replicate a demonic spiritual archetype. This is done to counteract and counterfeit the true temple of God, Mount Zion, the faithful, believing remnant.

In Baal's temple, a staircase winds up to a skylight window. This window of the cosmic sanctuary provides the exit and entryway for Baal to manifest his terrifying storm capabilities.	The anti-temple of the satanic cult must have passageways for demonic entry and exiting to execute acts of destruction on humanity, especially to persecute genuine followers of Yahweh.
The erection of Baal's temple incites another banquet, this time with the seventy territorial offspring of El and Asherah.	The construction of the universal satanic temple is constructed with the help of demonic powers who preside over their allotted territories (Deut.32:8ff.).
The courageous Baal falls to the clutches of Mot, the underworld's god of death, and the result is drought upon the land of Canaan.	Satan is defeated by Christ's death on the cross and believers are given delegated spiritual authority to overcome demonic oppression and harassment, to ultimately restore believers in Christ.
When harvest time finally arrives, Anath destroys Mot and Baal is resurrected.	Satan appears to survive the effects of the death and resurrection of Jesus Christ and resurrects his plan for a new world order.
The yearly ritual harvesting of Mot (death) induces Baal to resurrect and excites him to perform. Baal's rituals focus primarily on sexual perversion that is closely associated with human and animal sacrifices with chambers set up on the high places for cultic prostitution.	The cultic use of both male prostitutes (*kedeshim*) and female sacred harlots (*kedeshoth*) (1 Kgs.14:23,24; 2 Kgs.23:7) makes the worship of Satan a most violent, pornographic, bisexual cult—one that, of course, reflects the fullness of Satan's character quite well. John reveals that in the latter days the occult will be rampant for "by [the harlot-queen of heaven's] sorcery all the nations were deceived" (Rev.17; 18:23).
As Baal resumes his erotic behavior, he rapes Anath when she is in the form of a heifer and produces a male bull.	As the plan of Satan unfolds throughout history, the latter days are clearly marked as the age of antichrist. Satan's false messiah, the man of sin, will be revealed (2 Thess.2:3-12; 1 Jn.2:18; Rev.13)

Selected Bibliography

Ackerman, Susan. "'*And the Women Knead Dough*': *The Worship of the Queen of Heaven in Sixth-Century Judah*," Gender and Difference in Ancient Israel, Peggy L. Day, ed., Minneapolis: Augsburg Fortress, 1989.

Albright, W.F. "The High Place in Ancient Palestine," *Supplement Vetus Testamentum*, IV, Leiden: E.J. Brill, 1957.

———. *Yahweh and the Gods of Canaan*, A Historical Analysis of Two Contrasting Faiths, Garden City: Doubleday and Co., 1968.

Augustine. *City of God*, New York: Doubleday, 1958.

Barrick, W. Boyd. "The Funerary Character of 'High Places' in Ancient Palestine: A Reassessment," *Vetus Testamentum*, vol. 25, Leiden: E.J.Brill, 1975.

Beasley-Murray, G.R. *Jesus and the Kingdom of God*, Grand Rapids: Eerdmans, 1986.

Berkhof, Louis. *Systematic Theology*, Grand Rapids: Eerdmans, 1984.

Blenkinsopp, Joseph. *Gibeon and Israel, The Role of Gibeon and the Gibeonites in the Political and Religious History of Early Israel*, Cambridge: Cambridge University Press, 1972.

Block, Daniel. *The Book of Ezekiel, Chapters 25-48*, New International Commentary on the Old Testament, Grand Rapids: Eerdmans, 1998.

Boyd, Gregory. *God at War, The Bible and Spiritual Conflict*, Downers Grove: InterVarsity Press, 1997.

Brownlee, W. H. "From Holy War to Holy Martyrdom," *The Quest for the Kingdom of God*, Studies in Honor of George E. Mendenhall, ed. H.B. Huffmon, F.A. Spina, A.R.W. Green, Winona Lake: Eisenbrauns, 1983.

Bruce, F.F. *The New Bible Dictionary*, ed. J.D. Douglas, Grand Rapids: Eerdmans, 1979.

Budge, E.A. Wallis. *Egyptian Religion: Egyptian Ideas of the Future Life*, London: Routledge and Keegan Paul, 1972.

Clements, R.E. *God and Temple*, Philadelphia: Fortress Press, 1965.

Clifford, Richard J. *The Cosmic Mountain in Canaan and the Old Testament*, Cambridge: Harvard University Press, 1972.

Cloud, H., Townsend, J. *Boundaries: When to Say YES, When to Say NO To Take Control of Your Life,* Grand Rapids: Zondervan, 1992.

Cohn, Robert. *The Shape of Sacred Space, Four Biblical Studies,* AARSR 23, Chico: Scholars Press, 1981.

Culcan, W. "A Votive Model," *Palestine Exploration Quarterly* 108, 1976.

Day, John. *Molech, A god of human sacrifice in the Old Testament*, Cambridge: Cambridge University Press, 1989.

de Voux, Roland. *Ancient Israel, Vol.2, Religious Institutions*, New York: McGraw-Hill, 1961.

Dumbrell, W.J. *Covenant and Creation,* Nashville: Thomas Nelson, 1984.

Edwards, Jonathan. *Religious Affections*, ed. James M. Houston, Minneapolis: Bethany Pub. House, 1996.

———. *Thoughts on Revival*, New Haven: Yale University Press.

Eichrodt, Walter. *Old Testament Theology*, Philadelphia: Westminster, 1975.

Eliade, Mircea. *The Myth of the Eternal Return or, Cosmos and History*, Princeton: Princeton University Press, 1974.

Eliade, Mircea. *Patterns in Comparative Religion*, Cleveland: World Publishing, 1968.

Emerton, J.A. "'The High Places of the Gates' in 2 Kings XXIII 8," *Vetus Testamentum*, vol. 44, No. 4, Leiden: E.J.Brill, Oct. 1994.

Erb, Paul. *The Alpha and the Omega*, Scottdale: Herald Press, 1955.

Fee, Gordon, Stuart, Douglas. *How to Read the Bible for All Its Worth*, Grand Rapids: Zondervan, 1993.

Goldingay, John. *Word Biblical Commentary, Daniel*, 30, Dallas: Word, 1989.

Gowen, Donald. *Eschatology in the Old Testament,* Philadelphia: Fortress, 1986.

Gutmann, Evarose Rich. *Mountain Concept in Israelite Religion*, Ann Arbor: University Microfilm International, Ph.D. dissertation, Southern Baptist Theological Seminary, 1982.

Habel, Norman C. *Yahweh Versus Baal, A Conflict of Religious Cultures*, New York: Bookman Associates, 1964.

Hagner, Donald. "*The Old Testament in the New Testament,*" *Interpreting the Word of God*, ed. Samuel Schultz and Morris Inch, Chicago: Moody, 1976.

Haran, Menahem. *Temples and High Places in Biblical Times*, Colloquium in Honor of the Centennial of Hebrew Union College-Jewish Institute of Religion, Jerusalem: Hebrew Union College-Jewish Institute of Religion, 1981.

Harris, R., Archer G., Waltke. B., editors. *Theological Wordbook of the Old Testament*, vol. 1 & 2, Chicago: Moody Press, 1984.

Hauer, Christian E. "*Who was Zadok?*" *Journal of Biblical Literature*, 82, 1963.

Hislop, Alexander. *The Two Babylons*, Neptune: Loizeaux Brothers, 1959.

Johnson, David, VanVonderen, Jeff. *The Subtle Power of Spiritual Abuse*, Minneapolis: Bethany, 1991.

Kaiser, Walter, Silva, Moises. *An Introduction to Biblical Hermeneutics*, Grand Rapids: Zondervan, 1994.

Keil C.F., Delitzsch F. *Commentary on the Old Testament*, vol. 2, Joshua, Judges, Ruth, 1-2 Samuel, Grand Rapids: Eerdmans, 1985.

———. *Commentary on the Old Testament,* vol. 9, Ezekiel, Daniel, Grand Rapids: Eerdmans, 1985.

———. *Commentary on the Old Testament,* vol. 7, Isaiah, Grand Rapids: Eerdmans, 1986.

Kline, Meredith. "*Death, Leviathan, and the Martyrs: Isaiah 24:1-27:1,*" *A Tribute to Gleason Archer,* Kaiser and Youngblood editors, Chicago: Moody, 1986.

———. *Kingdom Prologue,* vol.1-2, 1985.

Koch, Kurt. *Occult Bondage and Deliverance*, Grand Rapids: Kregel, 1976.

Kramer, S. N. *The Sumerians*, Chicago: University of Chicago Press, 1963.

Kuenen, A. *The Religion of Israel to the Fall of the Jewish State*, translated by Alfred H. May, London: Williams and Norgate, 1882.

Ladd, G.E. *The Presence of the Future*, Grand Rapids: Eerdmans, 1974.

Leupold, H.C. *Exposition of Isaiah*, vol. 1, Grand Rapids: Baker Book, 1988.

Levenson, Jon. *Sinai and Zion*, Minneapolis: Winston Press, 1985.

Lewis, C.S. *Mere Christianity*, New York: MacMillan, 1960.

Marshall, Paul. *Thine is the Kingdom, A Biblical Perspective on the Nature of Government and Politics Today*, Grand Rapids: Eerdmans, 1984.

Miller, Patrick. *The Divine Warrior in Early Israel*, Cambridge: Harvard University Press, 1973.

Morris, Henry. *The Genesis Record*, Grand Rapids: Baker Book, 1982.

Murray, John. *Principles of Conduct*, Grand Rapids: Eerdmans, 1981.

Ollenburger, Ben C. *Zion, the City of the Great King, A Theological Symbol of the Jerusalem Cult,* JSOT Sup.41, Sheffield: JSOT Press, 1987.

Ottosson, Magnus. "*Eden and the Land of Promise*," Supplement to Vetus Testamentum, Vol.40, 1988.

Parrot, Andre. *The Tower of Babel*, trans. by Edwin Hudson, "Studies in Biblical Archaeology, No. 2," London: SCM Press, Ltd., 1955.

Petrie, W.M. Landers. *The Pyramids and Temples of Giza*, London: Histories & Mysteries of Man, 1990.

Reed, William L. *The Asherah in the Old Testament*, Fort Worth: Texas Christian University Press, 1949.

Renz, Thomas. "*The Use of the Zion Tradition in the Book of Ezekiel,*" *Zion, City of our God,* ed. Richard S. Hess and Gordon J. Wenhem, Grand Rapids: Eerdmans, 1999.

Roberts, J.J.M. "*The Davidic Origin of the Zion Tradition,*" *Journal of Biblical Literature*, 92, 1973.

―――. "*Zion in the Theology of the Davidic-Solomonic Empire,*" *Studies in the Period of David and Solomon and other Essays,* ed. Tomoo Ishida, Winona Lake: Eisenbrauns, 1982.

Robertson, O. Palmer. *The Christ of the Covenants,* Phillipsburg: Presbyterian and Reformed, 1984.

Rowley, H.H. "*Zadok and Nehushtan,*" *Journal of Biblical Literature*, 58, 1939.

Ryken, L., Wilhoit, J., Longman, T., editors. *Dictionary of Biblical Imagery*, Downers Grove: Intervarsity Press, 1998

Sawyer, John. *From Moses to Patmos, New Perspectives on Old Testament Studies,* London: SPCK, 1977.

Schaeffer, Francis. *The Complete Works of Francis Schaeffer, Vol.2,* Westchester: Crossway, 1982.

―――. *Genesis in Space and Time*, Downers Grove: InterVarsity, 1975.

Schaeffer, C. *The Cuneiform Texts of Ras Shamra-Ugarit,* London: Oxford University Press, 1936.

Sire, James W. *Scripture Twisting, 20 Ways the Cults Misread the Bible*, Downers Grove: InterVarsity, 1980.

Spence, Lewis. *Ancient Egyptian Myths and Legends*, New York: Dover, 1990.

Spencer, Aida Besancon. *Beyond the Curse, Women Called to Ministry*, Nashville: Thomas Nelson, 1985.

Thompson, Carroll. *Alienation: Dealing with the Basic Problem of Man*, Dallas: CTM Publishing, 1994.

———. *Possess the Land*, Dallas: CTM Publishing, 1977.

Thurneysen, Edward. *Eternal Hope*, translated by Harold Knight, London: Lutterworth, 1954.

Vannoy, J.R. *Covenant Renewal at Gilgal*, Cherry Hill: Mack Publishing, 1978.

Vaughan, Patrick H. *The Meaning of 'Bama' in the Old Testament*, A Study of Etymological, Textual and Archaeological Evidence, Cambridge: Cambridge University Press, 1974.

Wales, H.G. *The Mountain of God: A Study in Early Kingship*, London: Bernard Quaritch, Ltd., 1953.

Ward, William H. "*The Asherah*," *American Journal of Semitic Languages*, XIX, 1902.

Whitney, J.T. "'*Bamoth*' in the Old Testament," *Tyndale Bulletin*, 30, Cambridge: Tyndale House, 1979.

Wilder, E. James. *The Red Dragon Cast Down, A Redemptive Approach to the Occult and Satanism*, Grand Rapids: Chosen Books, 1999.

Wilson, John A. "Egypt," *Before Philosophy*, Hammondsworth: Penguin Books, 1949.

Wolf, Herbert M. *Interpreting Isaiah, The Suffering and Glory of the Messiah*, Grand Rapids: Zondervan, 1985.

Yadin, Yigael. "*Beer-sheba: The High Place Destroyed by King Josiah*," *Bulletin of the American Schools of Oriental Research*, 222, Missoula: Scholars Press, April, 1976.

Spiritual Reality
Order Form

Please send *Spiritual Reality* **to:**

Name: _____

Address: _____

City: _____ State: _____

Zip: _____

Telephone: (_____) _____

Book Price: $16.99

Shipping: $3.00 for the first book and $1.00 for each additional book to cover shipping and handling within US, Canada, and Mexico. International orders add $6.00 for the first book and $2.00 for each additional book.

Order from:
ACW Press
5501 N. 7th. Ave. #502
Phoenix, AZ 85013

(800) 931-BOOK

Also available at:
Christianbook.com
Amazon.com
BarnesandNoble.com

or contact your local bookstore